JAMES LUTHER MAYS

MICAH

THE OLD TESTAMENT LIBRARY

General Editors

JAMES LUTHER MAYS

MICAH

A Commentary

THE WESTMINSTER PRESS
PHILADELPHIA

Published by The Westminster Press®
Philadelphia, Pennsylvania

PRINTED IN THE UNITED STATES OF AMERICA

Library of Congress Cataloging in Publication Data

Mays, James Luther.
Micah : a commentary.

(The Old Testament library)
Bibliography: p.
1. Bible. O.T. Micah—Commentaries.
I. Bible. O.T. Micah. English. 1976.
II. Title. III. Series.
BS1615.3.M39   224'.93'07   76-2599
ISBN 0-664-20817-7

Because she made the years of its writing
such good years
this book is dedicated to
Mary Will Mays

CONTENTS

PREFACE

THE BOOK OF Micah has not received the attention it deserves in publications in English. That may be partly because of the challenge it presents to the interpreter. In some parts of the book the text is in bad condition. There is not much homogeneity in the style and content. It reflects a variety of circumstances and was formed over a rather long period for such a short book. In many respects it is a miniature of the book of Isiah, but without sufficiently large blocks of material to provide the same amount of data to bring to bear on particular problems. In this commentary I hope some justice has been done to all dimensions of the book. It has been my intention to provide the user with a guide to the individual sayings, to the way they were understood and used as they were gathered into large complexes and integrated into the growing collection, and to their role in the final form of the document. I am convinced that the book is not just a collection of prophetic sayings, but is the outcome of a history of prophetic proclamation and is itself in its final form prophecy. The material can and ought to be heard as prophecy in the various settings which belong to the history of its formation.

The translation of the text in the commentary is part of the comment, and not offered as an alternative to the several good translations of the Old Testament published in recent years. It undertakes to display those features of the Hebrew text which are pertinent to the comment, rather than literary polish. Biblical chapter and verse numbers follow the English Bible to avoid complicated citations; the reader is reminded at the beginning of each unit where the verse numbering of the Massoretic Text differs. Names cited in parentheses within the comment are those of commentators or authors of major works listed in the Bibliography or previously cited in footnotes on the particular passage. The Bibliography is, of course, only a selection. Other items relevant to particular problems are listed within the commentary.

Among those whose interest and encouragement have helped in the preparation of the commentary, some must be named. My colleagues, John Bright and Patrick D. Miller, Jr., have never failed to respond to requests for their judgment and advice. The hospitality and assistance of Walther Zimmerli during a recent sabbatical in Göttingen is remembered with gratitude. Hannah Clark, ruling elder in the Presbyterian Church and secretary of the Biblical Department, gave her enthusiasm and competence during the early stage of work on the manuscript. Before it was completed she died suddenly and left those of us who had worked with her a sense of loss that will not diminish. Arlene Jones helped greatly at the end.

ABBREVIATIONS

ANEP   *The Ancient Near East in Pictures relating to the Old Testament,*
          ed. J. B. Pritchard, 1954
ANET   *Ancient Near Eastern Texts Relating to the Old Testament,*
          ed. J. B. Pritchard, 1955[2]
ATD   Das Alte Testament Deutsch
BA   *The Biblical Archaeologist*
BDB   F. Brown, S. R. Driver and C. A. Briggs, eds., *A Hebrew*
          and English Lexicon of the Old Testament, rev. ed., 1957
BH   *Biblia Hebraica,* ed. R. Kittel, 1937[3]
BHS   *Biblia Hebraica Stuttgartensia* 10, 'Liber XII Prophetarum',
          ed. K. Elliger, 1970
BK   Biblischer Kommentar
BO   Bibliotheca Orientalis
BZAW   Beihefte zur *Zeitschrift für die alttestamentliche Wissenschaft*
CAT   Commentaire de l'Ancien Testament
FRLANT   Forschungen zur Religion und Literatur des Alten und
          Neuen Testaments
G   Septuagint
GKa   Gesenius-Kautzsch, *Hebrew Grammar,* 1910
HAL   L. Koehler and W. Baumgartner, *Hebräisches und aramäisches*
          Lexikon zum Alten Testament, 1967[3]
HAT   Handbuch zum Alten Testament
HK   Handkommentar zum Alten Testament
HTR   *Harvard Theological Review*
IB   *The Interpreter's Bible*
ICC   The International Critical Commentary
IDB   *Interpreter's Dictionary of the Bible*
Int   *Interpretation: A Journal of Bible and Theology*
JBL   *Journal of Biblical Literature*
KAT   Kommentar zum Alten Testament
KHC   Kurzer Hand-Commentar zum Alten Testament
MT   Massoretic Text
OTL   Old Testament Library
S   Peshitta

SAT   Die Schriften des Alten Testaments
SBT   Studies in Biblical Theology
TDNT   *Theological Dictionary of the New Testament* (Eng. trans. of
           TWNT), 1964ff.
THAT   *Theologisches Handwörterbuch zum Alten Testament*, ed. E.
           Jenni and C. Westermann, 1971ff.
ThB   Theologische Bücherei
TWNT   *Theologisches Wörterbuch zum Neuen Testament*, ed. G. Kittel,
           1932ff.
VT   *Vetus Testamentum*
WMANT   Wissenschaftliche Monographien zum Alten und Neuen
           Testament
ZAW   *Zeitschrift für die alttestamentliche Wissenschaft*
ZDMG   *Zeitschrift der deutschen morganländischen Gesellschaft*
ZDPV   *Zeitschrift des deutschen Palästina-Vereins*

I

INTRODUCTION

Micah (*mīkāh* 1.1, or *mīkāyāh* Jer. 26.18) is the short form of the Hebrew name that means 'Who is like YHWH?' (*mīkāyāhū* or *mīkāy͏ehū*). The name is in fact an exclamation of praise, an expression of adoration and wonder at the incomparable God of Israel. The name belonged to a man from the village of Moresheth in Judah who was called by God to be his spokesman. His mission gave the originating impulse to the formation of the prophetic book which bears his name.

The name is appropriate for a book whose range reflects the greatness of God. It is difficult to imagine a document which could offer in seven chapters a more comprehensive testimony to YHWH. Diametrically opposed aspects of the activity of God and his revelation finds expression in the sayings collected and arranged in the book. In the sayings YHWH speaks and is described as God of Israel and of the nations, Judge and Saviour, majestic in wrath and astonishing in compassion, worker of justice and promiser of forgiveness. He scatters his people and collects them as his flock; he destroys Zion and 'resurrects' her; he threatens the nations with humiliation and offers them peace.

There is a corresponding richness in the style and genre of language in the book. It contains announcements of judgment, oracles of salvation, controversy sayings, a lawsuit speech, instruction, laments, prayer, a proclamation of YHWH's appearance, a hymn. The historical setting of the sayings extends from the second half of the eighth century BC to the end of the sixth. In its variety and historical scope the book of Micah is a miniature of the book of Isaiah to which it is related in so many ways.

This variety and historical scope sets the task for a commentary on the book of Micah. A commentary must undertake first of all to identify the individual sayings collected in the book and to determine their original historical setting so that each can be heard in its own right. It must attempt to trace and follow the stages in which the sayings were collected and seek to discern the way they are to be understood as the word of YHWH in the new and broader context in which they were set. Was the process of collecting and arranging more or less arbitrary and based only on a concern with the past and its tradition, or did it grow out of a perception of the meaning and coherence of larger groupings as a testimony to YHWH? A commentary must also seek to do justice to the present form of the book as the final stage in the shaping of a prophetic witness to YHWH. What is its coherence? Is there a prophetic intention which pervades the whole and makes the book itself an instance of prophecy as well as a hermeneutical context in which its parts are to be heard? The last question involves more than simply a consideration of the final stage of redaction. It asks whether the book itself can be read with a measure of continuity and unity as prophecy in a larger sense, heard as 'the word of YHWH' in a fashion that does justice to the title.

In the following discussion, the last question is dealt with first in hope that an awareness of the content, arrangement, and integrating features of the book will provide a point of vantage for dealing with the mission of Micah as the book's origin and then with an attempt to discern the history of its formation. The comment on single passages will point to the way the sayings are related to their literary context as part of the whole and to their place in process of forming the book.

1. THE FORM OF THE BOOK

Like the other prophetic books Micah is a collection of brief literary units. These units with their own structure, style, and theme have for the most part been maintained in the collection in their distinctiveness. It is generally possible to recognize these units for individual study and to ask about their original historical setting. This analytical approach is essential to any grasp of the material of which the book is composed. Dealt with in this fashion the units lose their context in the book and are understood in relation to a reconstructed historical situation.

When the book is studied carefully with an interest, not in what makes it come apart, but in what holds it together, then a variety of integrating features begin to appear.[a] Catchwords and repeated motifs connect units which lie in sequence in the arrangement, and sometimes those which lie in different parts of the book. Units are sometimes arranged according to similar style and subject. Passages are placed in sequence so that their contrasting or complementary messages may be heard in relation to each other. Introductory rubrics are repeated to link units into larger complexes. Transitions lead from one unit into the next. These features are identified and discussed in the comment on particular passages.

Beyond these features there is an arrangement of the material which employs them in a movement of proclamation that flows through the entire book. The structure of this arrangement does not, of course, have the clarity and coherence of an original composition where the movement of thought creates the material. But there does seem to be a discernible pattern in the material which is the result of an accumulative and sustained intention to say something which incorporates all the smaller parts into a larger message.

The book is composed of two major parts, 1.2–5.15 and 6.1–7.20. Each part opens with an introductory summons to hear which identifies its audience (1.2 and 6.1a). Each is arranged so as to unfold a revelation of YHWH's way in the world. The first part is addressed to a universal audience of all peoples. It combines YHWH's judgment of Samaria and Jerusalem (1.3–3.12) and his redemption of Zion and Israel (4.1–5.9) into a witness to the nations that YHWH's coming kingdom faces them with a choice between submission (4.1–4) and punishment (5.10–15). The second is addressed to Israel. It portrays an Israel that lives under the inescapable judgment of God (6.1–7.6) and yet stands before the promise of the salvation of God (7.8–17), an Israel who must and may expect that salvation (7.7) only through the forgiveness of God (7.18–20). Each section is rounded off by a passage which concludes its movement, the first with the threat of YHWH's vengeance on the disobedient nations (5.15) and the second with a hymn to the compassion of God. Within each section there is evidence in the arrangement and shaping of the material that a persistent intention has been at work to bring the individual units under the control of broader kerygmatic purposes.

[a] For studies of the literary form of the book, see: E. Nielsen, *Oral Tradition* (SBT 11), 1954, pp. 79–93; B. Renaud, *Structure et Attaches Littéraires de Michée IV–V* (Cahiers de la Revue Biblique 2), 1964; J. T. Willis, 'The Structure of Micah 3–5 and the Function of Micah 5. 9–14 in the Book,' *ZAW* 81, 1969, 191–214; id., 'The Structure of the Book of Micah,' *Svensk Exegetisk Årsbok* 34, 1969, pp. 5–42.

Part One: 1.2–5.15

On first inspection the arrangement of ch. 1–5 seems to be based on the familiar principle of alternating blocks of oracles of judgment and prophecies of salvation with a resulting arrangement of 1–3 and 4–5. There are two passages which will not yield to this analysis. The first is the apparent promise of salvation to the remnant of Israel in 2.12f. The other is the announcement of YHWH's punishment in 5.10–15. Further, the analysis does not take account of the many inner relationships within the two blocks and the significance of the content of one for the other.

The summons to all the peoples to hear YHWH's witness (1.2) and the warning of his vengeance for those who do not hear (respond appropriately, 5.15) signal the kerygmatic focus. The section is concerned with universal history, with the nations and their power as the context in which YHWH's reign will be established.

The pivot of movement, the point at which a breathtaking shift occurs with the chapters, clearly lies between 3.9–12 and 4.1–5. The announcement that Jerusalem will be totally destroyed and disappear is followed by the proclamation that Jerusalem will be the capital of YHWH's reign to which the nations shall repair. The sayings in 1–3 lay the foundations for the lead up to 3.12, and those in 4–5 support and expound 4.1–5.

1.3–3.12 unfolds a message of YHWH's judgment on Israel. The proclamation of the advent of YHWH (1.3f.) sounds the overture for the sequence. The reason for his wrathful intervention is the rebellion of Israel (1.5a). Verse 5b distributes this guilt to the cities of Samaria and Jerusalem, the capitals of the northern and southern kingdoms. This identification of the guilty is the clue to a basic way in which the rest of the section is arranged. It corresponds to the 'Samaria and Jerusalem' of the title (1.1) and states the formula for the programme of God's punishment which is then developed. In chs. 1–3 there are only two sayings which speak specifically of God's action against these cities. The announcement of Samaria's destruction (1.6f.) is set immediately after the introductory proclamation. The memorable saying on the end of Jerusalem is heard at the conclusion (3.9–12). Similar descriptive motifs in each make one echo the other. Between the two which represent the onset and climax of the terrible work for which YHWH appears, the material is arranged to move from beginning to culmination and portray the execution of the Samaria-Jerusalem programme. The rest of ch. 1 (vv. 8–16) voices a throbbing lament which narrates the movement of a divinely sent disaster across the land of Judah to the very gates of Jerusalem (vv. 9, 12) and breaks off with a call to mourn the population going into exile (v. 16). But the announcement of the fall of Jerusalem itself is reserved to make room for the exposition of the rebellion of Jacob which is punished by the loss of the land (ch. 2) and the end of Jerusalem (ch. 3).

The material collected in ch. 2 turns around the theme of Israel and its land. Avarice for possession of the land as property is the crime which draws judgment (vv. 1f., 8f.). Loss of the land will be the appropriate punishment (vv. 4f.). A call is heard to depart from the land because it no longer serves the purpose for which God gave it (v. 10), a second summons to exile (cf. 1.16). The land which lies around the centre of Jerusalem is in focus. It is the sphere where Israel lives under the reign of YHWH, and rebellion against that reign defiles it. The corresponding punishment is its loss. The apparent salvation oracle in 2.12f. is in fact a disclosure that the exile is the work of YHWH (see the comment). He himself gathers Israel like a flock in a fold, breaks down the gate, and leads them away. It brings to a climax the references to exile already heard (1.16; 2.3, 10) by the assertion that Israel's removal from the land is no alien event, but a manifestation of YHWH's sovereignty. The saying has a clear counterpart in 4.6f. which tells how YHWH reverses 2.12f. by gathering the remnant, making them a great nation, and ruling over them in Mount Zion. The whole drama of exile and return, judgment and salvation is a revelation of YHWH's kingship.

Chapter 3 shifts the focus to Jerusalem and its leaders. Three rather similar sayings move toward the climax in v. 12. All are addressed to leaders who exploit their status and vocation for ends inimical to the reign of YHWH (vv. 3, 5, 9). All three announce the same punishment on these leaders; there will be no answer from YHWH when they cry out in need (vv. 4, 7) and events will disclose that their hope in him is empty (v. 11). Together the three sayings distinguish between the use of power in the government of Jerusalem and the reign of YHWH. The spirit-endowed prophet word alone represents the reign of YHWH and it reveals the reason for YHWH's coming (cf. v. 8 and 1.5). This claim prepares the way for and authenticates the incredible sentence upon Jerusalem. That city under these leaders will cease to exist (v. 12). There will be no connection between it and any city of God in the future.

With the announcement of the destruction of Jerusalem, the first phase of the Samaria-Jerusalem drama is complete, and the purpose of YHWH's appearance in wrath has been fulfilled. This arrangement of the sayings transposes an entire era of history into a unified drama of judgment, the whole an expression of the theophany. Samaria is destroyed because of idolatry, and drops from sight, to be heard of no more in the book. The land of Judah is ravaged and its population exiled because the land is defiled by injustice. Jerusalem falls because of the treachery of the leaders. The whole is the first element of YHWH's witness to the nations. The humiliation of Israel in the midst of history is proclaimed to all nations as a testimony to the reign of YHWH whose rule brooks no idolatry and overlooks no rebellion.

4.1–5.15 is the second element of the witness of YHWH which the nations are summoned to hear (1.2), a summons rephrased as warning in the last line (5.15). At its very beginning it points to 'the latter days which shall be', so its message concerns the future now being created by YHWH's work (4.1). Three recurrent motifs identify the structural concerns: many peoples/nations (4.1–3, 5, 11, 13; 5.15), Zion (4.2, 7, 8, 10, 11, 13), and remnant (4.7; 5.7, 8). The sequence sketches a drama of the way in which YHWH will establish the capital of his reign in Zion, reclaim and transform the scattered remnant into an invulnerable manifestation of his power, and so create the theopolitical reality by which the nations will find peace or punishment. As a sequel to 1.3–3.12 this section shows that the fall of the capital cities, Samaria and Jerusalem, serves the establishment of YHWH's capital in Zion, that the end of Jerusalem is not the end of the reign of YHWH, that the judgment of Israel is the work of YHWH on the way to the manifestation of his kingship among the nations.

The section opens and closes with paired prophecies which raise alternative visions of the nations under the coming reign of YHWH. 4.1–5 promises a Zion which has become the centre of the world because it is the place from which YHWH reigns. Where he reigns by the instruction of his word, nations end their rebellion and peace takes over. 5.10–15 announces the purge of YHWH, how he will cut off the tools and buildings of war and destroy every idol as the vengeance of his kingly anger against civil and cultic rebellion. That is his way with the nations who do not listen to this word which goes out from Zion, from the holy temple of the Lord (cf. 1.2 and 4.2).

The body of the section contains two complexes (4.8–5.4; 5.5–9) identifiable by particular motifs, stylistic devices, and subjects. 4.6f. serves as a unifying prelude to both because it states in anticipation the theme of each. Verses 6–7a promise that YHWH will rescue the exiled remnant and transform them into a strong nation. The second complex develops that theme with a series of sayings about the future Israel that shall live unthreatened and invulnerable in the midst of the nations. Verse 7b promises the unending reign of YHWH from

Mount Zion over this Israel of the future. The first complex develops that theme with three prophecies of the way in which YHWH will turn the crises of the present into a new dominion from Zion over its population. So 4.6f. is an oracle which announces *in nuce* what the body of the section unfolds. It may also furnish a transition from 4.1–5, which without mentioning Israel speaks of YHWH's glorious reign from Zion, to the body which reveals the central role the population of Zion and the exiled remnant of the nation will play in YHWH's new kingdom. Seen from this vantage, it may also be a clue to a correspondence between the two complexes of salvation prophecy and the two phases of the history of judgment portrayed in ch. 1–3. The first complex on the future of Zion answers the judgment of Jerusalem in ch. 3. The second on the invulnerable remnant in the midst of the nations transcends the loss of the land and the exile of the population in ch. 1–2.

4.8–5.4 contains four sayings all of which feature the motif 'daughter of Zion' (4.8, 10, 13; on the motif in 5.1 see the commentary). The first is a terse promise that the former dominion shall be returned to Zion (4.8). The other three are constructed on a similar pattern. Each begins with the adverb 'now' and speaks of the tribulation of that present (4.9–10a, 11; 5.1) and then goes on to disclose the way YHWH will turn that tribulation into the coming of his reign (4.10b, 12f.; 5.2–4). Together the three are a cumulative prophecy of how the promise in 4.8 will be fulfilled. The suffering helpless population of Zion will be redeemed from Babylon by YHWH (4.9f.). The attacking nations surrounding Zion will be overwhelmed in a victory that reveals who is lord of the whole earth (4.11–13). The humiliation of Israel's king will be followed by the inauguration of a new ruler whom YHWH will make great in the midst of the whole earth (5.1–4). The sequence is not a chronological succession of logically ordered events; yet each prophecy proclaims an achievement of YHWH's salvation that fills out a broad vision of the restoration of the people who live in and around Zion as a manifestation of the reign of God.

5.5–9 contains three sayings (5.5f., 7, 8) and a concluding promise (5.9). The beginning of each of the sayings is marked by an introductory 'and (subject) shall be' (*wehāyāh* plus subject). The common theme is Israel in the midst of the nations. When 'Assyria' (see the comment) threatens, that classic adversary will come under the hegemony of Israel (5.5f.). The remnant of Jacob will exist among the peoples mysteriously and powerfully (vv. 7 and 8). The promise in v. 9 gathers up and summarizes the effect of the sayings; all who lift their hand against Israel shall be cut off. The permanence and power of the coming reign of YHWH will be expressed in the invulnerability of the future Israel. It is possible that the demonstrative 'this' in the first line of the complex (v. 5) refers to the coming regent of YHWH (5.2–4) so that this new power of Israel is understood as the consequence of the regent's reign.

But this promise of such incredible power and security to the remnant of Jacob is not to be heard apart from the concluding prophecy of the section, which maintains its sequence with the foregoing with its own opening $w^e h\bar{a}y\bar{a}h$ (5.10–15). In direct address which must still have the Israel of the promises in mind, YHWH threatens to cut off every weapon and fortress as well as every relic of pagan faith. Israel's identity and power will paradoxically and mysteriously be wholly an expression of the power and identity of YHWH. Neither Israel nor the nations will be allowed their own power or own gods in the kingdom of YHWH.

The first part of the book has thus been shaped to serve as a prophetic proclamation of YHWH's reign over the nations, announced from his holy temple (1.2) on Zion where he shall be enthroned as royal judge of all peoples (4.1–4). It opens with the narrative of his coming from his heavenly palace to intervene in the affairs of earth (1.3f.) in a drama of punishment (ch. 1–3) and deliverance (ch. 4–5). As King YHWH will rescue Israel and reign over them from Mount Zion (4.7). The former dominion shall be restored to the daughter of Zion (4.8) through the regency of a new ruler of Israel whose power extends to the ends of earth (5.4). The wealth of all who oppose this future government will be turned into booty for the Lord of all the earth (4.13).

The establishment of this reign is accomplished by both the judgment and salvation of God. The two do not appear in a simple sequence, but are related in an on-going dialectic of action. The proclamation is heard in Israel and concerns her as one of the nations. YHWH's salvation of the remnant of Israel and of Zion will be the revelation that the nation's existence and role is wholly the work of his purpose and power. Zion's security and the nation's prowess among the peoples will mysteriously be effected apart from any of the usual instruments of power. And the message of Israel's judgment stands as warning that idolatry and unrighteousness are excluded from those who live under YHWH's rule.

The proclamation is a word to all nations. The judgment that came on Israel will be extended to them. All opposition to the kingdom which YHWH is establishing through the Zion and Israel of the future will be met by inexorable destruction of the enemies. All idolatry and trust in war will be cut off as it was in Israel. But the purpose of this judgment is to bring all to the peace and prosperity created by YHWH's reign from Zion, a reign of word and instruction.

Part Two: 6.1–7.20

The first part of the book began with the proclamation of a theophany which inaugurates YHWH's coming to establish his reign over the nations. Here the message begins with a trial scene (6.1–5), covenant proceedings between YHWH and his people to settle an estrangement between them. The different scene signals the distinctiveness of the two parts right from the start. The second is concerned directly and intimately with the relationship between YHWH and Israel, with judgment and salvation as God's struggle for the soul of his people.

The organizing features of the arrangement are clearly discernible. There is a general introductory summons to hear all that follows as the message of YHWH (6.1a). There are two major sections distinguished by mood and content. The first portrays the estrangement between YHWH and Israel (6.2–7.6) and the second deals with their reconciliation (7.8–20). The two are connected by an assertion of trust and hope in 7.7 where an amazing shift from weariness and despair to confidence sets in. The sequence of the two sections cannot be described simply as a juxtaposition of prophecies of judgment and salvation. There is in fact only one true oracle of judgment (6.9–16) in the first section, and the second contains only one promise of salvation (7.11–13). The accents of judgment and salvation are indeed present, but they are sounded as part of a movement which has interrelatedness and coherence as a whole.

As chs. 6–7 are read, an antiphonal alternation of voices is heard. YHWH speaks first to his people (6.3–5). An 'I' responds (vv. 6f.) and is answered in turn by a voice which uses the vocative 'man' to address the 'I' (v. 8). Then YHWH speaks to 'the city' (vv. 9–16) and again in human voice begins to speak in first person singular at 7.1 and continues through v. 10. In vv. 8–10 the gender of the pronouns shows that the speaker is feminine, and suggests that it is the personified city of 6.9, who responds to 6.9–16 in the entire sequence of 7.1–10. In 7.11–13 a voice (YHWH) addresses the feminine figure. The exchange is concluded by a congregational 'we' speaking directly to YHWH (7.14–20). Though speakers and addressees cannot be consistently identified in this way at earlier stages of the history of the tradition of these sayings, in the present literary composition the alternation of voices can be read as a dialogue between YHWH and an Israel who appears in a montage of identities (singular people, representative Israelite, city, corporate congregation). In the course of the dialogue YHWH's partner in the verbal struggle is brought from weariness with him (6.3) to a tireless and patient hope in him as saviour (7.7–10), from anxious searching for some means of placating God (6.6f.) to exuberant praise of his compassionate forgiveness (7.18–20).

Each saying in the whole seems to play a part in this movement. 6.1b is YHWH's summons to Israel to participate in this controversy which vindicates YHWH's way with his people and sets the relation between them right.

6.2–5 is YHWH's opening argument against the complaint of his people that he has wearied them. He appeals to the salvation history that brought them from bondage to the promised land and calls them to recognize anew his righteous acts. His deeds of salvation created the reality upon which their life should be based and vindicate his right to sovereignty over their existence. The argument serves to put God in the right and Israel in the wrong, and so establishes the relation in which the rest of the dialogue is conducted.

6.6–8 contains both a mistaken acknowledgment of God's claim and the right statement of what the claim is. In response to YHWH's proclamation of his righteousness, a 'man' representing Israel acknowledges his sin and lists an extravagant agenda of sacrifices as proposals to achieve atonement. The proposals are simply and flatly ignored by one who speaks for YHWH to summarize what he has always required: justice, loyalty, and a life that is wisely lived in submission to God. This threefold definition of YHWH's requirement establishes the assumptions on which both the following announcement of judgment (6.9–16) and confession of sin (7.1–6) are based. Both in turn lay bare the absence of justice and loyalty in the life of the people. In 7.7 the human partner in the controversy turns to a humble waiting on YHWH which responds to the requirement for a submissive confirmation of life to the way of God.

6.9–16 is YHWH's word of judgment. It is addressed to 'the city', a designation which shows incidentally that the Israel with whom God struggles is a population whose identity is focused in Jerusalem. Justice and loyalty are violated in their corporate life (vv. 10–12, 16a). That is the basis for the punishment already begun (v. 13) and under whose deprivation they live (vv. 14f.). Their devotion to the ways of the rejected kings of the northern state of Israel instead of loyalty to YHWH is the cause of their humiliation before the peoples around them (v. 16).

7.1–10 is the response of the city, speaking as a personified woman. In a lament (vv. 1–6), which serves in the context as penitential confession, she bewails the violation of justice and lack of loyalty among her people, and so in their name acknowledges the rightfulness of the punishment under which they suffer (7.4b). She abandons the complaint of weariness with the way of YHWH and turns to the strength of hope in his salvation (7.7). In the confidence of that hope she breaks out into a song of salvation (7.8–10). She has sinned and will bear the indignation of YHWH (7.9) until he changes his work from jugment to salvation and brings the very enemies who serve his punishment to the same humiliation she suffers.

7.11–13 is a divine promise addressed to the personified city. It raises a vision of the very salvation for which the city waits. Her walls shall be rebuilt, the boundaries of her territory extended, and her scattered population returned. The punishment which came on the city for her sin will fall upon the entire world because of its deeds. This general judgment will create the opportunity for the restoration of the city.

7.14–20 is the concluding response of YHWH's partner in dialogue, who now speaks as the corporate congregation of YHWH's people. First, they pray for the promise to be fulfilled and their salvation enacted (vv. 14–17). They appeal for a resumption of the historic deeds of YHWH which originally brought them into the land (vv. 14f.), the very saving deeds which YHWH had recited at the beginning of the controversy as the true basis of their relation to him (cf. 6.4f.). And they ask that this new activity of YHWH on their behalf be at the same time a revelation to the nations which shall turn them to him in recognition of his power (vv. 16f.). Second, the congregation praises YHWH for that characteristic of his way which is the basis of their hope that he will surely transform the history of judgment to salvation (vv. 18–20). Though they are sinners, justly under punishment, YHWH is incomparable as the one whose forgiveness is more powerful than their sins. He delights in mercy and will not persist in anger. Their salvation depends, not on them, but on something in him. So at the end the people who vacillated between complaint against him and feverish activity to propitiate him sing of their wondering joy at being wholly in his hands. The dialogue concludes. Its purpose is accomplished. Affairs between YHWH and Israel are set right. The dialogue has recreated Israel as a people who live prophetically, under God's judgment for their sin and in hope of his salvation.

The coherence which holds together this collection of disparate material is created through the alternation of voices, described above, the sequence of words from YHWH and his human partner which portray a steady progressive shift in the relation between the two. It is surely significant for this characteristic of the complex that at the beginning (6.1f.) and in the centre (7.9) the theme of *rīb* (complaint) is used to identify the proceedings taking place between YHWH and Israel in the verbal exchange. The word can designate a specific complaint which one person has against another, and also the procedure for making and settling the complaint, particularly in a legal setting. The classical prophets employed the *rīb* as a type of oracle in which YHWH's 'covenant lawsuit' against Israel was proclaimed and prosecuted. It was a verbal image for YHWH's historical activity in which he held Israel to the terms of the Sinai covenant and judged its conduct by the covenant's norms. 6.2–5 is an example of the type. The term also came to be used in the vocabulary of salvation for the intervention of YHWH against his enemies and those of Israel (Jer. 50.34; 51.36; Lam. 3.58; Isa. 51.22; Pss. 43.1; 74.22; 119.153; etc.). 7.9 is a case of this usage. The juxtaposition of the two in the two sections of the sequence expands the function of the *rīb* to the larger purpose of YHWH's way with Israel in which both judgment under the norms of the covenant and salvation to vindicate his promise and election of Israel are integrated in a linear movement. The introduction of the *rīb* motif at beginning and centre provides a dramatic setting for the alternation of voices and interprets it as the verbal struggle in which YHWH brings Israel to justice and to justification.

2. MICAH THE MORESHITE

The Sayings of Micah

An account of the mission and message of Micah depends upon a decision about which of the sayings collected in the book derive from him. There is general agreement that some of the sayings were not spoken by the Moreshite, but broad disagreement over which belong to Micah and which have been added in the growth of the collection. [b]

[b] The point of departure for discussion of the question is B. Stade's conclusion that Micah's sayings are to be found only in chs. 1–3 ('Bemerkungen über das Buch Micha,' *ZAW* 1, 1881, pp. 161–72). In their commentaries K. Marti (KHC, 1904) and W. Nowack (HKAT, 2nd ed. 1922) reached largely the same conclusions. Since then opinions have varied between variations of Stade's position (e.g., T. H. Robinson, HAT, 2nd ed. 1954) and claims that almost all the book came from

This commentary reaches the conclusion that Micah's sayings are found only in the first three chapters: 1.3–5a, 8–15 (with additions); 2.1–5 (revised); 2.6–11 (v. 10 is revised); 3.1–4, 5–8, 9–12. Generally speaking, the conclusion rests on these considerations: (a) Micah is remembered in Jeremiah's time as the prophet who announced the destruction of Jerusalem during the reign of Hezekiah; (b) Micah gives a quite specific description of the purpose of his mission in 3.8 which is consistent with these texts and inconsistent with most of the other material in the book; (c) these sayings display a continuity and consistency of style, setting, and message; (d) the language, setting, and message of the rest of the material suggests it consists of sayings and redaction which date from the late seventh century on.

In the year of Jehoiakim's accession (609/608) Jeremiah was arrested and hastily brought to trial for his life because he had prophesied against Jerusalem and the temple (Jer. 26; see also ch. 7). During the trial certain 'elders of the land' testified in his defence by recalling the prophecy of Micah, the Moreshite, who in the time of King Hezekiah had announced the coming destruction of Jerusalem. They were able to cite the very words of Micah from the conclusion of the oracle preserved in Micah 3.9–12. This remarkable instance of the quotation of a prophet's words in an *ad hoc* situation a century after they had been spoken shows what an impression Micah's oracle had made on some men in his time and identified the distinctive message for which he was remembered. He was apparently the first prophet to proclaim the unconditional judgment of YHWH upon Jerusalem. The elders obviously knew no tradition about what Micah had said which would compromise his usefulness as testimony that a prophet had already announced the destruction of Jerusalem without being punished.

At the conclusion of his oracle against corrupt prophets (3.5–7) Micah makes an assertion about the validity and purpose of his own vocation (v. 8). He has been especially endowed for a mission. He has the charisma of justice, accompanied by power and might, and is equipped thereby to declare to Jacob/Israel what his crime and sin

---

Micah (B. A. Copass and E. L. Carlson, *A Study of the Prophet Micah*, 1950). A. Weiser in his widely used commentary (ATD, 3rd ed. 1959) claimed everything for Micah except 2.12f.; 4.1–5; the final form of 4.6–5.1, which contains some reworked fragments from Micah; 5.7–9; and 7.8–20. He was largely followed by W. Beyerlin, *Die Kulttraditionen Israels in der Verkündigung des Propheten Micha* (FRLANT 72), 1959. The writer began his work on this commentary with the assumption that Weiser was correct, but has been forced away from that position by his examination of the material and its redaction.

are. In 1.3–5a there is a proclamation of the coming of YHWH in wrathful theophany because of the crime and sin of Jacob/Israel. This correlation between the purpose of YHWH's appearance and Micah's mission is crucial evidence for Micah's understanding of his role. He was the herald and interpreter of an intervention of YHWH to deal with the offences in Israel against his will. The correlation defies the extent of the material which can be attributed to Micah. It confirms the tradition of Jer. 26 in which he is remembered as a prophet of judgment.

The sayings which are consistent with Micah's understanding of his role are collected in chs. 1–3. They are remarkably homogeneous in style and message and in the social and historical situation which they assume. 2.1–5 (in its original form), 3.1–4, and vv. 9–12 are addressed to a particular group, the leaders of the nation who by virtue of power and position are responsible for what happens to the rest of the people in the social order. The complaint against them is that they reject justice and practise violent wrong in their own self-interest. The punishment announced is a catastrophe in which they will have no help from God. 2.6–11 is a controversy saying in which Micah answers their rejection of his prophecy. 2.5–8 is an oracle against false prophets which is quite similar in design to those against the leaders. The lament in 1.8–15 is a poetic narrative of the historical form which the theophany (1.3–5a) assumes as God brings the catastrophe. As a group these sayings compose a highly plausible record of the proclamation of Micah during the Assyrian crisis in the reign of Hezekiah, addressed to the civil and religious officials of the nation who are responsible for the absence of justice, and foretelling a disaster for them which will culminate in the fall of Jerusalem.

None of the rest of the material in the book can be fitted into a description of Micah's mission without disturbing its coherence. All the other sayings reflect different concerns and later situations. They have been brought into the Micah collection in the process of its continuing use (see the following section on 'The Formation of the Book'). The salvation prophecy in 4.1–5.9 and 7.7–20 is primarily concerned with the restoration of Zion as the centre of YHWH's reign. 6.1–5, 6–8 are addressed to an audience in a quite different mood and situation from that of Micah's audience. The lament in 7.1–6 does not sound like the prophet of 3.8. The oracles of judgment in 1.6f. and 5.10–14 are focused on idolatry and contain a vocabulary and perspective absent from the other oracles of judgment which can be ascribed to Micah. 6.9–15 is the most difficult to assess; it could be fitted into the picture of Micah's mission. But its literary setting and distance from the more certain material in the book argue against its inclusion. 2.12f. was inserted into the Micah collection after it was already in literary form.

The Man

In the two appearances of the prophet's name (1.1; Jer. 26.18) he is called 'Micah the Moreshite'. The name Micah was common enough in Israel throughout the centuries of the Old Testament period. It is perhaps significant that this Micah is distinguished by an epithet which identifies him with a town. Neither a family name ('son of . . .') nor a title is used. Like Nahum the Elkashite and Amos from Tekoa, he was known by his place of origin. Two inferences may be drawn from the name-type. Such an identification would be given a man away from home by others who marked him with the name of the place from which he came. So Micah must have entered history's traditions away from Moresheth, probably in Jerusalem. It is also likely that the experiences and perspectives which infuse his sayings are due in part to the vantage of a man from a town like Moresheth.

Moresheth is probably the Moresheth of Gath mentioned in 1.14 (see the comment). The site has been identified with Tell el-Judeideh, a rather imposing mound some twenty-five miles south-west of Jerusalem. It stands on the edge of the Shephelah overlooking the coastal plain; the road from Azekah south to Lachish runs through it. Since Rehoboam had fortified the place as part of his defence system to guard the western approaches to Jerusalem, it must have been much more important than a pastoral village. Military and administrative officials would have frequented the town and brought the interests of the Jerusalem government to bear on the community's life.

Except for his name and home, nothing is known directly about the man. The rest of his silhouette must be sketched from suggestions and hints drawn from his sayings. The book lacks any narrative which tells of him or his activity. The tradition allows us to know him only as spokesman for YHWH. According to the title (1.1) he was active during the reigns of Jotham (742–735), Ahaz (735–715), and Hezekiah (715–687/6). This 'dating' allows a maximum period of forty-six years for the span of his public activity. But the small number of sayings which can be attributed to him are so similar in their concern and in the circumstantial setting which they presuppose that a career stretching over such a long period seems unlikely. The sayings suggest a period of activity which lasted a relatively short time.

There are no historical references to persons or events in the sayings which settle the question of date with certainty. But the dirge bewailing the disaster devastating the towns of western Judah (1.10–16) can be associated with the campaign of Sennacherib against Judah in 701 during Hezekiah's reign. Twice, Micah's audience argues with the prophet that disaster will not befall them (3.11; 2.7). They could be responding only to the disaster foretold by Micah, but it could well be that their need to debate the message grew out of anxiety over a visible Assyrian threat. Jer. 26.18f. dates Micah's prophecy of Jerusalem's fall (3.9–12) in the days of Hezekiah and attributes Jerusalem's relief from the Assyrian siege to Hezekiah's repentance because of the oracle. It seems likely that 3.9–12 was the climax and latest of the series of sayings preserved in ch. 2–3, and that 1.8–16 belongs to the period of the Assyrian campaign. Thus the probable period for Micah's activity was 701 and the months immediately before Sennacherib's invasion.

The way in which Micah identifies the addressees of his message sayings suggests that they were spoken in Jerusalem. Without exception his audience is characterized as those who possess power and authority, and most often their power is associated with a particular office (2.1f., 8f.; 3.1, 5, 9, 11). Chiefs and leaders are said to build Jerusalem by bloody violence (3.9f., 1). He speaks twice of prophets who have commercialized their vocation (3.5, 11) and priests who have done the same (3.11). Such a concentration of officials is likely only in Jerusalem. He spoke to those who administered legal and economic affairs, to the priests and prophets who were assembled around the temple. It would have been in Jerusalem that he came to be called 'the Moreshite'.

Doubtless Micah knew the ways of the officials from Jerusalem through experiences in Moresheth, and the perspectives of his home shaped his concerns. When he describes the exploitation of the ordinary people of the land by the powerful, his words contain a sympathy with the suffering of the oppressed and an anger at their oppressors which indicate a deep personal identification with those who lost land and home and self-respect (2.1f., 8ff.; 3.2f.). The radical changes in the economic structure which brought inequality, commercialization, and centralization of power in the hands of one class had set in with a vengeance during the long and prosperous reigns of Jeroboam II in Israel and of Uzziah in Judah. These shifts in the social process took effect more slowly in Judah than in the northern state. We hear echoes of them in the sayings of Micah's great contemporary, Isaiah, whose indictments are often quite similar to those of Micah (cf. Isa. 1.23; 3.12, 15; 5.8; 10.1f.). But Micah did not share the wide range of concerns manifest in the messages of Isaiah whose setting in life and in tradition were Jerusalem. He said nothing about cultic apostasy or international policy, took no notice of the royal court and its place in Judah's life. He was gripped with a single-minded concentration on what was happening because of the leaders' consecration to acquisitions and their lack of concern for justice. Early in his reign King Hezekiah had inaugurated a reform of Judah's life, but it dealt only with the cult (II Kings 18.3ff.). Indeed, Micah's audience rejected his charges of sin and judgment with a righteous confidence in themselves and YHWH which could have been nurtured by the reforms (2.6f.; 3.11). They were certain that YHWH would allow no evil to come upon them. But Micah knew they were sinners. He did not share their faith that YHWH was in their midst because he had chosen Zion. He viewed them and his times with a consciousness apparently untouched by the religious traditions which prevailed in the temple and court of Jerusalem. Like Amos and Hosea he was from the villages where the old traditions of YHWH and the tribal league continued to inform the faith of those who were loyal to YHWH.

The Mission of Micah

The basic clue to Micah's understanding of his role and to the foundation of his proclamation is the correspondence between the purpose of YHWH's imminent intervention in history (1.5a) and the commission he received through his endowment with special powers by God (3.8). He was the herald who announced that YHWH was about to come down from his place to deal with Jacob's crime; he was the interpreter who identified what that crime was and declared it to Israel. All his oracles of judgment (2.1–5; 3.1–4, 5–7, 9–12) were spoken in carrying out that commission. In them he identified the sinners and their sin and announced what the consequences of YHWH's intervention would be for the sinners.

Micah's statement about his vocation gives no information about its place in his personal history. The statement is not a report about the past, but a claim attached to an oracle against prophets who mislead the people (3.5–7). The claim simply asserts that he is the recipient of a special charisma which equips and authorizes him to say what he is saying. But his consciousness of the endowment must have been created in some experience which inaugurated his mission and was similar to the experiences reported in the stories of the call of prophets like Isaiah, Amos, and Jeremiah. That experience must have had an intimate connection with the dawning of the conviction that

YHWH was about to intervene in the affairs of Israel. His announcement that YHWH was coming is expressed in the form and language
which was traditional for speaking of a theophany in which YHWH
enters the course of historical events to deal with his enemies. But
Micah knew, not only that YHWH was about to appear, but that his
wrath this time would be directed against the sinners in Israel.That
knowledge was an integral dimension of his experience of vocation,
because it was on the basis of this awareness that he announced the
inescapable punishment that would come on the sinners in Israel,
defended his vocation with vehement resolution against the opposition
of his audience (2.6–11), set his conviction against the faith and theology of civic and religious leaders (2.7; 3.5, 11), and even proclaimed
the end of Jerusalem (3.12). This combination of knowledge and
endowment could lie behind a peculiarity in the style of Micah. There
is only one line in his sayings where he uses the divine first-person
style and speaks the very words of YHWH (2.3; see the comment on
3.5). The rest are formulated as his own words. Though he does not
speak for himself, he is the spokesman. He is less the messenger and
more the representative, a style which could be the expression of an
understanding that the assignment to declare Israel's sin had been
given into his hands.

Micah lists three capacities given (or evoked?) in the divine endowment. Two, might and power, are quite similar in effect and
belong to the physical and psychological ability to do what he had to
do. The other gift, justice, is of a different order. It is specifically
cognitive and social. It involves a knowledge of a tradition about
what is right in the legal and economic and civil process. Endowment
with justice (*mišpāṭ*) must have meant a focus of all Micah's personal
concern and conviction on the tradition, and an elevated capacity to
grasp and articulate its critical meaning for the society he observed.
In two of his four oracles of judgment the term appears as the primary
norm of indictment (3.1, 9). In his other sayings he employed normative terms which serve as synonyms and antonyms of justice. In so far
as it is possible for one notion to be the central critical factor in a
prophet's consciousness and speech, *mišpāṭ* was that notion for Micah.

Micah's announcements of judgment are composed on the structure which is characteristic of the type as a prophetic saying. They
have two primary components, an indictment or indication of wrong-
doing and a proclamation of punishment. The structure is developed
in a pattern which can serve as an outline of his message.

The sayings begin with an identification of those to whom they are
spoken. The addressees are always a particular group, and never the

corporate nation. 3.1 and 9 name the heads of Jacob and leaders of Israel. They are the successors to heads or chiefs of clans who were responsible for the local administration of justice, the officials of the monarchy who now carried out the policy set in Jerusalem (see the comment on 3.1). 2.1 characterizes instead of naming, but these men who dream up wickedness at night because power to do what they want lies with them are undoubtedly the same class of officials. In 3.11 priests and prophets are grouped with the civil leaders and 3.5–7 is addressed to certain prophets. The basis for including these priests and prophets with the leaders is economic; they are accessories in Jerusalem to the corruption of the right order of things in Israel. Though the corporate names, (house of) Jacob and (house of) Israel, are used for the people whose crime Micah is to declare (3.8), his sayings in execution of that commission particularize. Both indictments and punishments concern the leaders of the nation. Micah speaks of his audience in Jerusalem with the traditional names Jacob and Israel as a way of symbolizing the identity in which they are addressed. He sees the officials as leaders responsible to the ethos and tradition of the patriarchal heritage and the tribal league. Micah mentions the king once and then only in passing (1.14); his sayings never refer to the existence of the monarchy. He may well have regarded the king as no more than one of the heads of Israel and included him in the general category; surely some of the deeds attributed to the heads could not have been carried out apart from royal policy (e.g. 3.10).

The indictments begin with a general characterization of conduct using normative terms (2.1a; 3.1b, 2a, 5a, 9b) and then itemize specific deeds (2.2; 3.2b–3, 5b, 10f.). The pivotal criterion among the normative words is justice; the rest are words and expressions employed to describe the violation of justice: 'to pervert the straight (way)' (3.9). 'to hate good and love evil' (3.2), 'iniquity' (2.1). Such language belongs to the ethical vocabulary of Israel and is at home in general usage as well as the instructional tradition of wisdom. Its function in Micah's language is to heighten the wrongness inherent in wilful misjustice. *Mišpāṭ* itself is the tradition of values and guidelines which govern conduct in economic and social affairs and decisions of the courts of elders and heads which managed this realm of life. The focus of Micah's indictment was the wilful violation of this tradition in both conduct and courts (cf. 3.11) on the part of those who were responsible for the administration of justice.

The specific deeds listed in the indictments against the leaders concern the use of office and power for gain at the expense of the people. Land and houses were being expropriated (2.2). Families were driven out of their homes and left as terrorized and helpless as if an invader had ravaged their village (2.8f.). The greed of the leaders had become an insatiable hunger that devoured the people for whom they were responsible (3.2f.). The capital city was being built up at the cost of bloodshed and violence (3.10). In this culture fascinated with money, prophets and priests had commercialized their ministry (3.5, 11). In listing these deeds as culpable Micah did not call directly upon laws and commandments, though specific traditions about YHWH's will lay behind his indictments (see the individual comments). In all the descriptions of what the officials were doing there is a common feature; it appears in the reiteration in various ways of the theme of unrestrained self-interest. Micah's concentration on the theme assumes that leaders, prophets, and priests had by virtue of their roles a preempting obligation to YHWH. He saw and judged the officials in terms of the old ideal of Israel as a society governed and preserved by YHWH. His indictments uncovered a fundamental shift of fealty. Though they still engaged in pious talk (2.7f.; 3.11b), the officials had found another authority which ruled their actions. It was wealth. In their dedication to their new 'sovereign,' neither God nor neighbour had much chance.

The punishments which Micah announced in his oracles are closely correlated with the indictments. The punishment would fall on the particular groups who had sinned, and would correspond to the deed. The various announcements can all be seen as expressions of the formula: what you have done to others, YHWH will bring upon you. The deed will return on their own heads. YHWH plans evil against those who plan evil; the land they seized in arrogance will be stripped from them in humiliation (2.1–4). Those who devoured their helpless victims will be reduced to crying out in their helplessness (3.1–4). The prophets who sell their services will be put in a situation in which their words are worthless (3.5–7). Because of those who have built Jerusalem with violence, the city will be reduced to rubble (3.9–12). In this last saying, the punishment falls on a place instead of a group. The saying makes it clear that Micah regarded Jerusalem as the urban incarnation of the crime he was commissioned to indict. The city was the institution in whose setting official power was perverted to evil purpose. In 1.9 Micah calls Jerusalem 'the gate of my people', a phrase which means the place where the administration of justice was centred. But the city had come to be an institution of injustice, and so would disappear in the same blow of YHWH which would humiliate and discredit its wicked officials. Micah did not say what concrete historical form the evil planned by YHWH would take.

But all his descriptions of punishment point to a military crisis in which Jerusalem would be destroyed and the leadership of the country displaced. The leaders would lament to YHWH for help with no answer (3.4). The false prophets would seek a word of salvation with no answer (3.6f.). The estates of the powerful would be broken up (2.4). The lament in 1.8–15 sketches the progress of a divinely sent disaster which moves across the villages to the west of Jerusalem and reaches to Jerusalem. The invasion of Sennacherib in 701 BC was the most likely occasion for the lament and would have created the crisis Micah anticipated in his announcements.

The city of course was not destroyed by the Assyrians, and Micah's most famous and daring prophecy was not fulfilled. It must have seemed at the time that his opponents who said, 'YHWH is in our midst and no evil shall come upon us,' were vindicated (3.11). Micah's prophetic activity must have concluded with Jerusalem's escape. He had carried out his commission 'to declare to Israel his sin.' Vengeance belonged to the Lord and fulfilment of prophecy had to be left to him. But the end of Micah's career was only the beginning of what was inaugurated by the word which came to him. His sayings were remembered and cherished among the country people whose lives were most threatened by the sins he denounced. Certain elders of the land who spoke at Jeremiah's trial still cultivated the tradition of Micah. They did not think his prophecy had been invalidated, but attributed to him the repentance of King Hezekiah which gave YHWH reason to relent and spare the city. At the very time of Jeremiah's trial the prophecies of Micah were assuming a new relevance, a relevance that was sensed and articulated by those who gave his collection of sayings their first new shape for re-use.

3. THE FORMATION OF THE BOOK OF MICAH

The sayings which can be attributed to Micah with confidence are collected in chs. 1–3. They were spoken during the period of his activity in Jerusalem toward the end of the eighth century BC. The latest material in the book comes from the post-exilic period after the temple had been rebuilt (515 BC). Early in the fifth century seems a likely *terminus ad quem* for the completion of the book in its present form. During that interval the tradition of Micah's message was cherished in faith, interpreted and applied, elaborated and extended in a process which was the expression of a confidence that Micah's

words were the word of YHWH, the announcement of a divine purpose which transcended Micah's time and moved toward the establishment of YHWH's reign in the world. The profile of that confidence is the proclamation of the book as a whole.

The problem of reconstructing that process is as difficult as the
undertaking to reconstruct the history of Israel and its faith during
the period when the book was emerging.[c] The latter can be accomplished in broad outline but much detail remains uncertain.
Many questions cannot be answered, even though the biblical and
extra-biblical evidence available for reconstructing the history is
greater and firmer. The growth of the book of Micah was one current
within that larger stream of history. Its movement remains even more
opaque to the historian's view, its stages and directions more hidden.
Yet the history of the two centuries involved and the period of the
book's formation span those traumatic crucial events which brought
Israel's history in the OT period to its climax: the Assyrian invasion
of Judah, the Babylonian siege and the fall of Jerusalem, the exile,
and the restoration. These events compose the structure of Israel's
history in the period and are reflected in the range and variety of the
book. The book is in truth one chapter in the history of prophecy during those two hundred years and a sweeping prophetic vision of the
meaning and goal of that history.

The creation of the book seems to have taken place in all its phases
as a self-conscious act of prophetic work. That is to say, not only are
the units collected in the book primarily of prophetic genre, but the
discernible stages of its growth reflect an intention to maintain a
focus on the proclamation of YHWH's reign as the purpose of the
emerging whole. This sustained intention is a guide to following the
course of the book's creation. While details of sequences and procedures by which redaction occurred remain inaccessible, it is
possible to sort out the major layers of development. Each reflects a
major concern or interest appropriate to its historical setting which is
expressed in themes, motifs, and language. When the chapters have
been analysed by the techniques of form criticism and literary criticism, the units and redactional material fall into stages.

The analysis of the present form of the book shows that it is com-

---

[c] Besides the works listed above in note a, studies on the process of the formation
of the book include: T. Lescow, 'Redaktionsgeschichtliche Analyse von Micha
1–5', *ZAW* 84, 1972, pp.46–85; and 'Redaktionsgeschichtliche Analyse von
Micha 6–7', *ZAW* 84, 1972, pp.182–212; Jörg Jeremias, 'Die Deutung der Gerichtsworte Michas in der Exilszeit', *ZAW* 83, 1971, pp.330–354; Ina Willi-Plein,
Vorformen der Schriftexegese innerhalb des Alten Testaments (BZAW 123), 1971.

posed of two parts, chs. 1–5 and 6–7. Each part has its own distinctive
arrangement and purpose. It turns out that the formation of each
part can be traced on its own. The unifying linkages, motifs, and
patterns of arrangement do not run from one to the other, except for
some hints that the final redactions of both parts shared common
perspectives and used similar motifs. The two parts seemed to have
received their final shaping at the stage at which they were brought
together (see below, p. 33).

Part One: chs. 1–5

The Sayings from Micah
The creation of the book began with the arrangement and preserva-
tion of a collection of sayings spoken by Micah of Moresheth.
Chapters 1–3, apart from a few additions and a number of revisions,
represent the collection (on the critical questions involved see the
comment; the coherence and character of the material is discussed
above, pp. 13ff.). The three announcements of judgment in ch.3
(3.1–4, 5–8, 9–12) were doubtless grouped because of their formal and
thematic similarity; all three are addressed to the leaders whose
corruption invokes an appropriate punishment from YHWH. 3.9–12
comes last so that its final word against Jerusalem would be heard at
the conclusion. (Only the phrase 'with the spirit of YHWH' in v.8
and the introductory formula in v.5 have been added to the original
words.) Chapter 2 opens with another oracle of judgment against
those who build estates by oppression (2.1–5, of which vv.3–5 have
been revised), followed by a controversy saying (2.6–11, which includes a revised v.10). The two are paired to give an example of the
basic message of Micah and the strife it provoked. In ch.1, the proclamation of YHWH's appearance to deal with the sins of Israel
supplies an impressive opening (1.3–5a). The lament over the disaster
brought by Sennacherib's invasion (1.8–15, with additions in vv.12b,
13b) portrays the form which YHWH's theophany takes. Proclamation and lament may have been a rhetorical unit, or could have
been placed in sequence because of the catchwords, 'all this' and 'for
this,' appearing in vv.5a and 8.
    The collection may have had as title, 'The Word of YHWH that
came to Micah of Moresheth.' At 3.1 there is an introductory rubric,
'But I said . . .', which connects the end of the controversy saying
(2.11) with the following oracles of judgment. This simple report
form in the first person gives the oracles in ch.3 the role of stating
what kind of response Micah made to the opposition of his audience,

and is a clue to the intention to order the sayings in the collection in a
sequence which has a logical pattern. The collection begins with the
theophany of YHWH to judge Israel, identifies the historical form of
the divine appearance, addresses the sinners upon whom judgment
comes, portrays their obstinate rejection of the message of judgment,
repeats the message three times over and concludes with the prediction of Jerusalem's destruction. The collection could have been the
work of Micah himself and may well have been composed and transmitted orally.

The Use of the Micah-Collection during the Babylonian Crisis

The prophecies of Micah were not fulfilled in his time. The
Assyrians did sweep across Judah to the very gate of Jerusalem.
Doubtless the upheaval and suffering accompanying the invasion did
affect many of the guilty against whom he spoke. But the cruel economic oppression of the poor and the corrupt civil and religious
leaders did not disappear. And Jerusalem did not fall. None the less,
there were those who revered and remembered his words, and must
have believed their potential for fulfilment was not exhausted. We
hear them speak at Jeremiah's trial. They know Micah as the prophet
of Jerusalem's end, and they have an understanding of the delay in
the realization of his announcement. Hezekiah repented and YHWH
relented (Jer. 26, see especially vv. 17ff.). This appeal to Micah's prophecy at Jeremiah's trial demonstrates that Micah's words were living tradition in certain circles almost a century after he had spoken
them.

At this point Judah's history had reached a stage in which the
words of Micah became resonant with the realities of the times. The
same sins of which Micah spoke were rife. As the Babylonian crisis
deepened, the possibility that Micah's prophecies would be fulfilled
heightened. But there were also new factors at work in the environment and in the consciousness of those who preserved the Micah collection. Not least of these were the Josianic reform under deuteronomic influence, the work of Jeremiah, and the experience of a calamity
that in the fall of the city and the exile created a new insight into the
possibilities inherent in Micah's prophecy. By revision, expansion,
and additions the collection was applied to the new situation. This
're-use' of Micah's prophecy of judgment makes up the second major
stage in the formation of the book. The evidence does not point so
much to one consistent systematic literary revision, but rather to an
ongoing process whose cumulative effect was to re-set the tradition
without obscuring its original character. The process is visible in a

number of features whose style, language, and concern correlates with the period of the Babylonian crisis.

(a) The 'Samaria-Jerusalem programme'. The calamity brought by the Babylonian invasion is seen as an event which is the counterpart of Samaria's fall. The Samaria oracle (1.6–7) is composed and set immediately after 1.3–5a, to which it is linked by v. 5b. The title (1.1) is expanded to show that Micah's message of judgment concerns the entire history of judgment beginning with Samaria and ending with Jerusalem. 1.12b was inserted as a reminder that YHWH's first appearance to punish reached to Jerusalem's very gate. The first three chapters are thus turned into a prophetic drama of the history of punishment. They reveal the continuity of YHWH's purpose and show that the Assyrian and Babylonian crises define the limits of the work which YHWH came in wrath to do.

(b) The basis of punishment. In Micah's oracles, the sin to which he pointed was the activity of a specific group in the social and economic sphere. Now the indictment is broadened to include a comprehensive notion of cultic and political idolatry—the practice of pagan religion and trust in military security. The new agenda of sin is apparent in 1.5b–7, 13b; 5.10–14; and the reworking of 2.10.

(c) The nature of judgment. In line with (b) God's punishment will be corporate. Micah foresaw disaster for the groups who were guilty and the institutions they maintained. The re-working of 2.3–5, 10 expresses the new understanding that the whole people is involved. 5.10–14 was added to re-define the intent of the punishment. Where Micah's 3.9–12 looks for the end of Jerusalem, 5.10–14 sees judgment as a purge to strip away the idolatry of cult and state.

(d) The time of punishment. At several places temporal phrases are added to the language of Micah to point to a future beyond the period in which he spoke and so to locate the fulfilment of his words in the period when this prophecy is being applied (2.3f.; 3.4).

At this stage of its development the Micah collection had largely been reworked by the revision of its language at a few places, and brief expansions inserted in the sayings. Two new sayings had been added, 1.5b–7 and 5.10–13. The collection was still, indeed more than before, a revelation of YHWH's judgment upon Israel and Judah, which was understood as living prophecy as the conclusion of the drama of punishment broke on Judah. The collection probably concluded with 5.13 ('. . . and you shall never bow down again to the work of your hands'). That sentence as a final statement of YHWH's intention was threatening, but it also opened on a future in which a people purged and purified would be freed from idolatry to worship YHWH alone.

The exilic prophecy of salvation for Zion

Except for 5.10–13 (with its two expansions in vv. 14f.), chs. 4–5 are a collection of oracles of salvation assembled to form the counterpart of the prophecies of judgment in chs. 1–3. The collection appears to have developed in two major stages. The first resulted in the complex 4.8–5.4 (minus 4.13; 5.3). The complex is identifiable by style, theme, and pattern of arrangement. The entire complex is composed in the style of direct address to Zion as place or population. The theme is the restoration of Zion to its role as the historical locus of YHWH's reign. There are three units which begin with an introductory 'now,' address the population personified as the feminine 'daughter of Zion' in a situation of distress, and promise the help of YHWH (4.9f.; 4.11f.; 5.1f., 4). 4.8 is addressed to the place where Zion stands, using masculine names; it introduces the complex with a basic promise which states the theme of the whole, the restoration of the former dominion of Zion. 5.2, 4 is similar in type to 4.8, a promise of restoration addressed to a place (masc.). It plays a double role, serving both as the promise which relieves the distress described in 5.1 and as a concluding counterpart where the type and style reverts to that of the introduction. The complex can be heard as a whole. It announces the restoration of Zion's former dominion (4.8) and then unfolds a vision of the way in which YHWH will fulfil the promise. The daughter of Zion must go to Babylon, but YHWH will rescue her from there (vv. 9f.). Though she is surrounded by hostile nations, they have been gathered by YHWH for judgment (vv. 11f.). Though her king has been humiliated, YHWH will raise up another ruler whose reign will bring Zion everlasting security (5.1f., 4). In the reign of that ruler YHWH's kingship will be manifest to the ends of the earth. The complex was probably assembled originally as an oral compilation of salvation prophecy for use in the small exilic community left in Jerusalem at times when they worshipped at the ruined sanctuary. All parts of the complex reflect the exilic situation; the travail of the fall of the city is fresh in the language of the sayings, but no restoration or rescue has yet occurred.

Indeed, some elements of the complex seem to reflect the humiliation of the last days of Jerusalem's anguish so directly, that they may have existed as independent doleful taunts (4.9–10ab; 5.1; 1.16 must have been inserted in the process of assimilating such elements; its style of feminine imperatives and its theme are similar). They have been filled out and equipped with promises appropriate to the distress they express. Perhaps 4.11f., a saying which undoubtedly was an original unit, furnished the model. 5.2, 4 with its promise to Bethlehem Ephratha would also have been an independent unit, juxtaposed to 5.1 to fill out the pattern (see the comment on the parts of the complex for discussion of all these possibilities).

The complex was joined to the revised Micah collection as a way of showing that the drama of judgment it unfolds does not exhaust YHWH's purpose with Israel. The election of Zion to be the place where God's reign is manifest on earth will be fulfilled. The judgment is not rejected or ignored. Its suffering is incorporated in each of the three larger units as a fact which determines the present. The confident promises express the trust that YHWH will resume his former way with the daughter of Zion by redeeming, protecting, and raising up a ruler who will be the shepherd of Israel to keep them in the strength which comes from God. The primary theological traditions which shape and inform the prophetic complex are the election of Zion and David.

Perhaps at this stage of the formation of the book 5.10–13 stood immediately after 3.9–12. Then 4.8 would make a stirring sequel to '. . . you shall bow down no more to the work of your hands'. The complex addressed to a people under judgment then raises a vision of the way the site of the old Zion would become the centre of a marvellous new history of renewal. 5.4 would make an appropriate conclusion to the new shape of the collection.

YHWH and the Nations

The last stage of the formation of chs. 1–5 reflects a concentration on the relation between YHWH and the peoples or nations, and, as an aspect of that concern, on Israel in the midst of the peoples. An intense interest in universal history enters the developing prophecy which began with Micah. The first two stages dealt with YHWH's judgment upon Israel and Judah, Samaria and Jerusalem. The third announced the restoration of Zion's former dominion. Now the prophetic vision of the growing corpus is expanded to address the question of the relation between that drama of judgment and restoration and the rest of the world.

The remainder of the material in these chapters is marked by this interest. The theme of the 'nations/peoples' is stated directly or indirectly. The theme of the remnant (the scattered remnant of Israel among the nations, or the remnant Israel living in the midst of the peoples) overlaps and accompanies the first theme. The material includes independent sayings collected because they feature these themes and additions which belong to the redactional work of fitting the sayings into their present literary context. (*a*) Sayings featuring nations/peoples: 4.1–4 with its liturgical response, v.5; 5.5f. ('Assyria' is a type of the nations who threaten Israel); 5.7 and 8; 4.13, a prophetic summons to battle which has been attached to 4.11f., by the catch-word 'thresh'. (*b*) Redactional strands featuring the same theme: 1.2 and 5.15. (*c*) Sayings featuring the remnant: 2.12; 4.6–7a; 5.7 and 8. (*d*) Redactional settings related to (*c*): 2.13; 4.7b; 5.3 (an apologetic insertion in 5.1–4 to co-ordinate the appearance of the new ruler with the return of the scattered remnant); 5.9 (to link vv. 10ff. to v.8).

The sayings are the oracles of prophets spoken during the late exilic and post-exilic periods. Their collection and arrangement as part of the book of Micah would have occurred sometime after 515 BC. 4.1–4 probably assumes the existence of the second temple, and 1.2 certainly does. As a group the oracles are quite various in outlook and presumably in historical setting. Note the contrast in the attitude toward the peoples in 4.1–4; 4.13; and 5.8. The way in which the term 'remnant' is used shifts: Israel is left a remnant (2.12), the scattered will be made the remnant (4.7), the remnant lives invunerable in the midst of many peoples (5.8). Yet this various material has been arranged and at places revised to integrate it into the movement of chs. 1–5 so that it can be read and heard within the witness with which YHWH confronts the nations (1.2).

Simply by placing the general summons to all the peoples of earth to hear YHWH's witness against them (1.2), chs. 1–3 are turned into prophecy to the nations; YHWH's judgment of Samaria and Jerusalem is the first part of the witness that he is King and his kingdom is coming. 2.12f. was inserted between 2.11 and 3.1 to show that it was YHWH himself who breached the walls of Jerusalem and led the remnant away. An oracle promising rescue to the remnant (v. 12) has been converted into a saying of judgment by the addition of v. 13 for this purpose (see the comment).

In chs.4–5, two blocks of material (4.1–7 and 5.5–8) have been set around the complex 4.8–5.4 so that they form its introduction and conclusion and become its literary setting. The blocks feature the introductory rubric *wᵉhāyāh* ('and it shall come to pass . . .'; 4.1; 5.5. 7, 8, 10). The introductory words of 4.1 state the temporal point obvious about all the events announced in chs.4–5; they will occur 'in the latter days', the time which is not yet, the future of the full manifestation of YHWH's kingship in the midst of the world.

4.1–4 with the liturgical response (v. 5) is set at the beginning as
YHWH's other word about Zion, the counterpart of 3.12. YHWH's
reign on Mount Zion will be recognized by all the peoples and his
royal decisions will create universal peace. 4.6–7a is YHWH's
announcement of what he will do for the congregation which asserts
its loyalty in v. 5. The introductory formula ('in that day, an oracle of
YHWH . . .') refers back to the time of 4.1 and connects 4.6–7a with
the time of YHWH's reign from Zion (cf. the formula used again in
this way at 5.10). YHWH will make those whom he afflicted into a
strong nation (cf. 4.3!), a promise which is the basic theme of 5.5–8.
4.7b has been added to the remnant saying (cf. 2.13 as expansion of
2.12) to identify this transformed remnant as the true and everlasting constituency of YHWH's reign on Mount Zion. It also serves
as a transition to the following complex 4.8–5.4 which as sequel now
portrays the acts by which YHWH's reign over Zion will be restored.
4.13 states both themes of the redaction: Israel's strength against the
peoples and YHWH's world-wide reign. It has been attached to 4.11f.
because its address to the daughter of Zion fits the style of the complex and because the catchword 'thresh' makes it an appropriate
sequel to v. 12. On the insertion of v. 3 in 5.1–4, see the comment.

All three sayings in 5.5–8 express the theme of the remnant made
strong among the peoples. 5.5f. has been revised so that it could be
attached to 5.1–4; the opening 'And this (one) shall be peace . . .' probably is intended to identify the coming ruler of v. 4 as the one whose
power will prevail over 'Assyria'. 5.9 was composed as a transition to
5.10ff., using its thematic motif 'cut off'. In the redaction, the formula
already used in 4.6 is employed to introduce 5.10ff. as the final saying
of the revision. It was probably displaced from a position just after
3.12 by 4.1–4. Now it stands as the concluding word of YHWH concerning the abominations which will not be permitted in his reign
over Israel, and the world! Verse 15 turns the threat of vv. 10–14
against the nations who do not heed his witness laid down in all of
chs. 1–5. It is the final contribution of the redactors who see in the
prophetic document they are completing the revelation of YHWH's
movement toward dominion over all the world.

Part Two: chapters 6–7

The analysis in the comment reaches the conclusion that chs. 6–7 are
composed of eight originally independent units (6.2–5, 6–8, 9b–15;
7.1–6, 8–10, 11f., 14–17, 18–20). The units represent a selection of
various types of sayings of which only three are distinctly prophetic in
genre (6.2–5, 9b–15, and 7.11f.). It is possible to infer the general

period in which some were composed; others are more difficult to
locate in a particular historical context.

There is general agreement in recent study that the four pieces in
7.8–20 could not have come from the prophet Micah because they all
point to circumstances after the fall of Jerusalem in the late exilic and
post-exilic history of Judah. (See the special introduction to 7.7–20
on pp. 152ff.) 7.8–10 is a song of trust sung by personified Jerusalem
when she is under the power of an unidentified foe. 7.11f. is an oracle
of salvation addressed to Jerusalem, promising a day when her walls
will be rebuilt and her population returned. 7.14–17 is a lament of
the congregation appealing for an intervention of YHWH to restore
Israel's territory by deeds that will put the nations in awe of him.
7.18–20 is a congregational hymn of praise to YHWH who will keep
his oath to the fathers and triumph over the congregation's sins in
victorious forgiveness.

It is much more difficult to assign the material in 6.1–7.6 to
historical settings. 6.2–5 is a covenant lawsuit speech in which YHWH
vindicates himself against a complaint of Israel. 6.6–8 is a *tōrāh* exchange which deals with the question of the way in which a sinner
can put himself right with God. 6.9b–15 has the form of an announcement of judgment by YHWH. 7.1–6 is a lament in evil times sung by
one of the pious faithful. None of these units contain overt clues which
demand any one of several possible historical backgrounds. Decisions
about the most probable setting have to be made on the basis of
language and content and the relations which can be discerned between them and other literature as well as the known course of
Israel's history.

There is a kind of general continuity between the sayings of Micah
in chs. 1–3 and these units, especially the first three. The sovereign
claim of Yahweh upon Israel, the demand for obedience to moral
norms, and the proclamation of judgment for violation of these norms
are common to both. Of course, such themes are common to most
prophecy. On these grounds all of the first four units have been assigned by some critics to Micah. But in specific language, stance and
style, these units are unlike the sayings which can be claimed for
Micah with high probability. Moreover, they contain features, discussed in the comment, which point to a period later than that of
Micah. 6.2–5 is addressed to an Israel that is weary with YHWH's
way and contains language that is characteristically deuteronomic;
the saying was probably composed in the late pre-exilic or exilic
period. 6.6–8 looks back on the prophetic insistence on justice and
loyalty as a revelation which has long since settled the question of

what Yahweh requires. The lament in 7.1–6 expresses the anguish of a *ḥāsîd* (faithful man) at circumstances which are probably those of the late exilic or post-exilic community. 6.9b–15 are best assigned to the very end of the pre-exilic era. The units thus represent a range of time that could run from the last years of Judah before the fall of Babylon down into the first decades of the fifth century.

The work of those who selected and arranged these sayings to create chs. 6–7 is apparent in sentences and phrases in the chapters which must belong to that process itself, because they serve to organize the larger complex by introducing, linking, and elaborating.

6.1a is an introductory summons to the entire sequence.

6.1b calls for and anticipates the response of Israel (vv. 6f.) to Yahweh's *rîb*-saying (vv. 2–5), and so provides a sequential continuity for vv. 2–5 and vv. 6–8.

6.9a is composed of a formula introducing a divine saying to 'the city' and a reverent observation addressed to Yahweh. The latter probably was an addition to the completed literary form of the book. The former picks up 'city' as addressee from the summons to hear (v. 9b) and introduces the exchange between Yahweh and the 'city' which takes place in 6.10–7.12.

6.16 expands the preceding announcement of judgment. First, it adds the accusation against the city that its inhabitants have followed the ways of Omri and Ahab, and so accuses them of apostasy. It also describes a judgment of humiliation before the people of the world which has echoes in 7.13 and 7.14–17 where the concern with the nations as the context of salvation and the extension of judgment to them comes into play.

7.7 unites the lament (7.1–6) and the song of confidence (vv. 8–10) and identifies the speaker in the lament as the feminine personification of the city who speaks in the song.

7.13 expands the oracle of salvation to the city (vv. 11f.) with an announcement of judgment upon the whole earth and makes the transition to the congregational prayer for Yahweh to exalt himself against the nations.

7.17b contains a phrase 'unto Yahweh our God', which states the confessional identity of the deity to whom the following hymn is addressed.

There are, then, redactional components scattered throughout the entire collection which link and interpret the individual units. It appears that the collection formed through their use emerged in two major phases.

There is an inner block of material organized by the theme of 'the

city', 6.9–15; 7.1–12. The song of confidence sung against a particular
enemy (7.8–10) and the oracle of salvation (vv. 11f.) both feature the
feminine personification of the city. These units are not linked by any
redactional connection. The genre of this smallest complex suggests
it had a setting in the cult of the destroyed Jerusalem, perhaps in the
early post-exilic years of harassment by Edom. 7.7 was composed in
the style of the song of confidence and used to attach 7.1–6, making
this lament in the first person continuous with the style of the song,
so that the feminine figure of the song becomes the one who laments.
The announcement of judgment (6.9b–15) was set in the beginning
of the complex and equipped with v. 9a ('Hark! Yahweh cries to the
city') as an introduction to the whole. The result is a sequence whose
first and final units are messages from Yahweh; it begins with judgment and ends with salvation. Between the divine speeches is a
response of the personified city which begins with lament at its human
helplessness and turns to reliance on the salvation of Yahweh after
she shall have undergone his punishment. The organizing pattern of
the movement which gives coherence to the final form of chs. 6–7 is already present in this first complex. The sequence could have been
used liturgically with speakers representing God and city in the cult
of the early post-exilic period in Jerusalem. Twice, the language used
to speak of the punishment upon the population can be read as a
description of disasters and disorder whose effects continue at the
period of composition (6.13–15; 7.4b). The composition creates a
balance of judgment and salvation within the scope of an expanded
perspective. To the original focus of 7.8–12 on a present of suffering
which is to be relieved by salvation in the future is added a background of judgment and lament which show the nature of the sin for
which Jerusalem suffers and how the suffering leaves her cast on
Yahweh alone.

The second major phase of the formation of chs. 6–7 was accomplished by setting the rest of the material around the first composition
to create the second part of the book of Micah. The format of an
alternation of divine and human voices between Yahweh and the
city was already established. That format was extended by adding
another exchange at the beginning. This compiler may have thought
that a lawsuit saying by Yahweh (6.2–5) was an appropriate introduction to the exchange; the theme of *rīb* (controversy) was already
present at 7.9. By adding 6.1b, the response of the human partner in
6.6f. is prepared for and the entire following dialogue interpreted as
part of the *rīb*.

At the end the congregational prayer for salvation (7.14–17) and the hymn of praise (vv. 18–20) were added. Verse 13 was composed to make the transition between the oracle of salvation (vv. 11f.) and the prayer; its concern with the whole earth prepares for the prayer's petition that Yahweh vindicate himself before the nations. By its addition the oracle now speaks of both the salvation of the city (vv. 11f.) and the judgment of the earth (v. 13) and so contains both movements of the attached petition, prayer for salvation of Yahweh's flock (vv. 14f.) and for the humiliation of the nations (vv. 16f.). In v. 17 the compiler inserted the phrase 'to YHWH our God' to identify clearly the one to whom praise is addressed in the hymn. The hymn supplied an explicit theological basis for the hope that YHWH will move from judgment to salvation.

6.16 contains features which belong to the interests of the final redactor. The verse places Israel's punishment by God in the context of the peoples and describes it with motifs of the judgment which shall come upon the nations in the course of YHWH's future salvation of his people. Just as the city and its inhabitants have been made desolate (šammāh) because of their acts, the whole world will be made desolate (šᵉmāmāh) because of their deeds. This interest in the world setting of YHWH's history of judgment and salvation is a feature of the compilation of ch. 1–5, where the future of Jerusalem in the midst of the peoples is a major concern. The redactor prefers 'peoples' to 'nations,' a term which appears in the unit he had at hand (7.15), a preference which is a characteristic of the final stage of chs. 1–5. Also, the use of 'mountains/hills' in 6.1b instead of the pair 'mountains/foundations of the earth' present in 6.2 may echo the influence of the first pair in 4.1. The concern to connect the judgment of Jerusalem with that of Samaria by introducing a connection with Omri and Ahab (6.16) could be related to the 'Samaria-Jerusalem programme' expressed in the redaction of ch. 1–5. And of course the selection of the block which features 'the city' means that chs. 6–7 like 1–5 are, though in a more subdued way, Jerusalem prophecy.

All these clues suggest that ch. 6–7 were given their final shape by the same concerns which shaped chs. 1–5. They are literary compilations designed to expand and complete the book of Micah.

BIBLIOGRAPHY

COMMENTARIES IN SERIES

K. Marti, 1904 (KHC)
J. M. P. Smith, 1911 (ICC)
H. Schmidt, 1923² (SAT II/2)
W. Nowack, 1922³ (HK III/4)
E. Sellin, 1929³ (KAT XII/1)
T. H. Robinson, 1954² (HAT 14)
R. E. Wolfe, 1956 (IB VI)
A. Weiser, 1959³ (ATD 24/1)
R. Vuilleumier, 1971 (CAT XI/b)

INDIVIDUAL COMMENTARIES AND BOOKS

W. Beyerlin, *Die Kulttraditionen Israels in der Verkündigung des Propheten Micah* (FRLANT) 72), 1959

B. A. Copas and E. L. Carlson, *A Study of the Prophet Micah*, 1950

J. Lindblom, *Micha literarisch untersucht*, 1929

B. Renaud, *Structure et attaches littéraires de Michée IV–V*, 1964

S. J. Schwantes, *A Critical Study of the Text of Micah* (unpublished dissertation, Dept. of Religion, John Hopkins University), 1962

G. A. Smith, *The Book of the Twelve Prophets* Vol. 1, rev. ed. 1928

J. Wellhausen, *Die kleinen Propheten* (Skizzen und Vorarbeiten V), 1893

Ina Willi-Plein, *Vorformen der Schriftexegese innerhalb des Alten Testaments* (BZAW 123), 1971

ARTICLES

H. Gunkel, 'The Close of Micah. A Prophetical Liturgy' in *What Remains of the Old Testament*, 1928, pp. 115–149

A. Jepsen, 'Kleine Beiträge zum Zwölfprophetenbuch 2', *ZAW* 56, 1938, pp. 96ff.

E. Hammershaimb, 'Einige Hauptgedanken in der Schrift des Propheten Micha', *ST* 15, 1961, pp. 11ff.

Jörg Jeremias, 'Die Deutung der Gerichtsworte Michas in der Exilszeit', *ZAW* 83, 1971, pp. 330ff.

A. Kapelrud, 'Eschatology in the Book of Micah', *VT* 11, 1961, pp. 392ff.

T. Lescow, 'Redaktionsgeschichtliche Analyse von Micha 1–5', *ZAW* 84, 1972, pp. 46ff.

—'Redaktionsgeschichtliche Analyse von Micha 6–7', *ZAW* 84, 1972, pp. 182ff.

L. P. Smith, 'The Book of Micah', *Int* 6, 1952, pp. 210ff.

J. T. Willis, 'The Structure of the Book of Micah', *Svensk Exegetisk Årsbok* 34, 1969, pp. 5ff.

II

COMMENTARY

1. THE TITLE: 1.1

1 The word of YHWH which came to Micah the Moreshite in the days of Jotham, Ahaz, and Hezekiah, kings of Judah, which he saw concerning Samaria and Jerusalem.

The title informs the reader that the book which it introduces contains YHWH's word, by whom the word was spoken, when, and whom it concerned. The title is composed of three elements which appear in various arrangements in the titles of other prophetic books: (*a*) 'the word of YHWH which came to . . .' (Hosea; Joel, Zephaniah, Malachi, see also Jeremiah, Jonah, Haggai, Zechariah), (*b*) 'in the days of . . .' (Isaiah, Hosea, Amos, Zephaniah, see Jer. 1.2f.), (*c*) 'concerning . . .' (Isa. 1.1; 2.1; Amos). The common presence of these elements in superscriptions shows that they belong to the genre of the book, not the prophets' words, and are contributions of those who preserved and transmitted the collections.[a]

The first element indicates what the tradents regarded as the most important fact about the collection. The primary title is 'the word of YHWH'; all else in the verse is subordinate to that identification. It is God's word which the book contains and provides. The formula, 'the word of YHWH came to . . .' appears first in narratives about prophets from the time of the early monarchy which must have been cultivated and passed on by prophetic groups (I Sam. 15.10; II Sam. 7.4; 24.11; I Kings 12.22; 13.20; 17.2, 8; etc.). Though it was not used by the earlier canonical prophets in their sayings, it reappears in

---

[a] See, among others, the discussion by W. Rudolph, *Hosea* (KAT XIII/I), 1966, pp. 35ff.; H. Wildberger, *Jesaja* (BK X/I), 1969, pp. 88ff.

titles like this one.[b] The formula is the expression of a specific theology of the word. The word occurs as event; it comes, happens.
It transcends the existence and experience of its spokesman, and has
an independent self-contained reality and a power to actualize itself.
Yet it is not a generality or a supra-historical entity. It takes form
through a particular individual at specific times and for a special
purpose. The title claims that the entire book is the result of the event
of the word of YHWH.

The man to whom the word came was Micah (*mīkāh*); he is
spoken of elsewhere only in Jer. 26.18 (where the *kᵉtīb* is *mīkāyāh*).
Both times he is identified by the epithet 'the Moreshite'; he was
known by the town from which he came. The town Moreshah is
likely the Moresheth of Gath mentioned in 1.14, some twenty-five
miles south-west of Jerusalem (see the comment on 1.14, and the
Introduction, pp. 15f.).

It is possible that element (*a*) was set at the beginning of the earliest
collection of Micah's sayings as a double signature to identify the
tradition as both YHWH's word and Micah's words. The other two
elements stem from the circles of the late seventh century into whose
hands the collection came. The list of the kings of Judah during
whose reigns Micah is said to have prophesied is identical with the
list used to date Hosea and Isaiah (where Uzziah is added because of
Isa. 6.1). This dating allows a maximum span of some forty-six years
for Micah's career. He is also said to have prophesied concerning
Samaria as well as Jerusalem. This rather long period and the limiting designation of the subject of his prophecy do not correspond to
the character of the sayings which can be attributed to Micah with
any degree of certainty. The one oracle against Samaria in the book
(1.6f.) appears to have been composed and set in its place as part of
the first major redaction of the Micah tradition toward the end of
the seventh century when his prophecy was being applied to the
circumstances leading up to the fall of Jerusalem. Both the dating
and the description of the subject of his prophecy are features of the
'Samaria-Jerusalem programme' conceived by the tradents to
portray YHWH's judgment on Israel and Judah as one unified action
of God (see the introduction to 1.2–16 below). The dating creates an
amply long context for the Samaria oracle before 722 BC 'Concerning
Samaria and Jerusalem' corresponds to the first and last oracles of
judgment in the present arrangement of chs. 1–3 (1.6f.; 3.9–12).

b W. Zimmerli, *Ezechiel* (BK XIII/I), 1969, pp. 88ff.

2. CAPITAL PUNISHMENT FOR THE CAPITAL CITIES: 1.2–16

In its final form, 1.2–16 is a complex of sayings designed to introduce chs. 1–5 of the book of Micah. The complex as a whole has a
purpose within the larger literary context which can be obscured if it
is interpreted only by an examination of its components. The section
should be read both as a resultant unity as well as a collection of
smaller units. (On the plan of the book as a whole and the role of
1.2–16, see the Introduction, pp. 2ff.)

The section unfolds in four movements discernible by style and
content: v. 2, a summons to all the peoples of earth to hear YHWH's
witness against them; vv. 3–5, the proclamation of the coming of
YHWH in cataclysmic majesty to deal with the sin of Jacob-Israel
which lies in the cities of Samaria and Jerusalem; vv. 6–8, the
announcement of Samaria's destruction; vv. 9–16, a lament describ-
ing a disaster which moves across Judah, engulfing many of its towns
and reaching to the gate of Jerusalem. The thematic continuity of
vv. 3–16 is apparent. YHWH comes to punish Samaria and Jerusalem;
the punishment of Samaria is described; punishing disaster stands at
the gate of Jerusalem. The imminent threatening but uncompleted
work of YHWH on Jerusalem opens on the next two chapters; the
completed punishment is described in 3.9–12. So vv. 3–16 composes
the first and organizing movement of an arrangement which reaches
its first climax at the end of ch. 3. It reflects the Samaria-Jerusalem
conception of Micah's prophecy expressed in the title (1.1). Verse 2, on
the other hand, points forward to chs. 4–5. The summons is addressed
to all the peoples of earth to hear a witness against them. It is in
chs. 4–5 that a concern with peoples and nations reappears. There
they furnish the context in which YHWH establishes his reign on earth
through the salvation of Jerusalem and rescue of his people. So the
function of v. 2 is to set the entire course of YHWH's way with Jerusalem in a universal setting as a message to all the peoples of earth.

Beyond this overall pattern and purpose, 1.2–16 is held together
by a number of integrating links. Verse 3 is connected to v. 2 by the
conjunction 'for', making YHWH's coming the occasion for the
summons to all peoples. 'All this' in v. 4 is resumed by 'for this' in
v. 8, relating vv. 8–16 back to v. 5 across the intervening Samaria
saying. Verse 12b echoes a theme of the theophany from v. 3 and
applies it to Jerusalem. Verse 13b employs the crime/sin vocabulary
of v. 5a. The most important of unifying features is the shift which
occurs in the names in v. 5. 'Jacob' is understood to mean the country

of which Samaria is the capital. 'House of Israel' is changed to 'Judah' of which Jerusalem is capital. This transition in v.5 is the seam which organizes and holds the chapter together.

The pattern of relations between ch.1 and the rest of the book suggests by itself that this opening complex is the achievement of those who arranged and redacted the book. But conclusions about the literary analysis of the materials and the origin of its components have varied, with differences about the number and limits of the sayings included, their origin and historical setting, and redaction.[a] The text is divided for comment into the sections suggested by the present arrangement. At one point this division conflicts with a widely held conclusion that v.9 is the end of one saying and v.10 is the beginning of another. But the clear intention of v.5 is to anticipate sayings which deal with both Samaria and Judah-Jerusalem, and there can be little doubt that vv. 8f. broach the latter theme.

The formation of ch.1 is a work of theological synthesis of considerable magnitude. It takes prophecies which deal with two separate crucial events in the history of Israel and Judah and makes them part of one continuous drama whose inner meaning is revealed in the introductory proclamation of a theophany. The fall of Samaria to the Assyrians in 722/21 BC and Sennacherib's invasion of Judah in 701 BC are merged into one panorama of judgment which takes place in the course of YHWH's intervention because of their sin. That panorama furnishes the setting in which the sayings in ch.2 and 3 are to be heard and reaches its climax in the prophecy of Jerusalem's destruction (3.9–12). Verse 2 presents the entire drama as a witness of the Lord, YHWH, against the nations, for it manifests to them the power by which he will fulfil in their midst the unfinished work of establishing his reign (ch.4–5). The redaction turns individual prophecies dealing with particular acts of YHWH into a larger prophecy in another key which speaks of the whole strategy of the God who comes.

3. LET THE WORLD HEAR THE WITNESS OF THE LORD: 1.2

2 Hear, O peoples, every one;
　　listen, O earth, and all who are in it;

[a] For studies of ch. 1 and its problems, see G. Fohrer, 'Micha 1' in *Das Ferne und Nahe Wort*, Festschrift L. Rost, 1967, pp.65–80; T. Lescow, *ZAW* 84, 1972, pp.54–61, 70, 82–84. Fohrer includes a survey of the problems and positions which have been taken.

that Lord[a] YHWH may be a witness against you,
the Lord from his holy palace.

At the very beginning of the book all the peoples of earth are
summoned to hear YHWH witness against them from his holy palace.
This opening cry sets the scene and creates the context in which the
following prophecy is to be understood. Like the summons which
introduces the second part of the book (6.1f.), this call convenes a
judicial process. 6.1f. announces YHWH's case against his people, but
here it is the whole population of the earth that is drawn into judgment. YHWH sits as King of the earth in his holy palace to hold court,
and the affairs he adjudicates concern everyone. He bears the title
'Lord' (*'adōnāy*), the one who is superior and to whom everyone else
is servant. 'Earth, and all who are in it', a favourite phrase of hymnic
language (Deut. 33.16; Isa. 34.1; Pss. 24.1; 50.12; 89.12), is used in
praise of YHWH as creator and owner of the earth. He officiates in
'his holy palace' (*hēkāl qādōš*), the royal residence sanctified by his
presence. In Ps. 11.4 the phrase designates the heavenly palace where
YHWH sits in judgment over men on earth. Elsewhere it is used of the
Jerusalem temple, usually as the centre toward which Israel's prayer
and devotion is directed (Pss. 5.8; 65.5; 138.2; Jonah 2.5, 8; cf. Ps.
79.11). The latter is its reference here (cf. 4.1–4). YHWH's role as
witness shows that the convocation is judicial in character. Where
YHWH is 'witness against', he acts both as giver of evidence and
accuser (Jer. 29.33; Mal. 3.5; cf. also Ps. 50.7; I Sam. 12.5). That the
Lord of all the earth is also Judge goes without saying.

Verse 2 was inserted between the title and the following theophany
announcement by the redactor whose concern with people and
nations as a feature of Israel's future under YHWH is so evident in
chs. 4–5. Nothing more is heard of the universal audience addressed
here until the eschatological sayings of chs. 4–5 in which 'peoples/
nations' are a recurrent theme (4.1, 2, 3, 5, 7, 11, 13; 5.7f., 15; also
in 7.16 and 6.16 as emended). A summons of two parallel cola calling
upon an audience to hear a saying, announcement, or discourse is
common in prophetic, didactic, and liturgical literature. But a
summons to all peoples based on the way YHWH's reign will affect
them is not present in prophetic literature before Jer. 31.10 and Isa.
34.1 (cf. Ps. 49.1). As noted above, much of the vocabulary of vd. 2 is
psalmic, pointing to a liturgical setting and function for its composition. The composer thinks of the entire sequence of sayings in chs. 1–5
as YHWH's witness against the peoples of earth. There it is revealed

---

[a] 'Lord' lengthens the metre; *'adōnāy* is an added qere for YHWH.

how YHWH judges his own people and will restore them in a process of judging the nations—all as the manifestation of his rule as Lord of the earth. 4.1–4 shows what blessing can come to the nations who heed the call to hear. 5.15 threatens YHWH's vengeance against those who do not hear, and is a redactional counterpart to v.2 by which the witness is concluded. The summons has been connected to the following theophany (vv. 3f.) by the conjunction 'for' making it the occasion of the summons. In the classic portrayal of a theophany in II Sam. 22.7=Ps. 18.7 (cf. Isa. 18.4; 63.15; 66.1) YHWH comes from his heavenly *hēkāl*. The juxtaposition of v.2 and vv. 3f. set Jerusalem temple and heavenly palace in functional identity. The witness who speaks from the temple by this prophecy to announce his coming reign over earth is the one whose awesome intervention from above will shatter earth with his majesty. In the faith of the redactor the purpose of YHWH's coming is still being worked out, and the prophecy he introduces is still on the way to fulfilment.

4. THE COMING OF THE LORD: 1.3–5

> 3 For, see! YHWH comes forth from his place;
>   he descends and treads upon the heights of earth.
> 4 Mountains dissolve under him,
>   and valleys split,
>   like wax before fire,
>   like water spilling down a slope.
> 5a For the crime of Jacob is all this,
>   for the sins[a] of the house of Israel.
> 5b What is the crime of Jacob?
>   Is it not Samaria?
>   And what are the high places of Judah?
>   Are they not Jerusalem?

This solemn proclamation announces that YHWH is coming to earth in awful majesty in order to punish the sin of Jacob/Israel which lies in the capital cities of Samaria and Judah. Verse 3 is the announcement proper; v.4 describes the cosmic effect of his

---

[a] The MT of v.5 contains irregular shifts which violate what would be expected in synonymous parallelism: why does 'sins of the house of Israel' change to 'high places of Judah'? The text is often corrected to reach the expected sequence in dependence on G. But G was the first corrector of the problem. The irregular shift results from redaction and expansion. See the comment.

appearance; v.5 discloses the purpose of his intervention in the affairs of earth. The proclamation is closely connected to its literary context. The initial conjuction 'for' in v.3 makes God's appearance the occasion for the summons to all the earth (v.2). 'Samaria' and 'Judah-Jerusalem' in v.5b name the subjects of the two following sayings (vv.6f. and vv.8–16). Both of these connecting links belong to the redaction of ch.1; 'for' was added with the insertion of v.2, and v.5b with the insertion of the oracle on Samaria (vv.6f.). The saying from Micah lies in vv.3–5a. It was set at the beginning of the first collection of his sayings because descriptions of YHWH's appearance seemed good introductions to prophecies of judgment (see Amos 1.2; Nahum 1.2–5). It was followed by the saying in vv.8–16 which could have been a continuation of this unit (see the comment on vv.8–16). The announcement itself gives no hint of the historical setting in which it was delivered, but its connection with vv.8–16 may be a clue, whether the connection was original or expressed a judgment of the earliest collector. Verses 8–16 have the invasion of Judah by Sennacherib in 701 BC as its background. The occasion of crisis and danger may have furnished the setting also for this saying. By announcing the coming of YHWH when the crisis was imminent Micah would have clothed the events with a theological significance of overwhelming magnitude, turning political and military strategems into theological drama.

Verses 3–4a contain the two characteristic elements of a description of a theophany, the coming of YHWH from his own particular sphere or residence (3) and the effect of his manifestation in awesome phenomena (4a); here the second element is developed by metaphors (4b). This two-element description is a literary type which appears in hymnic (Judg.5.4f.; Ps.18.8–16=II Sam.22.8–16; Pss.68.8–9; 77.17–20; 144.5f.) and prophetic materials (Nahum 1.2–6; Hab.3.3–15; Amos 1.2).[b] The type maintained its distinct identity from the earliest times of Israel's history throughout the Old Testament period; the earliest example is probably the hymn of victory found in Judges 5, and versions of it appear in post-Old Testament apocalyptic (Ethiopian Enoch 1.3–7; Assumption of Moses 10.3–6; II (4) Ezra 3.18; 8.23). Its vitality lay in its unparalleled usefulness as a presentation of YHWH as the one who comes from beyond the local human scene to intervene in the affairs of men with irresistible might. Its imagery clothes a past or expected occurrence with the drama of divine intervention. Most often the intervention is directed against YHWH's enemies for the deliverance of his people; and in later pieces, a

[b] On the type and its history see Jörg Jeremias, *Theophanie* (WMANT 10), 1965.

general judgment against the wicked in all the earth is the goal. But here the theophany comes upon Israel. Micah turns an instrument of Israel's confidence that Yahweh will save them against their religious security, just as Amos shifted the target of the hope for 'the day of YHWH' from the nation's enemies to Israel as YHWH's enemy (see Amos 5.18–20). YHWH comes, not to save Israel from its enemies, but to deal with them as he deals with his enemies, because of their sin (v. 5a).

[3] The description of the theophany begins with the exclamation 'See', directing attention to YHWH as centre and subject of the event already unfolding as the proclamation sounds forth—the coming of the God whose name is YHWH and therefore totally distinct from any other human or divine power, the God whose appearance always serves his purpose to be Ruler of his people and Lord of the world. 'Come forth' ($y\bar{s}$') with YHWH as subject emphasizes, not so much leaving a particular place, as going forth for a particular undertaking, for instance for war against the enemy, a setting in which $y\bar{s}$' is frequently found. With this meaning the verb is a typical item in the theophany description and its echoes (Judg. 5.4; Isa. 26.21; 42.13; Hab. 3.13; Zach. 14.3; Ps. 68.8; cf. also the reports of the battles of YHWH in Judg. 4.14; II Sam. 5.24). The location of the divine witness in v. 2 is the 'holy temple'; but here YHWH comes from 'his place' (elsewhere only in Isa. 26.21 which contains the entire sentence and may be an echo of this text). An older strain in the theophany tradition spoke of YHWH's departure from Sinai (Judg. 5.4; Hab. 3.3; Deut. 33.2); more often his own sphere is in the heavens (Isa. 26.21; 63.19; Jer. 25.20; Ps. 18.10; 144.5). 'Descends' (yrd, Isa. 63.19; 64.3; Pss. 18.10; 144.5) as a sequel to 'comes forth' shows the latter is the case here. It is often suggested that either 'descends' or 'treads' is an expansion of the original poetic line; 'treads' is missing from G, but it fits better with the prepositional phrase 'upon the heights' (cf. Amos 4.13, Job 9.8). YHWH's first contact is with the heights, the 'backbone' of the world whose bases reach down to the foundations of the earth; what moves them sends tremors through the whole universe.

[4] In the theophany descriptions the phenomena which manifest the appearance of YHWH are usually the fearful earthshaking features of the thunderstorm, earthquake, or volcanic eruption. Here there is a poetic portrayal of the way all the earth, mountain and plain, gives way and begins to disintegrate before the force of his appearance; the picture of mountains dissolving and plains splitting shows that the most permanent topography of the world cannot maintain itself when he appears. How much less men who oppose him!

Metaphors visualize the disintegration. Mountains dissolve like the melting wax before fire (Pss. 97.5; 68.3). Plains cleave like water that breaks into many currents as it spills down a rocky slope. What this cataclysmic appearance portends for man, and which men it concerns, is not yet said. Theophany descriptions tend to be self-contained and assume a function assigned by a particular literary context. Not until v. 5a does the prophet disclose whom this event, which Israel believed was directed against their enemies, concerns.

[5a] The first poetic line of v. 5 supplies the immediate context for the theophany description in vv. 3f. 'All this' refers to the coming of YHWH and the phenomena of his manifestation. The cause of YHWH's appearance is the 'crime of Jacob' and 'sins of the house of Israel'. The theophany, which is almost always an action against those who oppose YHWH's purpose, has become an action against the very people for whose deliverance he had acted in the past. The word-pair 'crime/sin' specifies the reason for the reversal. 'Crime' (*peša'*) means rebellion against YHWH's authority. Sin (*haṭṭā't*) means failure, missing the goal of the norms set by Israel's relation to YHWH. The pair constitute a comprehensive characterization of the people's conduct; their corporate identity is that of sinner, and in that identity YHWH comes to deal with them.[c] The word-pair appears in 3.8, where Micah states the purpose of his proclamation; he is endowed with strength 'to declare to Jacob his crime, and to Israel his sin'. (The only other occurrence of the pair in the book is in 1.13b, a redactional comment.) In Micah's language the names 'Jacob' and '(house of) Israel' are used for the audience to which he speaks, the people of Jerusalem and its surrounding territory in Judah. The name-pair clearly has this application in 3.9, to which 3.1 is an exact parallel; 3.8 fits this pattern of usage. Originally 'Israel' was the name for the sacral tribal league as a folk united under YHWH; it was more a religious than a political identification.[d] The prophets continued to use the name with this connotation to address any particular audience in the identity given them by their relation to Yahweh. The only text in the book of Micah in which 'Jacob' (2.7, 12; 3.1, 8, 9; 4.2; 5.7, 8; 7.20) or 'Israel' (1.13, 14, 15; 2.12; 3.1, 8, 9; 4.15; 5.1, 3; 6.2) designates the political entity of the northern kingdom is 'Jacob' in 1.5b. Micah announces a theophany already under way whose purpose is judgment upon the sin of Jerusalem and Judah. What the crimes and who the sinners are he specifies in the sayings in chs. 2–3.

c See R. Knierim, article ḥṭ' in *THAT I*, pp. 542ff.
d See M. Noth, *The Laws in the Penteteuch*, 1967, pp. 28ff.

[5b] The similarly formed second and third lines of v. 5 derive from the redaction of ch. 1 and are not the language of Micah; their setting is ch. 1 as a compositional unit. The second line points forward to the announcement of Samaria's judgment in vv. 6f., and the third line to vv. 8–16 and its lament over the plight of Judah and Jerusalem (v. 9). Each line begins with a question and concludes with a rhetorical question which answers it. The questions are really inquiries about the interpretation of v. 5a; they ask what the crime of Jacob and the sin of Israel's house are, and assume that the parallel measures of v. 5a have two distinct references. The questions and their rhetorical answers are formed so as to reinterpret the meaning of v. 5a. The second line says the crime of Jacob is Samaria, taking 'Jacob' as the name of the northern kingdom whose capital is Samaria. The third line replaces 'house of Israel' with Judah, the name of the southern state, and then cites Jerusalem as Judah's guilt, an opinion certainly in line with Micah's preaching (comment on 3.9–12). Judah-Jerusalem anticipate v. 9, where both appear. But the redactor also changes the expected 'sin of' to 'cultic high places of' (*bāmōt*), a shift which in its immediate context seems to make no sense. The translator of G apparently felt the problem so seriously that he reverted to the expected 'sin of'. But the subtlety of the redactor is apparent in this device. He expresses his interest in the offence of the Canaanized cult, the theme of the judgment upon Samaria in vv. 6–7, but a concern which appears elsewhere only in the later saying in 5.10ff. He probably chose the word because of its appearance in 1.3 and 3.12. Thus he calls attention to the 'heights of (*bāmōtē* K) earth' upon which YHWH treads in his appearance (1.3) and the 'wooded height' (*bāmōt*) into which YHWH will turn Jerusalem by his judgment (3.12). (Note the *bāmōt 'āwen/ /ḥaṭṭa't yiśrā'ēl* in Hos. 10.8.) The word is to him a theme for the point of YHWH's attack, for the sin of Judah, and for the consequences of Jerusalem's sin. By these reformulations the redactor prepares the hearer or reader of the book for understanding the theophany as the event which brings about the fall of Samaria and the Assyrian incursion against Judah. The theophany becomes the theological interpretation of the crisis which came upon Israel and Judah in the latter part of the eighth century.

5. THE PUNISHMENT OF SAMARIA: 1.6f.

6 I will make Samaria into a ruin in the field,
a place to plant vineyards.

> I will pour her stones into the valley,
> and uncover her foundations.
> 7 All her images shall be smashed;
> all her Ashera[a] shall be burned by fire;
> all her idols I will lay waste.
> For she collected them as the fee of a harlot,
> so to the fee of a harlot they shall revert.

The city of Samaria will be razed to its foundations (v. 6) and all its idols destroyed (v. 7a). Verse 7b states a rather cryptic justification for the fate of the idols. The announcement of punishment is composed in divine first-person style. The subject and the style distinguish the saying from its surrounding context. The saying is anticipated in v. 5b where Samaria is identified as 'the crime of Jacob'. That indictment is the basis for the announcement of punishment. There is also a pattern of relations between the saying and the broader context of chs. 1–5. The title (1.1) says Micah prophesied against Samaria and Jerusalem; 1.6f. is the only oracle which deals with Samaria, so it fulfils this concept of Micah's mission, a concept expressed also in v. 5b. It corresponds to the prediction of Jerusalem's total destruction at the end of ch. 3 (3.12), where even some items of vocabulary reappear. The oracle opens the portrayal of the drama of judgment which begins with Samaria and reaches to Jerusalem. At the end of ch. 5 (5.10–15) there is another divine saying proclaiming the destruction of cities and idols, which stands there as a warning that the judgment which falls on Samaria and Jerusalem will come upon all the nations who do not listen to YHWH's witness. The unit is thus an important feature of the organization of chs. 1–5.

The city of Samaria was taken by the troops of Shalmaneser in 722/721. If the prophecy is Micah's prediction of that event, the oracle would have been spoken by him sometime in the preceding years and would be the only saying which would have to be dated so early in the reign of Hezekiah. Because of the connection with v. 5, vv. 6f. have been read as part of a longer oracle covering vv. 2–7 (Weiser) or vv. 2–9 (Fohrer) spoken by Micah in those years. Since idolatry is not a concern of any other saying which can be attributed to Micah, v. 7 (Marti, J. M. P. Smith; only v. 7a by Jörg Jeremias) has been attributed to a redactor. Others have denied the entire divine saying to Micah, seeing it as a misplaced fragment of Hosea material (A. Jepsen) or a contribution of an anti-Samaritan redactor

---

[a] 'a šhērēhā for 'etnānēhā, which was probably drawn from the next line to repair a damaged word in the text; it does not fit the sentence in which it stands or echo 'images/idols'.

who gave chs. 1–5 their final form in the fourth century (T. Lescow). The verses are clearly part of a redactional pattern whose concern is the Samaria-Jerusalem scheme of judgment specified in the title and introduced in v. 5b. The style and the concern with idolatry are found together elsewhere only in 5.10ff., itself a later piece. The language seems in part to have been drawn from material already at hand and it would also appear to have been composed as a companion piece to 3.12.

[6] YHWH speaks of what he himself will do to Samaria. The features of his action are those of a military conquest in which the conquering enemy turns the city into a ruin (Ps. 79.1) and razes it down to its foundations (Ps. 137.7). The slopes of the proud hill on which the city stood will revert to use as vineyards. There is no mention of any historical agent. In the literary context the destructive work is surely to be understood as the effect of the theophany portrayed in vv. 2–4. The fate of Samaria parallels that predicted in 3.12 for Jerusalem; the urban reverts to rural; the site reverts to agriculture. 'Ruin' ('$\hat{i}$) appears only in this text, in 3.12 and its quotation in Jer. 26.18, and in the lament in Ps. 79.1 ('they have made Jerusalem a ruin'); the word is singular (plural in other three occurrences) because of its grammatical grouping with 'in the field'. 'Field' also picks up a motif from 3.12. 'Pour' (ngr), which has 'stones' as accusative only here, draws on 'poured' in the theophany description (1.4). 'Planting place' (maṭṭā') occurs only in exilic and post-exilic texts (Ezek. 31.4; 17.7?; 34.29?; Isa. 60.21; 61.3).

[7] It is remarkable that, in a prediction of the devastation and disappearance of such a great city, only the fate of idols should be mentioned. The fact shows that these representatives of other gods are the real target of YHWH's action and the crime which he punishes. The prophet Hosea inaugurated the prophetic polemic against idols. Because of its corruption by the cult of Baal he called the religion of the northern state 'harlotry' (e.g., 4.10–15) and applied the term 'harlot's fee' (cf. Deut. 23.19) to the sacrifices by which devotees of the fertility cult hoped to ensure the fertility of fields and herds (Hos. 2.14; 9.1). The language of v. 7 seems to reflect Hosea's influence and that of the deuteronomic circles in which it was cherished. The 'Deuteronomist' orders that the images of the nations be 'burned by fire' (7.15, 25; 12.3). Hosea's polemic is picked up by Jeremiah (8.19; 10.3ff.; 10.14; etc.), and rises to a crescendo in Deutero-Isaiah (40.20; 44.8, 10, 15; 48.5, etc.). The focus on idols as the prime guilt is a heritage of Josiah's reform and a feature of the deuteronomistic view of Israel's history (II Kings 22; 21.7) YHWH's

smashing (*ktt*) of the idols carries out a pattern of action against the images used in Israel's cult which is narrated in the deuteronomistic history (Moses smashes the golden calf, Deut. 9.21; Hezekiah the bronze serpent, II Kings 18.4; Josiah, the images and Asherim, II Chron. 34.7).

What v. 7b means precisely is not clear, because the reference of 'harlot's fee' (*'etnan*) is obscure. Somehow, the idols will go the same way they came; their fate will be like their guilty origin. In the only other uses of *'etnan* beyond this text and Hosea, the term is applied to political (Ezek. 16.31ff.) and economic relations (Isa. 23.17f.) as a characterization of gifts or profits. Perhaps what is meant in v. 7b is that the idols have been acquired and established in securing relations with other nations, and will be broken up and carried away by one.

6. A WAIL OVER THE WOUND OF THE LORD:
1.8–16

> 8 ªOver this I will mourn and wail;
>   I will go strip-ped ᵇ and naked.
> I will raise a mourning like jackals,
>   a grieving like the ostrich,
> 9 that the wound of YH(WH)ᶜ is incurable,
>   that it has come to Judah.
> He has reached to the gate of my people,
>   to Jerusalem.
> 10 *In the gardens of Giloh* ᵈ rejoiceᵉ not;
>   weep, only weep.ᶠ

ª The text of the following verses, especially vv. 10–16, has been seriously damaged in its transmission. The above translation draws on two major studies of the problem: K. Elliger, 'Die Heimat des Propheten Micha', *ZDPV* 57, 1934, pp. 81–152; also in *Kleine Schriften zum Alten Testament*, (ThB 32), 1966, pp. 9–71; and S. J. Schwantes, 'Critical Notes on Micah I 10–16', *VT* 14, 1964, pp. 454–61. So that the reader can readily see the extent of the difficulty, the translation based on conjectural reconstruction is italicized.

ᵇ *šōlāl* with qere.

ᶜ *makkat yh(wh)* with Elliger for *makkōteyhā* to go with the singular *'ᵃnūšāh*. Taking the final two consonants as an abbreviation for *yh(wh)* supplies an antecedent for the masc. verb 'he has reached' in the following line.

ᵈ With Elliger, *bᵉgannōt gīlōh*, for *bᵉgat*.

ᵉ *tāgīlū* for *taggīdū*, cf. P; Schwantes explains the *tagdīlū* assumed by G's translation as a mixed form incorporating both MT and the proposed emendation.

ᶠ MT's negative particle *'al* may have arisen from a misunderstood emphatic *l* with the verb (Schwantes).

In the streets of[g] Beth-aphrah[h]
    roll[i] in the dust.
11 [j]*The Shophar they sound*[j] for you,[k]
    community of Shaphir.
[l]*From her city*[l] she comes not out,
    the community of Zaanan.
Raise[m] a mourning, Beth-ezel,
    they take from you[n] your[o] standing place.
12 *Who*[p] can hope[q] for good,
    community of Maroth?
For evil has come down from YHWH
    to the gate of Jerusalem
13 *You harness*[r] the chariot to the team,
    community of Lachish.
That was the chief sin for the daughter of Zion, for in you
    were found the crimes of Israel.
14 [s]*To you they give*[s] parting gifts,
    [t]Moresheth-gath.
The community[u] of Achzib has become a failing brook
    for the king[v] of Israel
15 *Shall*[w] still the heir come[x] to you,
    community of Mareshah?

[g] Adding $b^e\dot{h}\bar{u}\dot{s}\bar{o}t$ to fill out the line (Schwantes); Elliger, 'in the vineyards of'.
[h] The *l* in MT *bet l^e'aprāh* is out of place in the name-form.
[i] Reading the qere, cf. G.
[j] Adding *šōpār*, and reading MT '*ibrī* as *ya'ăbīrū* (B. Duhm); see the locution in Lev. 25.9.
[k] *lāk* for *l^{e}kem*.
[l] *mē'īrāh* for MT's '*eryāh*, and dropping the gloss *bōšet*; cf. G.
[m] Adding '^{a}*šēh* (Schwantes), the locution from 8b. Elliger concludes that the two measures of this line have each lost a beginning and reconstructs two lines.
[n] *mimmāk* for *mikkem*.
[o] MT has third masc. sing. suffix; see Schwantes' plausible explanation of the corruption here.
[p] *mī* for *kī*, see G.
[q] *yiḥ^{a}lāh* replacing a *y* before MT's *ḥālāh*.
[r] *r^{e}tōm* is dubious; on the assumption that the beginning of each line is damaged Schwantes sees in the consonants the remnant of '*āsart^e*, the specific verb for harnessing a team, e.g. Gen. 46.29; Ex. 14.6; II Kings 9.21.
[s] Vocalizing MT's consonants *lknttny* as *lāk nitt^{e}nū*.
[t] Removing the preposition '*al*, drawn into the sentence by the corruption of its beginning.
[u] Filling out MT *bty* to read *yōšebet*, with Elliger.
[v] Singular for MT's plural, created by dittography.
[w] Adding an interrogatory *ha-* (Elliger).
[x] *yabō'* for '*ābī*.

Never again[y] to Adullam will come
     the glory of Israel.
16 Shear off all your hair[z]
     over the children in whom you delight.
   Be bald as the vulture,
     for they have gone from you into exile.

In its present form and position this powerful and skilfully composed lament continues the portrayal of the effect of the theophany
proclaimed in vv. 3f. YHWH has appeared in wrath because of the
guilt of Samaria and Jerusalem (v. 5). Verses 6f. announce the punishment of Samaria. Now a lament describes how YHWH's wounding
blow falls upon Judah as a disaster which sweeps over one town after
another until it reaches to the very gate of Jerusalem. The piece
closes with a summons (to Jerusalem?) to mourn like a grieving
mother who has lost her precious children (v. 16). The lament is
linked to its foregoing context in several ways. The names 'Judah . . .
Jerusalem' in v. 9 correspond to their occurrence in v. 5b. The opening 'over this' echoes 'all this' in v. 5a, where the demonstrative refers
to the preceding theophany. In v. 12b 'evil has come down from
YHWH' picks up 'YHWH has come down' in v. 3.
     The relation of vv. 8–16 to the literary context is the work of those
who arranged and formed ch. 1 as part of the book (see the introduction to 1.2–16 above). The question of the rhetorical unity of
these verses and of their continuity with any of the preceding materials
as an original saying is disputed. Verses 8f. have been understood as
the conclusion of a saying which includes vv. 2–9.[aa] But if the conclusion reached above concerning the origin of the saying against
Samaria (vv. 6f.) is correct, that cannot be the case. Verses 8f. serve
as a natural introduction to the lament proper (vv. 10–15) identifying
the genre of the saying and its occasion. The mourning song can
stand on its own; it is self-contained with respect to type and theme.
Only the demonstrative 'this' at the beginning seems to point back;
but it could as well point forward to the content of the lament (v. 9)
in the way that 'Hear this', the abbreviated summons to attention,

---

[y] Adding *lō' 'ōd* (Schwantes).
[z] No subject for the feminine imperatives is identified; some insert 'daughter of
Zion' to create a 3+2 rhythm. See the comment.
[aa] So most recently G. Fohrer who divides the chapter into two units (vv. 2–9
and 10–16), understands 10–16 as a lament-song composed as an oracle of judgment on the Shephelah of Judah delivered before 711, and reconstructs a text with
2+2 lines ('Micha 1' in *Das Ferne and Nahe Wort*, Festschrift L. Rost, 1967, pp. 65–
80.

refers to the following 'word' (e.g., Micah 3.9; Amos 8.4; Hos. 5.1). The shift from 'Jacob . . . house of Israel' (v. 5a) to 'Judah . . . Jerusalem' (v. 9) could be a clue that the two were not originally connected.

On the other hand the theophany description (vv. 2–5a) may have been developed by Micah with the lament; otherwise the rather formal announcement of the theophany lacks any historical identification. The mourning song could provide a portrayal of its effect. [bb] Of course vv. 2–5a spoken in the crisis of 701 BC would have had an obvious historical relevance. Whether vv. 8–16 are its original sequel or not, they are complementary, and the arranger may have brought together what had a unity in the prophecy of Micah.

Conclusions about the literary analysis of vv. 8–16 are encumbered by the condition of the text. No plausible understanding of the MT, especially vv. 10–15, is possible apart from reconstructions and emendations. In the above translation, words based on reconstructions are italicized so that the user of the commentary may readily identify those for which conjectures are necessary. Once the text is arranged in poetic lines, the basic problem seems to lie in damage to the beginning of each line, where words have either been lost or obscured. This initial corruption may have drawn after it further disturbance of the original in the attempts of scribes to understand and adjust what was before them. The present state of MT does show that in vv. 10–15 most lines were constructed around a word-play on the name of the city. As would be expected in poetry of this type (the mourning song), the lines seem to have been composed of two measures, the first with three and the second with two accents, the *qīnāh* rhythm. These characteristics together with internal considerations, hints from the versions, and possibilities developed out of study of the geographical pattern suggested by the cities listed, are the basis for the proposed text. The basic study which developed these principles for reconstruction is the work of K. Elliger (listed in note a above). In spite of the textual problems, the saying repays every effort expended on its interpretation. It is a magnificent witness to Micah's literary ability, to the historical situation in which he spoke, and the profound emotion of his participation in the suffering of his people.

The prophet speaks throughout. Verse 8 introduces and identifies the saying as a mourning song. Verse 9 states the theme and basis of the lament, the fatal blow which has struck the country of Judah and

[bb] T. Lescow thinks that Jer. 25.30f. plus 34–38 furnishes a parallel of theophany followed by lament (*ZAW* 84, 1972, pp. 54f.). See Jer. 4.5–8, where a description of invasion is followed by a lament.

reached to its capital, Jerusalem. Verse 8 is composed in $3+3$ rhythm; v. 9 shifts to $3+2$, which is followed in the rest of the song. The lament proper extends from v. 10 v. 16. In vv. 10–15 there are eleven poetic lines which name a city and develop a word-play in its name. Each evokes a swift glimpse of the desperate plight of the city's population. Most of these lines are built around the phrase 'community of . . .' (11a, b, 12a, 13a, 14b, 15a; in 14a, the name of the city, *mōrešet gat*, reproduces the sound of *yōšebet* . . . and takes its place). The other four (10a, b, 11c, 15b) vary the arrangement, probably to achieve the desired play on the city's name. Within vv. 10–15 the pattern of the lines is interrupted twice. At midpoint in the sequence v. 12b restates v. 9. Verse 13b comments that chariots and teams, mentioned in v. 13a, were the chief sin of the daughter of Zion. The concluding v. 16 also lacks the pattern; it is a summons to mourning expressed in feminine singular imperatives, which are probably addressed to the daughter of Zion of v. 13b. All three exceptions to the pattern are to be reckoned to the reinterpretation of Micah's prophecy in the exilic period.

The list of cities named in the poem can hardly be an arbitrary or accidental selection and must be a fundamental clue to the setting and function of the saying. Putting together the information which can be gained from archaeological investigation, the occurrence of the names in other Old Testament texts, and the identification of the sites by current Arabic names of ruins, a significant pattern for the location of the cities emerges. Within the Old Testament the city-lists of Joshua 15.20–62, which groups cities in administrative districts and probably dates from the reign of Jehoshaphat,[cc] and the report of the cities fortified by Rehoboam in II Chron. 11.5–12 are particularly helpful.[dd] The sixth city named in the lament is Lachish (tell ed-Duweir). In the eighth century BC it was a large fortress city in the Judaean defence system, located at the western edge of the Shephelah guarding the roads into the northern and southern hill-country of Judah.[ee] The cities named after Lachish are spaced in an arc curving away north-east into the Shephelah; Mareshah, Moresheth-gath, and Achzib in the next district to the north (Josh. 15.44), and Adullam at the southern edge of the next one (Josh. 15.35). All are neighbouring cities; the arc is about twelve miles in length. Lachish along with Mareshah and Adullam were rebuilt as fortress cities by Rehoboam,

    [cc] See J. Bright, *A History of Israel*, 1972², p. 248 and the literature cited in n. 65.
    [dd] On the historical value of the report and its interpretation, J. Bright, op. cit., p. 229 and n. 14.
    [ee] See G. E. Wright, 'Judean Lachish', *BA* 18, 1955, pp. 9–17; reprinted in *The Biblical Archaeologist Reader* 2, 1964, pp. 301–12.

and this holds for Moresheth-gath on the probability that it was the Gath of the list in II Chron. 11.5ff. The cities are not named in exact geographical order, Mareshah being south of Moresheth-gath. The latter was the home of Micah (1.1). Five of the cities listed before Lachish are named only in this text: Beth-aphrah, Shaphir, Zaanan, Beth-ezel, and Maroth. Of these, the location of Beth-aphrah alone is known; it has been tentatively identified with eṭ-Ṭaiyibeh between Lachish and Hebron in the hill country. Giloh, the only reconstructed name, lies also in the hill country farther south (Josh. 15.51). If these two can be taken as clues to the location of the others, the cities named before Lachish lie to the south-east running up into the hill country and not reaching beyond a distance of twelve to fifteen miles. The entire list occupies a quadrant to the south-west of Jerusalem, and includes Micah's home town. At least four are fortified cities in the system of defences erected to protect Judah from attack from the direction of the coastal plain.[tt]

In 701 BC, during the reign of Hezekiah, the Assyrian king Sennacherib concluded a military campaign along the eastern Mediterranean coast with an assault on Judah. The resulting destruction and suffering, which flowed over Judah to the very walls of Jerusalem, was the historical setting for Micah's lament. Sennacherib himself gave an expansive report of the campaign in his Annals,[gg] and had his siege of Lachish portrayed in reliefs on the walls of his palace.[hh] The Old Testament account of Judah's defeat stands in II Kings 18.13–16; the calamity was the setting for oracles by Isaiah (1.4–9; 22.1–14). Sennacherib moved against Judah from the west, overwhelmed Lachish and other 'strong cities', according to his count forty-six in all. The defence system of fortified cities in the Shephelah was certainly a focus of his attack. He also claimed countless villages. Two hundred thousand of the population were said to have been deported. Hezekiah was driven inside Jerusalem, held there as though in prison, and finally was spared only by submission and the payment of an impoverishing tribute.[ii] The defeat of cities including Lachish, the exiling of population (?), the 'wound' that reaches all the way to Jerusalem are all directly reflected in Micah's saying. Its language

[tt] For geographical orientation consult the references in Y. Aharoni, *The Land of the Bible*, 1967, especially pp. 297f. and pp. 337ff.

[gg] *ANET*, pp. 287f.

[hh] *ANEP*, plates 371–374; on the archaeological finds at Lachish, G. E. Wright, *Biblical Archaeology*, 1962², 167–75.

[ii] On history of the time and the importance of the event in Judah's history, see J. Bright, op. cit., pp. 277–86.

gives the impression of composition while the invasion was in full movement.

The poem is a skilled adaptation of the mourning-song used in the lament for the dead, a fact which the copyist who introduced the line from David's famous lament over Saul, 'Tell it not in Gath . . .', to reconstruct the beginning of v. 10, must have recognized (see note d). The prophets, portraying a city or a whole people as the bewailed dead, used the type to forecast the fall of a nation yet untouched by disaster (Amos 5.2), and to describe and interpret the demise as and after it occurred (Jer. 9.10–11, 17–22; Ezek. 19.1–14; Isa. 14). Many sections of the book of Lamentations employ the genre in mourning the fall of Jerusalem. Compare also Isaiah's announcements of mourning 'for the destruction of the daughter of my people' (Isa. 22.4) and his lament over wounded Judah (1.4–9). The language of Micah's introduction clearly identifies the function of his saying (see comment on v. 8). The individuality of this mourning song grows out of his use of the sequence of cities as a way to sketch the panorama of the disaster. The song contains no note of scornful mocking; the genre is to be taken in utter seriousness as a poignant outpouring of grief and consternation at the tragedy come over his home town and its neighbouring cities. Yet the personal pathos carries and expresses the prophetic vocation; the song reveals that the reality of the tragedy is the work of YHWH. It is Israel's God who is manifest in the ravaging power of the Assyrians.

[8] The language with which Micah introduces this saying characterizes it as a mourning for the dead. The defining verb (sāpad) and noun (mispēd) in nearly all instances occur in the setting of rites for the dead: sāpad ʿal (II Sam. 1.12; 11.26; I Kings 13.30; Zech. 12.10), sāpad lᵉ (I Sam. 25.1; 28.3; I Kings 14.13, 18; Gen. 23.2; Jer. 16.5, 6; 22.18; 34.5), sāpad (II Sam. 3.31; Gen. 50.10; I Kings 13.29; Ezek. 24.16; Eccles. 3.4; 12.5; Zech. 12.12), mispēd (Gen. 50.10; Zech. 12.10; Amos 5.16 with ʾēbel as here; Jer. 6.26; Esth. 4.3). The few exceptions are extensions of the language to songs and rites over calamity which brings death, or over cities and peoples personified as those for whom mourning rites must be observed (Jer. 4.8 with hēlil as here; 48.38; Ezek. 27.31 over Tyre; Isa. 22.12; 32.12; Zech. 7.5; 12.11; Joel 1.13 with hēlil; 2.12; Ps. 30.12). To 'go stripped (šōlāl qere; Job 12.19) and naked' is a sign of defeat (Amos 2.16; Job 12.19). Isaiah went naked and barefoot as a prophetic symbol of Egypt's defeat and humiliation (Isa. 20.2–4). Micah will sing his mourning song identified in appearance with those over whom he grieves, the conquered population of the cities named in his song. Jackal and

ostrich are frequently paired in descriptions of the wilderness (Isa. 34.13; 43.20; Jer. 50.39; Job 30.29); comparison with the jackal's familiar howl and the doleful moaning sound which the ostrich can make heightens the intensity of Micah's announcement.

[9] The subject and basis for Micah's mourning song is the punishing devastation wrought by YHWH in Judah and reaching even to Jerusalem. *makkāh* (blow, affliction, wound) is one of the words used for YHWH's action in punishment (I Sam. 4.8; Deut. 28.59; 29.21; Lev. 26.21) and is often applied by the prophets to the damaging conquest of an enemy (Isa. 1.6; Jer. 14.17; 19.8; 30.12; Nahum 3.19; see 'incurable wound' in Jer. 15.18). The southern state of Judah is like a man hopelessly wounded by YHWH. The historical event interpreted by this theological language is Sennacherib's attack on Judah and conquest of many of its cities, leaving king Hezekiah shut in Jerusalem. The situation suggested by the verse is the time when the conquest of the Shephelah and hill country is complete, and only Jerusalem remains. 'Gate of my people' as a term for Jerusalem appears also in Obad. 13. The meaning of the expression is suggested by Boaz's use of 'all the gate of my people' as a collective for those in Bethlehem qualified to sit in the court in the gate (Ruth 3.11). It is applied by Micah and Obadiah to Jerusalem as the capital where court and government for their people were centred.[jj]

The use of 'my people' ('*ammī*) in Micah deserves special notice. The term occurs nine times (1.9; 2.4; 8, 9; 3.3, 5; 6.3, 5, 16). In chs. 1–3, the antecedent of the first-person possessive is the prophet; see the comment on 3.5 and 2.4. In 6.3, 5, it is the familiar vocative for Israel as the '*am YHWH*; the text of 6.16 should be read '*ammīm*, 'peoples'. The term is of course common in the speech of one who refers to the folk who are his own kinship or local or political group (Gen. 23.11; 41.40; 49.29; Judg. 14.3; I Sam. 5.10; Ruth 1.16; etc.). Micah uses it for the population of Judah when he speaks of their suffering under their oppressors in Jerusalem and from the Assyrian invaders. Isaiah used 'my people' in a similar way (10.2; 22.4; possibly 5.13; see 26.20; 32.13). In Jeremiah and Lamentations 'daughter of my people' in laments over Jerusalem is frequent (Jer. 6.22; 8.19, 21, 22, 23; 14.17; Lam. 2.11; 3.48; 4.3, 6, 10). The setting of all these uses of 'my people' in laments over suffering and in indictments for oppression by the powerful indicates the identification

---

[jj] This explanation seems more likely on the available evidence than the suggestion that the term means the 'gate' through which an Assyrian army pressing south from Samaria must pass in order to overwhelm Judah; so A. Alt, *Kleine Schriften* III 1959, p. 373, n. 3.

in grief felt by the speaker. It seems that 'my people' in these contexts functions like the vocative 'Ah, my brother' in the mourning song.

[10a] The first measure of MT resembles a sentence in David's famous lament over Saul: 'In Gath tell it not' (II Sam. 1.20). Several things count against the originality of the text. There is no word-play on Gath. The Gath referred to is certainly the old Philistine Gath with which David was associated (I Sam. 27.1ff.). Its location is uncertain (Albright—Tell 'Areini; Aharoni—Tell es-Safi; Wright—Tell Shariʿah?; see G. E. Wright, *BA* 34, 1971, 76ff.); but all suggested sites lie west of the Shephelah, beyond the grouping of the other places listed in this poem. Its status in the time of Micah, whether it was an Israelite city or even in existence, is in doubt.[kk] The sentence from David's lament has probably been introduced to account for recognizable letters in the damaged text. P, and more distantly G, suggest the verb 'rejoice', which makes good sense in the context. Giloh would supply a name for the requisite word-play (assonance: *gīlōh—yāgīlū*). The city is located in the southern Judaean hill country by the administrative list in Joshua 15 (v. 51; see II Sam. 15.21). The second measure of MT contains a negative imperative, 'weep not', the opposite of the expected summons; a call to weeping is demanded by the context. With the line reconstructed, the lament begins with a call to replace the joyous celebrations of festive occasions with weeping, the expression of sorrow.

[10b] In v. 10 both name and word-play are clear. Beth-(le-)Aphrah, known only from this text, has been identified with eṭ-Taiyibeh, a site north-west of Hebron in the Judaean hill country. The name is echoed in the word 'dust' (assonance: *bēt leʿaprāh-ʿāpār*). Rolling in the dust is an extreme expression of grief, like putting dust on the head or lying in the dust (e.g. Josh. 7.6; I Sam. 4.12; Job 16.15; Jer. 6.26). A prepositional phrase like 'in the streets' (Elliger: 'in the vine-yards') is needed to fill the poetic line and correspond to v. 10a.

[11a] The location of the city Shaphir, mentioned only here, is unknown. The addition of the word 'Shophar' ('horn', usually from a ram, used for a signalling instrument) fills out the line and provides a word-play for the name (assonance: *šōpār—šāpīr*). Shophar has the advantage of fitting a verb partially reconstructed from MT's consonants (*ʿbr*). The horn was sounded at the approach of an enemy (Hos. 5.8; 8.1; Jer. 4.5; etc.) as a signal of danger. The horn is blown for Shaphir, under attack and soon to fall. The phrase 'community of . . .' (also in 11b, 12a, 13a, 15a) uses a feminine singular participle (*yōšebet*) with the name of a town as a collective which personifies the

kk W. F. Stinespring, 'Gath', *IDB* 2, pp. 355f.

population as a woman (the device is a favourite of Jeremiah, 22.23; 48.18, 19; 51.35, 36; also in Isa. 12.6; Zech. 2.11).

[11b] The name Zaanan is known only from this text, though Zenan is listed as a city in the Lachish district (Josh. 15.37). The form Zaanan is required, however, for the word-play with the verb 'she comes out' (assonance: ṣa'ᵃnān-yāṣᵉ'āh). The line means that Zaanan does not come forth to face the enemy because the struggle is hopeless, or because the city is destroyed already.

[11c] The existing text of v. 11c is clear, but the sequence of its two apparent measures in not. MT can be translated: 'The lament of Beth-ezel, they (Heb. sing., impersonal passive) take from you (pl.) his standing place.' On the assumption that the first word of the line is damaged, the imperative 'raise' can be supplied, and the name understood as a vocative and the pronouns corrected to this syntax. Beth-ezel is named only in this text and its location is unknown. The expected word-play is not so evident as in the previous lines. Perhaps there is a play on the meaning of the verb 'āṣal whose consonants are those of the name; 'āṣal means 'take away' in Num. 11.17, 25, a meaning echoed by the verb of the second measure (lāqaḥ min-). Beth-ezel is summoned to join in lament because its inhabitants have lost their place for standing against attack. Elliger concludes that the entire first measures of two poetic lines are lost and composes appropriate replacements:

> On every side is heard
>   the lament of Beth-ezel.
> O community of the fortress Esean,
>   they take away your support.

[12a] The name Maroth is also peculiar to this text and its site unidentified. The word-play, however, is clear. Maroth can be associated with mārar, mār ('be bitter, bitter') in contrast to 'good'. 'Who can hope for good, O community of bitterness!'

[12b] The following line (v. 12b) is a dependent sentence, developing the thought of 12a and so interrupting the sequence of independent poetic lines. It tells why Maroth cannot hope for help, and is connected directly with 12a by the word 'evil' (raʿ, 'disaster'), the antonymn of 'good' in the opposing word pair 'good/evil'. There is also a possible word-play in the contrast of sense between 'evil, disaster' and the name Jerusalem, whose second component (šlm) evokes šālōm ('salvation'). The entire verse would say something like: 'How can the community of bitterness hope for the good of help when the evil of calamity has come from YHWH to the very gates of the city of

salvation!' 'Come down' echoes the verb's appearance with YHWH as subject in the theophany description (v.3b). 'To the gate of Jerusalem' picks up a theme of the introduction to the lament in which it is said that 'Yahweh's devastation has reached to the gate of my people, to Jerusalem' (v.9b). This restatement of themes from other parts of the chapter suggests that the sentence is an expansion added to unify the material. It introduces motifs from the theophany and the introduction to the lament to be sure the reader understands that the disaster which causes the lament is the effect of YHWH's coming down and reaching in his wounding to Jerusalem's gate. The comment thus belongs to the redactional work of crafting ch. 1 into a unity.

[13a] Lachish, the most important urban centre in Micah's list of cities, lies on the western edge of the Shephelah, guarding the access to the network of roads, leading into the hill country of Judah. The word-play on the city's name appears in the word 'team' (lākîš— lārekeš). Reference to chariots is appropriate for a fortress city; Lachish was one of the citadels upon which Judah depended for defence of its western approaches. The line is an ironic cry of warning that teams should be harnessed and chariots made ready—for flight (cf. I Kings 12.18).

[13b] Verse 13b obviously disturbs the flow of the lament. A word-play, characteristic of the composition, is missing. Instead the sentence accuses and explains, elements otherwise lacking in the poem. It is prosaic and drops the style of direct address in its first clause. The line is a comment provoked by the mention of chariot and team in v. 13a. The chariot is 'the chief sin for the daughter of Zion'. Reliance on chariots and horses was regarded as an offence against YHWH by Hosea (10.13; 14.3) and Isaiah (2.7; 30.16; 31.1), and is forbidden in Deut. 17.16. Verse 13b interrupts the lament to comment that this was the chief sin also for the 'daughter of Zion', the population of Jerusalem. 'Daughter of Zion' is the antecedent of 'for you (fem.)' in the following clause; the crimes of Israel (here the name refers to the northern state) were present also in Jerusalem. The comment and accusation is the addition of the tradents who applied Micah's prophecy to the fall of Jerusalem a century later. Horses and chariots lead the list of the things which YHWH will cut off, enumerated in Micah 5.10ff.; 'daughter of Zion' is the characteristic motif of the complex of sayings in 4.8–13. Both came into the book in the process of its development.

[14a] Moresheth-gath was, according to the gentilic accompanying his name in 1.1 and Jer. 26.18, the home town of Micah. The city

is named only in this text. It can probably be identified with Tell el-
Judeideh on the road between Lachish and Mareshah on the way
north to Azekah, and must have been the 'Gath' fortified by
Rehoboam (II Chron. 11.8).[11] The word-play in the line seems to
involve a pun on the city's name. Moresheth, which is close to the
sound of *mōrāšāh* ('possession') received farewells, i.e., the residents of
the city are leaving. 'Farewell-gift' is used once (I Kings 9.16) for the
dowry of a bride (*meʾōrāšāh*, Deut. 22.23) as she departs to her hus-
band's house; that image could be the basis of the pun.

[14b] Achzib is named in the administrative list in Judges 15 (v. 44)
between Keilah and Mareshah. It has been identified tentatively with
Tel el-Beida north-east of Lachish. The word-play (assonance) on the
city's name lies in 'failing brook'; *ʾakzīb* has become an *ʾakzāb*. The
term *ʾakzāb* is used by Jeremiah for a stream that runs dry and so is
disappointing, unreliable (Jer. 15.18; cf. Isa. 58.11 and Job 6.15ff. for
other uses of the metaphor). The city of Achzib has failed the king of
Israel; he relied on it for defence, but the city disappointed him as a
dry brook betrays the thirsty man who comes expecting to find
water.

[15a] Mareshah is a city just north-east of Lachish, in the vicinity
of Achzib (Josh. 15.44). It was also one of the places fortified by
Rehoboam (II Chron. 11.8). The word-play is heard in 'heir' (assonance: *mārēšāh-yōrēš*). The loss of an heir means the end of life's
continuity, and no future (II Sam. 14.7; Jer. 49.1, where the synonym
is 'children'). Micah's rhetorical question implies that Mareshah has
lost its sons and can look for no existence of the community in the
coming generation.

[15b] Adullam, the last of the cities named by Micah, was located
in the administrative district north of the one to which Achzib and
Mareshah belonged (Josh. 15.35), and has been identified with Tell
esh-Sheik Madhkur east-north-east of Achzib. It was also fortified by
Rehoboam (II Chron. 11.7). The play on the name of the city appears
in the assonance in the word-sequence at the reconstructed beginning
of the line: (*haʿōd*) *ʿad-ʿadullām*. The expression 'glory of Israel' belongs to that group of phrases in which the 'glory' (*kābōd*) is that of
a particular land or people, and refers to the prestige of their existence,
their honour and importance apparent in wealth, population, military strength (Moab, Isa. 16.14; Jer. 48.18; Kedar, Isa. 21.16;
Assyria, 10.16; Hab. 2.16; Israel, Isa. 17.3f.; 62.2; 66.11). See the
lament after the ark was captured by the Philistines: 'The glory has
departed from Israel' (I Sam. 4.21f.). Adullam has no future; the

[11] See Y. Aharoni, *The Land of the Bible*, 1967, pp. 290f.

honour of children, wealth, power which belonged to Israel will never come to the city again (see Lam. 3.18!).

[16] The lament concludes with a summons to rites of mourning. Cutting off one's hair and shaving the head were defacements of the person used in rituals of mourning to display the diminution of life caused by death or disaster (Job 1.20; Amos 8.10; Jer. 7.29; 16.6; Isa. 22.12; Ezek. 7.18). The imperatives in the verse are feminine singular. Who is addressed and who are the 'children of delight' that have gone into exile? Perhaps Micah speaks directly to Jerusalem as a feminine figure and represents the captured towns of Judah as her children. Sennacherib's deportation of the outlying population could be already under way. It is more probably that the imperatives depend on v. 13b and refer to the daughter of Zion addressed there. In that case v. 16 is, like v. 13b, a later application of Micah's saying to Jerusalem after the city has fallen to the Babylonians.

7. THE PLAN OF MEN AND THE PLAN OF GOD:
2.1–5

1 Woe to those who plan iniquity,
   and to those who work at evil in their beds.
At morning's light they carry it out
   because it lies in their power.
2 They covet fields and seize them,
   houses and take them.
They oppress a fellow and his household,
   a man^a and his inheritance.
3 Therefore this is what YHWH has said:
   'See, I am planning against this family evil.
You shall not withdraw your necks from it,
   nor shall you walk upright,
   for it shall be an evil time.
4 In that day a taunt-song shall be raised over you;
   a lament shall be sung, ^b saying:^c
"We are utterly ruined.
   The property of my people is measured;^d
   ^eThere is none to return it^e again.

^a *w^e* is probably a dittography.
^b Omitting *nhyh* as a dittography after *wnhh nhy*.
^c *w^e'āmar*; see BHS.
^d *yimmad* for *yāmīr*; cf. G.
^e Reading *w^e'ēn mēšīb* (cf. G), and taking *lešōbēb* as part of this sentence.

Our fields are divided up."[f]
5 Therefore you[g] shall have no one
to cast the measuring line by lot in the assembly of
YHWH.'

Verses 1-5 are held together by a common theme, getting and losing property, and by the repetition of motifs. The saying concerns those who *plan* iniquity and *evil* which they carry out by seizing the *fields* of others (vv. 1-2). As punishment YHWH is *planning evil* for them (v. 3) and one day they shall wail when their *fields* are parcelled out to others (v. 4). Nor will they have any part in any future distribution of land among the people of YHWH (v. 5). The formal structure in which this thematic unity is expressed is rather complex. Verses 1-2 are a woe saying which characterizes those to whom the saying is addressed; it serves as the basis for the announcement of punishment in v. 3 which is connected by 'therefore', introduced by the messenger formula, and spoken in divine first-person style as direct address to an audience. Verse 4 is introduced by the temporal phrase 'in that day' which refers to the final sentence of v. 3, 'for it will be an evil time'. The style of direct address continues, and a lament which the addressees will sing in the time of punishment is quoted. Verse 4, then, continues the announcement of punishment. Verse 5, still in direct address, is attached by another 'therefore' and adds yet another element to the coming punishment. This complexity raises the question whether vv. 1-5 represent an original oral unit.[h]

The bulk of the sequence contains a saying whose purpose and pattern are quite clear and are characteristic of other sayings of Micah. The woe-saying (vv. 1f.) concerns a particular group, the greedy and powerful men who are expanding their landed estates at the cost of those who are vulnerable to their oppression (cf. 2.8f.; 3.1-3, 9f.). Their punishment will be directly correlated with their guilt; they who plan evil will suffer from it (v. 3), lose the fields they seized (v. 4), and be excluded from further acquisition of property (v. 5). Sayings addressed to a particular group and announcing a punishment which fits their guilt are characteristic of Micah's oracles of judgment in chs. 1-3. But there are elements of the present text which

[f] Pual for piel; cf. G.

[g] *l[e]kem* for *l[e]kā*; the *m* was lost by haplography.

[h] On the literary analysis and interpretation of 2:1-5 see especially A. Alt, 'Micha 2, 1-5. *GĒS ANADASMOS* in Juda', KS III, 1959, pp. 373-81; J. Jeremias, 'Die Deutung der Gerichtsworte Michas in der Exilszeit', *ZAW* 83, 1971, pp. 333ff.; T. Lescow, 'Redaktionsgeschichtliche Analyse von Micha 1-5', *ZAW* 84, 1972, pp. 50ff., 8of.

broaden the application of the punishment to the entire people and see the fulfilment of the prophecy in a time much later than Micah's. 'Against this family' (v. 3) and 'The portion of my people is measured; there is none to return it again' (v. 4) speak of a judgment falling upon the entire corporate group. 'For it shall be an evil time' (v. 3) and 'in that day' (v. 4) express a conviction that the prophecies take effect at a time which is later than that of their delivery. The lengthy prosaic character of v. 5 suggests also that its first line was expanded when the unit was reworked. All these elements belong to interpretation of Micah's prophecy as one which was fulfilled about a century later in conquest of Judah by the Babylonians. The revision of the oracle shows that the guilt to which it pointed persisted and was punished in a judgment that transcended the punishment foretold by Micah (see the Introduction, pp. 24ff.).

The woe-saying is a type of speech used frequently by the prophets (e.g., Amos 5.7, 10f.; 5.18–20; 6.1–3; the collection in Isa. 5.8–24; 10.1–4; Hab. 2.12–14, 15–17; Jer. 22.13–17).[1] The opening 'woe' (*hôy*) is a cry of grief familiar in laments over the dead;[j] in prophetic use it confronted the audience with the charge that their feet were already in the path that leads to the grave. The audience is not directly addressed; a participle (v. 1a) followed by third-person-plural verbs (vv. 1b, 2) depicts conduct; the style identifies the hearers by their deeds, not by name or office. They are sinners whose deeds violate the basic orders of life set by God and so destroy the health and wholeness of the community. Destructive conduct is frequently described in terms of broken commandments and departures from wisdom's instruction about the good way to life (see the comment on vv. 1.). When followed by an announcement of punishment, the woe-saying proper serves as the indictment of guilt which is the basis of YHWH's sentence.

Micah delivered the original saying in Jerusalem and spoke to the same audience to which all of his announcements of judgment were addressed, the business and political circles of the capital who were enriching the city and building estates by the oppression of the small farmers in the country of Judah (2.9; 3.1–3, 9–11). The woe-saying from Isaiah (5.8–10) is the counterpart to vv. 1–3 in type and theme. The time was the period before the Assyrian attack in 701, anticipated in the language of vv. 3f.

[1] See E. Gerstenberger, 'The Woe-oracles of the Prophets', *JBL* 81, 1962, pp. 249–63; C. Westermann, *Basic Types of Prophetic Speech*, 1967, pp. 189ff.
[j] G. Wanke, "*ʾwy* und *hwy*', *ZAW* 78, 1966, 215–18; W. Janzen, *Mourning Cry and Woe Oracle* (BZAW 125), 1972.

[1] In the customary dirge the opening 'woe' would be followed by the name of the bewailed dead. Instead, a characterization of conduct ensues, impersonal in style; but Micah and his audience know whom 'the shoe fits'. The portrait of men who spend the night planning the iniquity they will perform the first thing in the morning is like Amos's sketch of the entrepreneurs who cannot wait until sabbath is over to gouge their customers (Amos 8.4-6). Iniquity ('*āwen*) is a word from the Old Testament vocabulary for deeds which are destructive of the community's well-being; it identifies an act as the expression of a power intent on the violation of the order set by God to preserve and augment the life of individuals or their social group.[k] For '*āwen* with the verb 'plan' and its derivatives, see Jer.4.14; Ezek. 11.12; and Prov.6.10, where 'a heart that plans '*āwen* while on his bed' is listed as one of six things hated by YHWH. 'Planning '*āwen* while on his bed . . .' is a feature of the portrayal of the wicked in one of the wisdom psalms (Ps.36.5). 'And those who work evil' (*ūpōʿªlē rāʿ*) disturbs the movement of thought to v. 1b; the deed planned at night belongs to the morning. The verb in this context must mean something like 'work out in their minds'. In v.3 a motif from each of the measures and its appearance is used to state YHWH's immanent act: 'plan evil'. The men addressed by the 'woe' are members of the power structure in Judah's society. The source of their dreams is opportunity created by their power. Might has become their right; power corrupts them. The wisdom teachers warned, 'Do not withhold good from those who have a right to it, because it lies in your power to do so' (Prov.3.27).

[2] Verse 2 moves from a general characterization of conduct to a specific stipulation of deeds. The powerful are expropriating the property of small landowners through oppression. The engine which drives the enterprise is covetousness, breaking the instruction of YHWH to his people: 'You shall not covet your neighbour's house-(hold).' *ḥāmad*, self-centred desire, is primarily a word of the commandment tradition (Ex.20.17; 34.24; Deut. 28.32, cf. Josh. 7.21); v. 2 as a whole is a charge that this land-grabbing is a violation of the relation between neighbours ordained by YHWH. 'Oppress' ('*āšaq*) is also a theme of Israel's normative tradition; commandments forbid it (Lev.5.21; 19.3; Deut.24.14; cf. Samuel's declaration of innocence, I Sam. 12.3f.) and the teachers warn against it (Prov. 14.31; 22.16; 28.3). The contexts in which '*āsaq* appear (often with *gzl*, as here) show that the verb specifically means taking something away from another through an advantage of position or power. For those who

k R. Knierim, *THAT* I, pp.82-84.

lost their property, the result involved more than simple economic impoverishment. In Israel's social order a man's identity and status in the community rested on his household or family, dwelling place, and land. His inheritance in his father's family was his 'portion' in the family (Gen. 31.14). Lose it, and he lost all the rights which were based on its possession; he had no 'place' in the community and had left only the life of a wage-labourer or a slave. His life passed into the hands of others. The independence which came to him with his inheritance was gone.[1] The plight of the weaker citizens in Israel and Judah, referred to so often by the eighth-century prophets, was the result of an economic development which, supported by the policies of the royal court, had reached its climax in the eighth century. The rich and ruling classes were assembling estates in the country by skilfully managed loans and corrupt courts (3.1, 9). The old family properties around the villages were being broken up and the clan system pressed out of existence.[m] Micah, whose home was in one of the villages, must have known through bitter experience the anguish and humiliation of this economic progress. But he also knew that both motive and deed of those who prospered thereby was a violation of YHWH's will and would bring divine punishment upon them.

[3] 'Therefore' establishes the woe-saying as an indictment upon which the announcement of punishment is based (so lākēn in 3.12; see comment on 3.6). The messenger formula, 'this is what YHWH has said', introduces the very words of YHWH in direct address to the guilty: 'Since you plan iniquity, I plan evil, a catastrophe which will turn your power into powerlessness.' The nature of the catastrophe is not identified. Instead, the metaphor of a yoke on their necks is employed to describe how the powerful end up in the control of others. The metaphor is generally used as an image of servitude to a conquering enemy (Isa. 9.4; 10.27; 47.6; Jer. 27.8; 28.14; Ezek. 34.27). Whether Micah had the Assyrians in mind as he spoke cannot be known; their threat loomed on the horizon of his time. But it was not so much who, as what, that matters in the punishment. The powerful will be bowed by the yoke of a captor, and walk in humiliation. The guilty will suffer the same feeling of helplessness that they have brought on others. 'This family' as designation of those to be punished is unexpected; in such a context the term must refer to the entire people, all Israel (see Amos 3.2; Jer. 8.3). That would mean the judgment falls on a much broader group than the guilty described in the woe-saying. The punishment described is designed to fit the sin of the

[1] L. Köhler, Hebrew Man, 1956, pp. 149ff.
[m] A. Alt., op. cit.; R. de Vaux, Ancient Israel, 1961, pp. 72f., 166f.

guilty with appropriate precision. 'Against this family', which is placed awkwardly in the syntax of the sentence and is not in direct address style, must be an expansion. 'For it will be an evil time' appears also as a redactional comment on one of Amos' oracles (5.13). Read as part of the divine announcement it is rather anti-climactic and explanatory. It is best understood as the comment of a tradent who has lived through the fall of Jerusalem and believes that the calamity is the disaster of which Micah spoke.

[4] 'In that day' refers to the 'evil time' of the immediately pre-ceeding expansion and has been added along with it to 'date' the lament in the time of the tradent when he believes the prophecy is being fulfilled. The first poetic line introduces a song which those who are punished will sing. The quoted song is identified as a taunting song (māšāl) and a lament of grief (nᵉhī). Māšāl is a term applied to the broadest variety of sayings and songs.[n] Nᵉhī is quite precise; a frequent synonym for qīnāh, it names the funeral song sung in the rites of mourning (see Amos 5.16; Jer. 9.9, 17–19; 31–15). The nᵉhī was sung by professional mourners, skilled at the art (see the texts cited above); it is they who are pictured as the singers here, the subject of the verbs in third person.

The dirge is composed of four measures whose style and assump-tions differ. The first and fourth measures are composed in first- person-plural style in a two-beat rhythm, and are connected by play on the assonance in Hebrew between 'ruined' and 'fields' (šādōd nᵉšaddūnū/ šādēnū). 'Fields' picks up a motif from v.2. These two measures are the lament in the original saying. They carry out the scheme of the appropriate punishment, and the first-person-plural style has the second person plural 'you' of vv.3 and 4a as antecedents. The second and third measures are composed in three-beat rhythm in first-person-singular style and sparate the closely connected first and fourth measures. They speak of the loss of the 'portion' (the assigned terri-tory) of the whole people of YHWH. These intervening measures came into the text with the other expansions which understood the punishment to be the fall of Judah and Jerusalem. In Jer. 9.17–19 there is an oracle which speaks of a nᵉhī sung in that time. It contains the phrase 'How we are ruined' (šūdādᵉnū). That oracle of Jeremiah's may have been the specific provocation for connecting this one of Micah's with that time. The first-person pronoun in 'my people' may have been used because YHWH quotes the lament.

[5] If the textual change of 'you' from singular to plural is correct (note g), v.5 continues the style of the original oracle. The basic idea

[n] O. Eissfeldt, *The Old Testament, An Introduction* 1965, p.96.

expressed in the line is more consonant with Micah's expectation than with the situation of the redactor. Micah looked for YHWH to bring a yoke on the necks of the exploiters and strip them of their power. Then their ill-gotten fields would be taken away from them and the land redistributed among the general population. The present form of the verse is prose, and has probably been expanded in the re-working of the unit. The original might have been a line of 2+2 rhythm like the quoted lament in v. 4: 'You will have no one/to cast the measuring line.' The full expression 'to cast the line by lot' is peculiar to this text. For the use of the measuring line (*ḥebel*) to divide up land see Amos 7.17; *ḥebel* is the object of similar verbs in Pss. 78.55; 16.6; cf. II Sam. 8.2. 'By lot' is a variant which was pro-bably added under the influence of the tradition in Josh. 14–21 where the promised land was apportioned to the clans through a sacral allotment (see Josh. 18.8, 10). 'Assembly of YHWH' (*qāhāl YHWH*) as a designation of the sacred assembly of Israel appears first in Deuteronomy (23.2) and then in later literary contexts (e.g. Num. 16.3; 20.4; I Chron. 28.8; Neh. 13.1). The expansion 'by lot in the assembly of YHWH' relocates Micah's exclusion of the guilty from ownership of land in a future when the land which has been lost by the entire people will once again be redistributed after the pattern set in the deuteronomistic history. When that happens, those who were guilty of the crime described in Micah's oracle will have no rights in the sacral assembly.

8. DON'T PREACH SUCH THINGS: 2.6–11

6 'Don't preach', they preach.
   'They shall not preach about these things.[a]
   Disgrace shall not overtake[b] us.
7 Is the house of Jacob accursed[c]?
   Is YHWH impatient,
      or are these things his deeds?
   Do his acts[d] not benefit
      [e]the one who walks uprightly?'[e]

[a] Sellin vocalizes MT's consonants *le'ālāh*, 'about a curse'.

[b] *yaśśîg* for *yissag*, a confusion of sibilants.

[c] *he'ārûr* for *he'āmûr*; G. R. Driver sees a metathesis of letters, *ḥamû'ār*, which would result in the same translation.

[d] Reading *debārāyw*; MT has a first-person-sing. suffix resulting from confusion about the speaker, cf. G.

[e] The words in MT have been rearranged on the assumption that *'im* is the preposition of the preceding verb. Read *'im hôlēk yāšār*.

8 ʳBut you! againstʳ my people
   you ariseᵍ as enemy.
   Fromʰ ⁱthe peaceful
      their cloakⁱ you strip,
   ʲtaking away security,
      plotting war.ʲ
9 You drive the women of my people
      from theirᵏ comfortable houses.
   From theirᵏ children you take
      their dignityˡ for ever.
10 Arise and go,
      for this is no place of rest.
   Because of uncleanness ᵐyou shall be destroyed
      by ruinous destruction.ᵐ
11 If a man cameⁿ in the spirit,
      and deceived with lies,
   'I will preach to you about wine and beer'—
      he would be this people's preacher!

This saying opens a window on the reception given Micah and his message. Along with 3.11b it furnishes some information concerning the way his audience responded to his prophecy. Those to whom he addressed the announcement of YHWH's judgment found his message, not only personally offensive, but theologically inconceivable. The confrontation between prophet and audience concerned ultimately the question of their understanding of God. Like his fellow prophets of judgment in the eighth century, he was told to shut up (Amos 7.12f.; Hos. 9.7f.)

The verb 'preach' appears three times in the opening line (v. 6a) and twice in the concluding one (v. 11). This motif marks the upper

---

ᶠ Dividing MT's consonants *w'tml* to read *weʾattem le*.

ᵍ Reading *tāqūmū* for *yeqōmēm*; the verb was corrupted by the confusion at the beginning of the sentence.

ʰ Probably *mēʿal* for *mimmūl*.

ⁱ *šālēm hāʾderet*; taking the final *h* of *šalmāh* as article for the next word and pronouncing *šālēm*; a final *t* has been lost from *'dr* by haplography.

ʲ Assuming a *ḥ* and *m* have been lost by haplography, the sequence can be read with Schwantes; *maʿabīrīm beṭaḥ/hošebīm milḥāmāh*.

ᵏ Singular suffixes with plural antecedents.

ˡ Changing the first-person suffix to third; confusion about the speaker and influence of *hādār*.

ᵐ For *teḥabbel weḥebel* read *teḥubbelū ḥebel*, correcting the division of letters. In the comment a reconstruction of the line is proposed.

ⁿ *hālak* for *hōlēk*.

and lower limits of the saying. The collector of Micah's sayings probably placed this unit after vv. 1–5, because the coming punishment
sketched in them makes an appropriate antecedent for the demonstrative pronouns 'these (things)' of vv. 6f. The foregoing oracle of judgment illustrates the kind of preaching to which objection is made at
the beginning of this unit.

The MT of these verses is in poor condition. It cannot be understood without emendations and reconstructions. Part of the difficulty
in the transmission of these verses seems to stem from a confusion
about the speaker. The difficulty is apparent in v. 7. The first full line
refers to YHWH in the third person, but in the next line MT uses a
first person pronoun which can only have YHWH as antecedent:
'Do not my acts benefit the one who walks uprightly?' The presence
of the style of divine speech in MT is probably founded on the assumption that YHWH is the antecedent of the pronouns in the
expression 'my people' in vv. 8 and 9. But the clear parts of the text
and the characteristics of the entire unit can be best understood if the
passage is read as a saying of the prophet which has its setting in a
controversy with his audience. The saying unfolds in two major
movements: the characterization of the opponents (vv. 6f.) and the
rejoinder of the prophet (vv. 8–11). The first movement contains a
quotation of what the opponents say, which depicts their general rejection of the message from the prophets who preach judgment. The
quotation is probably a dramatic device to sum up the attitude of the
audience rather than a direct repetition of what has been said, though
it presupposes a situation in which the prophet has been verbally
attacked and rebuked. The audience rejects the prophecies about
judgment and regards them as inaccurate on the basis of what they
know about YHWH and the uprightness of their life. Most of their
remarks are in the form of argumentative rhetorical questions (v. 7).
Micah's rebuttal portrays his opponents as ruthless marauders who
despoil their helpless victims (vv. 8f.). They evict the weak from their
property (v. 10a was originally another quotation of what the
opponents say), by a cruel exploitation of the debt laws (v. 10b). The
saying concludes with a scathing comment about the kind of preaching that would suit them (v. 11). For other examples of sayings shaped
in the process of controversy, see Amos 3.3–8; 5.18–20; 7.14–17; Isa.
28.23–29.°

° On the type and its setting in the prophetic ministry, C. Westermann, *Basic
Types of Prophetic Speech*, 1967; H. Gunkel in *Die Schriften des Alten Testaments* II/2,
1915, pp. lxix–lxxi; J. Begrich, *Studien zu Deuterojesaja*, 1938, pp. 42–7. Also the

The identity of Micah's partners in discussion is clear from the description of them in vv. 8–10. They are the powerful men of Jerusalem who are seizing the property of the small farmers in the villages, the addressees of the other oracles of judgment (2.1f.; 3.1f, 9–11).

[6] The saying plunges *in medias res*. The opponents of Micah have already made their position clear with a vehemence reflected in his quotation of their statements. The issue is the message of those who announce YHWH's judgment upon Israel. The verb 'preach' (*hiṭṭîp*) occurs three times in the first line. In three of its four occurrences, 'preach' is a word for the speech of prophets and has 'prophesy' (*hinnābē'*) as synonym (Amos 7.16; Ezek 21.2, 7). Qal and one instance of hiphil (Amos 9.1) mean 'drip, flow with'; the association of the verb with prophetic speaking may have developed from the frenzy which came over the early charismatic prophets in a state of ecstasy. The verb could have a pejorative ring in Amos 7.16, something like 'rant, drivel'. Probably, like the word 'preach' in English, it could be used in a derogatory way, depending on the tone and intention of the speaker. The prohibition 'Don't preach' (*'al* with jussive) is plural; Micah pictures his partners in discussion as the opponents of a group. He does not let their hostility to him become the issue, but draws into the argument the whole record of the rejection of YHWH's messengers of judgment. All had been resisted by the leaders of the nation (see Amos 2.12; 7.16; I Kings 13.4; 18.4; 19.2; 22.8; II Kings 6.31). If there is any 'preaching' being done, it is the self-righteous, angry rebuke heard from those who attack YHWH's messengers; their order 'not to preach' is the worst kind of preaching itself. As the quotation resumes with 'they shall not preach', the opponents move from warning to outright prohibition (*lō'* with imperfect), assuming a stance of authority meant to end such prophecy once and for all. The demonstrative 'these (things)' has no antecedent, but its appearance in v. 7 shows it refers to the deeds of YHWH's punishment announced by prophets like Micah. Perhaps a little preaching was all right, but not about things like that!

With an absolute assertion of their feeling of security, Micah's opponents deny the relevance of judgment to them. The disgrace of humiliating catastrophe, any misfortune that would leave them exposed to the insults of those who behold their downfall, would never touch them (cf. Amos 9.10).

[7] This angry, defensive denial arises out of a conviction about

analysis of the 'controversy dialogues' in the tradition about Jesus in R. Bultmann, *History of the Synoptic Tradition*, 1968², pp. 12–54.

their identity and character, a theology of themselves set forth in a
series of argumentative questions. 'Is the house of Jacob accursed?'
Is it conceivable that the family of father Jacob who won the promise
and blessing from YHWH could possibly now stand under a divine
curse, the very opposite of blessing, and so be placed irrevocably
beyond the sphere of salvation to suffer the ills which express God's
rejection? (See the extended description of the effect of the curse in
Deut. 28.15–68.) So they wrap the cloak of their religious heritage
about them and stand unthreatened and secure as the heirs of Jacob
whose destiny it is to live out an unbroken history of God's favour (cf.
Matt. 4.9).

They appeal to the very character of YHWH himself. Is YHWH so
impatient and short-tempered as to act in anger? The question is
really an affirmation that YHWH is 'slow to anger'. The expression
(literally, 'short of spirit') appears with its opposite 'slow to anger'
('erek 'appayim, literally 'long in anger, temper') in Prov. 14.29. That
YHWH is 'slow to anger' is an established confessional motif (see
especially YHWH's proclamation of his character in Ex. 34.6, and
'erek 'appayim in Num. 14.8; Pss. 86.5; 103.8; 145.8; Joel 2.13; Nahum
1.3; Jonah 4.2; Neh. 9.17; also the variant in Jer. 15.15). Micah's
opponents find his message in irreconcilable contradiction to a confession of faith which has become their slogan, and turn what is true of
God's way into an absolute dictum that frees them from responsibility before God.

The rest of their argument follows from this proposition. YHWH
would not do 'these things' which Micah foretells (cf. v. 6). Such
deeds (ma'alāl, usually of wicked acts of men, e.g., Micah 3.4; of
YHWH's saving acts only Pss. 77.12; 78.7) are not expected from the
God in whom they believe. Quite the contrary; his acts (debārim,
which could mean YHWH's 'words', his announcements of his plans)
benefit 'those who walk uprightly'. That YHWH rewards the upright (yāšār) is a constantly repeated lesson taught by the wise (e.g.,
Prov. 2.7, 21; 11.3, 6, 11; 14.9, 11; etc.). The powerful take their
prosperity as a sign of YHWH's favour, and as a confirmation of their
righteousness. That wealth, however gotten, should contribute to a
feeling of being right, to self-justification, is not restricted to Micah's
time. Doubtless his opponents were sober, industrious, and chaste
citizens, and found satisfaction in living up to their selection of the
precepts for a righteous life. Success and self-righteousness are an
unshakable foundation for a theology against the prophetic word of
judgment. In 3.9 Micah charges the same people with the perversion
of uprightness (yešārāh).

[8] In v. 8 Micah begins his response, accepting the challenge of his opponents' argument. With an opening adversative, 'But you!', he puts the reality of their lives in evidence. One has only to look at what they have done. They are not upright; they are 'the enemy of my people', and have accumulated a record of successful oppression that would justify the wrath of God many times over. Micah calls those who suffer from their exploitation 'my people', affirming his identity with the folk whose existence is being destroyed by the greed of the powerful (see 'ammī in v. 9, and the comment on 1.9). Thus he drives a wedge in the total population of Judah, separating the weak from their oppressors, and excluding the latter from the group to which he belongs. They are not members of a folk whose solidarity with each other augments the well-being of each. They have made themselves 'the enemy' and, judged by their deeds, might as well be the Philistines or Assyrians.

The following lines (8b, c, 9) describe how Micah's opponents play the role of enemy. The text is so badly damaged at points that the sense must be guessed at. But enough is clear to make out a recitation of precisely those actions which would be expected from conquering invaders. The powerful, in their avid drive for property, even claim the cloak of those who only try to live in peace, earning their bread and keeping the ties of their community firm (8b).

[9] But the 'enemy' leaves them no security. They must live as those against whom war is waged (cf. 3.5). Women are driven out of modest homes, the pleasure and comfort of their simple lives is taken away. Their children are left in poverty, the dignity and honour of home and recognition in a community of their own lost for ever. For these children there is no future but slavery and servitude. The vehemence of these accusations and the anguish felt by Micah as he rehearses them are apparent in his language. Behind the items of Micah's rebuttal of their claim to uprightness is the new economic power of the urban 'capitalists' who were acquiring estates in the countryside of Judah and appropriating the property of the villagers in the process. See the comment on 2.1f.; 3.1–3.

[10] The present form of v. 10 (with the minor correction noted in footnotes to the text) reflects the application of Micah's prophecy to the situation in Judah at the beginning of the exilic period.[p] The first poetic line is a summons to people under judgment to depart because the place they live is no longer a place of rest and security (menūḥāh) for them. Menūḥāh is understood in the specialized sense it has in the deuteronomic vocabulary as a term for the land as a gift of

[p] See J. Jeremias, ZAW 83, 1971, pp. 339f.

YHWH's salvation, a synonym for 'inheritance' (Deut. 12.9; I Kings 8.56).[q] The second line tells why the 'rest' will be violated. The land can no longer be a place of rest because of 'uncleanness', a term for idolatry as in Jer. 19.13; Ezek. 22.5, 15; 24.13; 36.25, 29; 39.24. This concern with idolatry as Judah's basic guilt (cf. 1.7; 5.12f.) and the relation of Micah's prophecy to the fall of Jerusalem and the exile are features of the first redaction of the book (see the Introduction, pp. 24ff.). Originally the two lines in the saying of Micah (v. 10a) were another quotation of what the addressees said, their orders to the poor to get off the property being expropriated. Mⁱnūḥāh was used as in Ruth 1.9, a term for home as a place of security. Verse 10b was a description of the way in which the expropriation took place. The powerful were perverting the laws which dealt with securities and pledges given by debtors to those from whom they borrowed (Ex. 22.25–26; Deut. 24.12–13). The laws were meant to protect the debtor and keep him from falling into the power of the creditor.[r] The pledge was traditionally a symbolic sign of debt, never real property. But it appears that these avaricious creditors were taking land in pledge for the slightest debt and then seizing it at the first failure of payment, thus destroying the livelihood of those evicted. The original said:

> 'Arise and depart,
>> for this is no home (for you).'
> For the gain of the slightest thing you pledge
>> with a ruinous pledge.[s]

The reinterpretation is based on the special meaning which mⁱnūḥāh had for the tradents and on the homonym ḥbl which means both 'pledge' and 'destroy'.

[11] The saying ends with a scornful remark whose sarcasm and bitterness are calculated to conclude the controversy. Micah flings at his audience a job-description of the preacher they prefer. Such a preacher would be an enthusiastic charismatic in the old style of the spirit-filled prophets. He would lie. His preaching would intoxicate them in a drunkenness that freed them from facing reality. A man like that would be a preacher to please such people! The syntax of v. 11a poses problems. If 'spirit' is understood as an adverbial accu-

[q] G. von Rad, *Old Testament Theology* I, 1962, pp. 223f.

[r] On the practice of taking pledges as security for debt, see R. de Vaux, *Ancient Israel*, 1961, pp. 171f.

[s] In this reconstruction read *taḥbⁱlū ḥᵃbōl* for MT's *tḥblwḥbl*, and *mⁱʾūmāh* for the graphically similar *ṭāmⁱʾāh*.

sative of 'came', which makes for the best poetic arrangement, the line can be translated as above. A man 'coming in the spirit' is an allusion to the man of the spirit (*'iš rūaḥ*; cf. Hos.9.7), a title for a prophet which came from the ecstatic spirit-possession of the old *nebî'îm* (I Sam.10.6; I Kings 18.12; 22.21; II Kings 2.9, 16). The appearance of 'deception' (*šeqer*) in the sentence recalls the 'deceiving spirit' which came upon the prophets to lead Ahab to his fall (I Kings 22.22). It is possible to see *rūaḥ* as a member of a hendiadys which goes with the verb 'lie', and to translate, 'If a man came/and spun windy lies. . . .' The message which Micah puts in the mouth of this 'ideal' preacher is probably sarcastic metaphor; the man would talk about subjects that pleased the audience. Micah offers a more direct description of the practice of 'successful' prophets in 3.5. 'This people' has a derogatory ring. Isaiah used the phrase when he spoke of the disobedience and stubbornness of his audience (Isa.8.6, 11f.; 9.16; etc.). Here it marks off a people who are distinct from Micah's people (vv.8f.), the oppressors who reject the messenger of YHWH. In 3.8 Micah describes the fundamentals of his own vocation as a preacher-prophet in terms that stand in sharpest contradiction to 'this people's preacher'.

9. THE LORD WILL LEAD THE REMNANT AWAY: 2.12f.

12 I will surely assemble, O Jacob, all of you.[a]
   I will surely gather the remnant of Israel.
   I will unite him like a flock in the fold,[b]
   like a herd in the midst of the pasture.[c]
   And they shall be in commotion[d] because of man.
13 The 'breaker' shall go up[e] before them;
   (they break out and)[f] they shall pass through[g] the gate
      and go out by it.
   Their king shall pass through[g] before them,
      YHWH in front of them.

[a] G assumes *kullō*; MT's second singular is curious, and the direct address is not continued.
[b] *baṣṣîrāh* for MT's *boṣᵉrāh*.
[c] *haddōber* for MT's *haddābᵉrō*.
[d] *tehᵉmeynāh* for MT's *tehîmenāh*.
[e] *wᵉᶜālāh* for *ᶜālāh*.
[f] *pārᵉṣû* seems to be a superfluous repetition of *happōrēṣ*.
[g] Removing the initial *waw* as a dittography.

2.12f. appears to be an oracle of salvation. It promises that YHWH
will gather the remnant of Israel as a shepherd gathers his flock in
the fold (v. 12) and then lead them out by the gate, going before them
as their King (v. 13). The verses have been interpreted often as a
particular version of the drama of salvation proclaimed by Deutero-
Isaiah in which YHWH as King (Isa. 41.21) gathers his flock (40.11;
43.5f.), overwhelms their enemies (41.15f.; 45.2), and leads the
liberated people in a new exodus (49.9ff.; 51.10). The similarity of
Micah 2.12f. in vocabulary and form to the oracle of salvation in
4.6f. seems to confirm this general approach to its interpretation.

If 2.12f. is indeed an oracle of salvation, its presence at the end of
ch. 2 in the midst of an otherwise unbroken sequence of oracles of
judgment is an enigma. Every other promise of deliverance in chs. 1–5
appear in chs. 4–5. Why the exception? There is general agreement
that the oracle is a late addition to the Micah collection. Where the
question about its location in the book has been asked, two solutions
have been proposed. The oracle is said to have been displaced somehow from its proper location in ch. 4; but that explanation simply
calls for yet another.[h] It has also been explained as an oracle of
salvation which marks the conclusion of the first of three sections of
alternating sayings of judgment and salvation (chs. 1–2, 3–5, 6–7) which
reflect the redactional composition of the book.[1] But the separation
of ch. 3 from chs. 1–2 conflicts with the clear Samaria-Jerusalem patterns established in ch. 1 for chs. 1–3 (see the Introduction, p. 25).

The answer to the problem must be sought in the history of the
formation of the saying. It is not a rhetorical unity. The unexpected
third colon of the second poetic line of v. 12 is a comment on the
similes used in the line: 'They (i.e., fold and pasture) shall be in
noisy commotion because of man.' The style shifts in v. 13. In v. 12
YHWH himself speaks of Israel as a corporate singular. Verse 13
speaks about YHWH and refers to Israel with plural pronouns. The
movement of thought is uneven. Promises that YHWH will assemble
the scattered remnant of the nation usually have the gathering of the
dispersion back to Judah in mind. But v. 13 thinks of some walled
place, apparently a city, out of which YHWH will lead his people,
and seems to take 'fold' as a metaphor for this enclosed place, just as
the comment at the end of v. 12 does. The conclusion is that v. 12 is
an original saying which has been developed by both a comment and
expansion.

[h] See the discussion and literature cited by B. Renaud, *Structure et attaches
littéraires de Michée IV-V*, 1964, pp. 20ff.
[1] See the article by J. T. Willis cited in the bibliography.

[12] Verse 12 is the saying of a prophet who spoke during the late exilic period or afterward. It presupposes the scattering of Judah's population through flight and deportation. God speaks by the prophet of the future of the remnant left after judgment. He promises to perform the work of gathering which belongs to his role as the shepherd of Israel. The title 'shepherd' belongs to YHWH's identity as ruler of his people. The role of shepherd became prominent especially in exilic salvation prophecy when the predicament of the dispersion appeared to offer no future beyond the dissolution of Israel among the nations (e.g., Jer. 23.3; 31.8–10; Isa. 40.11; Ezek 34). Hope lay alone in the possibility that the title of shepherd represented a dimension of YHWH which transcended his wrath and judgment. Here the good shepherd promises to fulfil his office in sentences spoken as the firmest assertions. Not one of the flock will be lost; all will be sought and found and gathered together as one flock (Luke 15.4ff.). The comment at the end of the verse is obscure because of the opaqueness of the phrase 'because of man'. Clearly the similes 'fold' and 'pasture' are taken as literal references to a place which will be in commotion when the flock is gathered. Does the commotion occur 'because of such a crowd of men in one place', or 'because of a man or men who threaten the flock'? Is the latter an oblique reference to the human enemies who brought about the fall of Jerusalem and so a preparation for v. 13?

[13] The theme of v. 13 is 'YHWH before them'; the motif appears three times in four cola. Clearly YHWH as king leads his people from within some place out by the gate. As in the comment, the fold has become an assembly point for departure. But is the 'fold' understood as a place of captivity from which the flock must be delivered? The most probable answer lies in the verb used in the title given YHWH (*happōrēṣ*), and in the reference to the gate. YHWH is called 'the one who breaks out/through' only in this text, but the verb is used with YHWH as subject in two established contexts. YHWH 'breaks out' to slay any who violate the limits set by the sanctity of his presence, especially in connection with the ark (II Sam. 6.8· I Chron. 15.13; Ex. 19.22, 24; probably II Sam. 5.20 is to be understood this way). This pattern of usage does not fit v. 13 well, but a second one does. Twice in psalms which recite YHWH's acts, one of his deeds is breaching the walls of Jerusalem at the city's fall (Pss. 80.12; 89.40; cf. 60.1; Isa. 5.5). YHWH is not 'the breaker' who breaks walls of captivity to rescue his flock, but the one who breaks down the fortified gate of Jerusalem and leads them out through it. The otherwise obscure mention of 'the gate' must presuppose and allude to the two

references to the gate of Jerusalem as the focus of YHWH's assault on
Jerusalem in 1.9, 12. Verse 13, then, must be an expansion of the
salvation oracle of v. 12 which reinterprets it as a prophecy of the
gathering of the population into Jerusalem at the time of the Babylonian siege. It creates a larger unit which functions as an announcement of punishment. The siege and fall of the city is the work of
YHWH as King of Israel. The exile is a manifestation of his sovereignty and not his defeat.

The final form of the saying fits in with the prophetic view of
YHWH's plan for Israel which is developed in the arrangement of
chs. 1–5. It sees the entire sweep of Israel's history from the fall
of Samaria and Jerusalem, through the exile, to the restoration of Zion
as the strategy of YHWH to establish his reign in the world. Since v.
13 presupposes 1.9, 12, and since the formation of 2.12f. is similar to
4.6f., which plays a key role in the arrangement of·chs. 4–5, the
creation of 2.12f. and its insertion in the Micah collection in its present place must be the work of the final redactor of chs. 1–5 (see the
Introduction, pp. 27ff.). The oracle interrupts the apparent connection between 2.11 and 'But I said . . .' at the beginning of 3.1
(see the comment on 3.1–4). In its present literary context 2.12f. concludes the sequence of sayings which refer to the exile (1.16; 2.10)
with a climactic statement that the fall of the city and the capture of
its population is indeed the work of YHWH.

10. CANNIBALS IN THE COURT: 3.1–4

1 And I said,
  'Hear, you heads of Jacob
    and leaders of the house of Israel.
  Isn't it your part to know justice,
2a O haters of good and lovers of evil?ᵃ
3 Theyᵇ eat the flesh of my people,
  and strip their skin off them,
  and break their bones.

ᵃ The pronouns in v. 2b lack an antecedent, which ('my people') appears in v. 3a.
The lines have got out of order because the repetition of phrases and words confused a scribe ('skin off them' in 2b and 3a; 'flesh' in 2b and 3a; 'their bones' in 2b
and 3a). The best rearrangement is to move 2b after 3, and read *yigzᵉlū* for *gozᵉlē*.
See the comment below.
ᵇ There is no need to remove *waʾᵃšer*; it is used similarly in 3.5b and makes for a
balanced syllable count in this line.

They chop(them) up as if[c] for the pot,
   like meat to put in the cauldron.
2b [a]The skin will be torn off them,
   their flesh off their bones.
4 Then they will cry out to YHWH,
   but he will not answer them.
He will hide his face from them, in that time,
   since they've turned their deeds to evil.'

The leaders of Israel preside over an administration of injustice in the courts for which they are responsible. They flay and devour the plaintiffs instead of hearing their plea. In punishment YHWH will bring a plea to the leaders' lips—and be deaf. The oracle is an announcement of judgment in the style of a prophetic saying. It begins with a summons to attention, identifying the addressees (1a). The accusation (1b, 2a, 3) opens with an argumentative question (1b) in direct address which states the responsibility which the guilty have betrayed. Then shifting to participles and third-person verbs, the character (2a) and conduct (3) of the accused is cited. Verses 2b, 4, predict the punishment which will fall upon the guilty. In structure and theme the saying is similar to 3.9-12; like this counterpart it was spoken in Jerusalem to the officials who acted as judges in the provincial courts.

The opening phrase, 'And I said', poses a tantalizing problem. It introduces the oracle as though Micah were reporting at a later time what he had said to the leaders of the house of Israel. But no narrative setting for a report is given. The phrase appears in the report of the call stories of Isaiah and Jeremiah (Isa. 6.5, 8; Jer. 1.6), but there in dialogue with YHWH. G and S understood MT's consonants as a third-person verb (*we'āmar*, instead of *wā'ōmar*); in the third-person report of Isaiah's discussion with Ahaz, 'and he said' (7.13) translates *wayyō'mer*, and that would be the expected form here if the verb were in the third person. With so little evidence for guidance, explanations for the function of 'and I said' have been quite various.[d] It has been passed over as an enigmatic gloss (Wellhausen, Marti, J. M. P. Smith). Some have regarded it as the remnant of a first-person report which has been dropped in the book's redaction (Sellin, Weiser). Others have seen it as a connecting link between 2.6-11 and 3.1-4, originally a continuity in which Micah reports how he rejected the opposition of the magistrates to his preaching and

---

[c] For *ka'ᵃšer*, G read *kiš'ēr*, 'like flesh', an emendation often adopted.

[d] For a survey of the discussion and positions taken, see J. T. Willis, *ZAW* 80, 1968, pp. 50-54.

then spoke an oracle against them; 2.12f. was later inserted in the redaction of the book and broke the continuity (variously Ewald, Stade, Duhm). Amos 7.7–12 might furnish an approximate parallel. It seems more likely that the phrase was introduced by Micah in arranging a collection of his sayings as a connection between 2.6–11 and 3.1–4 to show that they were spoken to the same addressees, though not necessarily on the same occasion. It is his way of demonstrating what the true content of 'preaching' is in contrast with the kind preferred by the magistrates (2.11). In the oracle against the prophets (3.5–8) Micah sets the practice of the prophets in opposition to his own vocation, which he describes in the only other first-person report in the material which stems from him (3.8).

[1] The 'heads of Jacob' and 'leaders of the house of Israel' are public officials in Jerusalem, as the use of the titles in 3.9f. clearly indicate. Micah employs the frequently paired names, Jacob and Israel, as a way of addressing his audience in Judah in their identity as the people whose history is the work of YHWH and whose obligation is to his lordship (on Micah's use of these names, see the comment on 1.5a). The titles 'head' ($r\bar{o}$'$\check{s}$) and leader ($q\bar{a}\d{s}in$) are synonyms. In both appearances the titles are associated with the administration of justice (see 3.9, 11). The earliest use of 'head' as a title for leader in the Old Testament is Ex. 18.25 where it is applied to the 'able men' whom Moses appointed to serve as judges for divisions of Israel; they are also called officers ($\check{s}ar\bar{i}m$), which is the title Isaiah gives to the men in Jerusalem who are responsible for justice (Isa. 1.23). In the villages and towns, presiding over the court in the gate was traditionally the responsibility of the elders. But in Jerusalem, and probably in other cities fortified by the king, there were officials appointed by the king to serve as judges (II Chron. 19.4–11; Deut. 16.18–20).[e] Leader ($q\d{a}\d{s}in$) is a title that appears in only two settings. In the premonarchical life of Israel it was used for military leaders (Josh. 10.24; Judg. 11.6, 11 where $r\bar{o}$'$\check{s}$ is the synonym). The title surfaces again in eighth-century Jerusalem and is used by Isaiah (1.10; 3.6, 7; 22.3) and Micah for officials in Jerusalem.

With an accusing question Micah states their responsibility and his theme. It belongs to the office of the heads of Jacob 'to know justice' when they function as judges in the court. The verb 'know' means to be skilled in acquaintance with the normative legal traditions of justice and sound in recognizing their authority. Those who know justice will reach the right decision, the finding which upholds

[e] See R. de Vaux, *Ancient Israel*, 1961, pp. 152–5, for a full description of the organization and practice of courts in Israel.

justice (see *hammišpāṭ* in Deut. 1.17; 17.9, 11; I Kings 3.28; 7.7). The failure of justice in Jerusalem's courts is a recurrent motif in Isaiah and Micah (Isa. 1.17, 21–23, 26; 5.7, 23). Micah views these leaders in the light of traditions like those recorded in Ex. 18.13–27 and in Deut. 1.9–18, which define their obligation to be righteous judges, free from partiality and impervious to bribery. The right decision was the concern of God himself (Deut. 1.17), so the righteousness of a judge was an obligation to YHWH.

[2a] Alongside their responsibility Micah sets the reality of their conduct: they hate what is good and love what is evil. Compare his charge that 'they detest justice and pervert what is moral' in 3.9. The word-pair 'love/hate', used for personal preference in conduct, is a favourite device in antithetical proverbs (Prov. 1.22; 9.8; 12.1; 13.24); and the pairing of 'good/evil' as characterizations of conduct appears twice in the wisdom psalms (Pss. 34.14 and 37.27). For the eighth-century prophets the alternative patterns of conduct described by this vocabulary are a special issue in the courts of justice; Amos exhorts the elders who sit in the court in the gates to 'hate evil, love good, and uphold justice' (Amos 5.15); Isaiah has a similar exhortation (1.17). The place where the corruption of Israel's moral traditions, the ethical standards inculcated in the family and taught by the wise men, is showing in hideous clarity is the court, the very place where the issues of life and honour and property are settled.

[3] Their actual deeds are characterized by a long metaphor, sustained through three poetic lines. The heads of Jacob are portrayed as cannibals who skin their victims, strip their meat, chop their bones, and lump them in boiling kettles. The measures of the metaphor tumble out one after another, driven by a vehement revulsion from what is depicted. The sentences do not come in any logical order so as to construct a unified picture of a process of preparing food; instead the items emerge in snatches, with repetitions and *non sequiturs*. The rearrangement of MT's order proposed in the translation brings the sequence into better order. The metaphor uncovers the vicious nature of the economic and legal processes by which the powerless are devoured; compare 2.2, 9; 3.9f. The victims are called 'my people', the term Micah uses for the wronged and ruined folk with whom he confesses his identity in distinction from those who violate YHWH's order by their oppression of the weak. On Micah's use of *'ammī*, see the note at 1.9.

[2b] The repetition of the same tense in vv. 2b and 3 has led to the disarrangement of their lines. The repetition and the movement of thought in the entire saying are clarified if v. 2b is understood as the

first line of the announcement of punishment.[t] The same cruelty which the leaders have visited on the weak will come upon them. With v. 2b in this sequence, the adverb 'Then' in v. 4 has an antecedent to which it points. The circumstances described in v. 2b are those in which the leaders will cry out for help.

[4] The precise details of the punishment are not reported. Instead, Micah portrays a time in the future when circumstances will wring a cry of anguish from the guilty leaders. The fate of suffering they brought on their victims will come upon them.

'In that time' is an inserted phrase which takes the adverb 'Then' to be a temporal reference to a distant future. It is one of the additions by which the words of Micah are applied to events at the time of Jerusalem's fall; see the last sentence in 2.3.

The language predicting the punishment is drawn from the vocabulary of the laments of those who in distress turn to YHWH. For 'cry out' see the appeal ($zā'aq$) in Pss. 22.6; 107.13, 19; 142.6. The 'answer' of YHWH is the saving help that delivers, or the oracle promising salvation (Pss. 3.5; 4.2; 20.2). That YHWH 'hides his face' means the absence of his favour manifest in unrelieved distress (Pss. 13.2; 22.5; 27.9; 69.18). As so often in announcements of judgment, the description of the punishment is composed to correspond to the deeds of the guilty. The punishment fits the crime; those who prey on the helplessness of others will themselves know the terror of helplessness. The concluding measure echoes the indictment and states its significance as the basis for the future of Jacob's leaders; YHWH does not answer the laments of those who choose evil instead of good.

11. THOSE WHO SELL THE WORD SHALL LOSE IT:
3.5–8

5 This is what YHWH has said against the prophets:
who mislead my people.
When they have something to chew on,
they proclaim 'Peace'.
. Let a man fail to put something in their mouth
and they sanctify war against him.
6 Therefore,
it will be night for you without vision,
darkness[a] for you without divination.

[t] So J. Lindblom, *Micha*, 1929, pp. 70ff., followed by A. Weiser.
[a] Reading the noun $ḥašēkāh$ (cf. G) as a better synonym for 'night'; MT has a verb, $ḥašekāh$.

> The sun shall set for the prophets,
> the day go dark for them.
> 7 The seers shall be confounded,
> and the diviners in consternation.
> All of them will cover their beards,
> because there is no answer from God.
> 8 But I! I am filled
> with power, [b]with YHWH's spirit,[b] and justice and might
> to declare to Jacob his crime,
> to Israel his sin.

Conflict among the prophets was episodic in Israel's history. Alongside the messengers of YHWH's judgment stood prophets who contradicted their words with promises of weal and welfare. From the time of Elijah and Micaiah ben Imlah there were two prophetic words to guide Israel in its life under YHWH's reign. 3.5–8 stems from one engagement in the conflict and sets the two words in sharp contrast. It is an oracle against the prophets in Jerusalem. The saying unfolds in three stages: the indictment of the prophets for misleading the people (v. 5), the announcement of the punishment which would befall them (vv. 6f.), and a concluding declaration by Micah concerning the basis and purpose of his own mission (v. 8). This final claim which introduces the distinctiveness of Micah's vocation so emphatically and abruptly comes as an unexpected element after the announcement of judgment. This suggests that the saying was delivered to an audience of prophets who had called his word into question. The oracle derives from conflict between the lone man from Moresheth and the professional guild of prophets in Jerusalem.

There is only one other use of the messenger formula, 'This is what YHWH has said', in the book of Micah. In 2.3 the formula introduces the second element of an oracle of judgment, the announcement of punishment which is composed in divine first-person style. But this speech uses the style of a saying of the prophet throughout. The 'I' who speaks in v. 8 is clearly the prophet. Verse 7 refers to the deity in the third person. The expression 'my people' in v. 5 has the prophet as antecedent of the possessive pronoun in Micah's language (see the comment below). The original unit probably opened with the definite plural participle, 'The ones who mislead my people', a style used in woe-sayings with or without an introductory 'Woe!'[c] The first collector of Micah's sayings added 'This is what YHWH has said against

---

[b] An expansion of the text; overloads the metre and includes a superfluous '*et*-.

[c] See E. Gerstenberger, *JBL* 81, 1962, pp. 252f.

(*'al*) the prophets' to mark the beginning of a separate saying clearly.[d]
He probably understood 'my people' as a sign of divine first-person
style; the phrase 'against the prophets' was taken from v. 6.

[5] From the time of Micaiah ben Imlah (I Kings 22) the men
who announced YHWH's punishment charged that the prophets
misled the people (cf. Isa.9.12ff.; Jer.23.13, 14, 32). The prophet
(*hannābī'*) was the agent through whom YHWH communicated with
Israel to disclose his purpose and decisions in specific situations. The
office was set alongside that of the king so that the earthly monarch
and his subjects could know the policy and edicts of their divine
suzerain. Micah accuses the prophets he knew of corrupting their
office; what the people heard from them was based, not on YHWH's
way, but on self-interest. Clients were given calculating manipulating
words as the revelation of God. They heard words empty of divine
reality and were drawn by deceit into a swamp of professional avarice.
Micah's indictment sounds like a general condemnation of all he
knew who were called '*nābī*''; in 3.11 he speaks of the prophets in
Jerusalem without exception. In the tradition about Micah, he himself is assigned no title. The superscription of the book (1.1) and the
elders at Jeremiah's trial (Jer.26.18) call him simply 'the Moreshite'.
But the latter do speak of his language as 'prophesying', and Micah's
opponents take his messages for the speech of a *nābī*' (see the comment
on 'preach' in 2.6). Micah is, like Amos, another case of a man so
isolated and estranged by the contradiction between his message and
that of Jerusalem's prophets that he must speak of them in alienation.
The mission and message is a greater reality than the office. The
criterion of Micah's critique is first of all his knowledge of YHWH
(see v. 8), but the motivation for his assault on the prophets comes also
from his compassion for those whom they mislead. Micah calls them
'my people' in his sense of identity with them in contrast to their
oppressors, and in his passionate empathy with those who are betrayed
(see 3.3; 2.8f., and the note on *'ammī* in the language of Micah at 1.9).
By this phrase Micah places himself in the midst of those who are
misled and takes up their cause in a way that can be seen as a sym-
bolical act representing the God who hears the cry of the weak and
exploited.

In two scornful and derisive lines Micah uncovers the true source
of the prophet's words. What comes out of their mouths depends on
whether anything goes in. Feed them and you hear good words;
slight them and you hear of your doom. 'Jerusalem's prophets pro-

[d] T. Lescow assumes that the force of 'and I said' in v. 1 continues, and simply
omits the formula as redactional: *ZAW* 84, 1972, pp.48f.

duce divinations for money' (3.11). The old seers and prophets had
received gifts and fees for their services (I Sam. 9.6ff.; I Kings 18.19;
Amos 7.12). But in the history of the prophetic guild, the patronage
of the royal house and the support of the emerging commercial urban
class had turned the custom into the controlling concern of the prophets. The 'nouveau riche' in Jerusalem had drawn prophet and
priest into their own environment where money talked louder than
God. To those who supported them the prophets proclaimed 'Peace'
(šālōm). The term is broader in meaning than peace as the absence of
hostility; it connotes a state of well-being in life, security and satisfaction, free from enemies and misfortune. It is the wholeness of
living which goes with a life that is whole, of a piece with its environment in God and world.[e] From Micah we hear the word used for the
first time as a summary term for the content of false prophecy. In the
crisis years of Jerusalem's fall the term would become a slogan of the
struggle over the right word from God; Jeremiah and Ezekiel drew
the battle line against their prophetic opposition with the cry, 'There
is no peace' (Jer. 6.14; 8.11; 12.12; 30.5; Ezek 13.10, 16; the classic
case is Jeremiah's confrontation with Hananiah, Jer. 28). In Micah's
day the issue had not yet become the question of the 'salvation' of the
state of Judah. These prophets were promising well-being in the name
of God to those who paid them well, and so had made šālōm a matter
of a transaction between patron and professional. God supplied, but
the prophets kept the keys of the kingdom. Against those who did not
support them, they 'sanctified war.' Taken literally, the phrase refers
to the cultic rites customary as preparation for going to battle,
especially in holy war (see the phrase in Jer. 6.4; Joel 4.9).[f] Micah
appears to use 'sanctify war' as a metaphor for the hostility of the
prophets. See his portrayal of the oppressors of the weak as an enemy
who wages war in 2.8. Probably the prophets produced oracles of
misfortune against those who did not support them. In a culture in
which prophets were believed to be able to divine the plans of God
and whose words had the power to bring about what they foretold,
they had considerable power to threaten and undo the life of a man.

[6] The conjunction 'therefore' introduces the punishment to come
upon the prophets (similarly in 3.12 with a shift to direct address; in
2.3 with the messenger formula). The change of style to direct address

[e] See the full exploration of the richness of the word in Israel's vocabulary by J.
Pedersen, *Israel* I–II, 1926, pp. 263–335; and G. von Rad, '*eirēnē*', *TDNT* II, pp.
402ff.
[f] See the discussion in J. A. Soggin, *VT* 10, 1960, pp. 79–83; P. D. Miller, *VT*
18, 1968, pp. 103f.

in v. 6a shows that Micah speaks to an audience of prophets.[g] 'Night',
'darkness', 'the sun going down', 'the day growing dark' are a series
of images for the experience of distress and dereliction. The cause of
the distress will be the absence of any vision (*ḥāzōn*), the medium of
revelation or the revelation itself (Ezek. 13.16; 7.26; I Sam. 3.1).

[7] 'Seer' (*ḥōzeh*) is a title based on the practice of acquiring oracles
by visions (see the terminology and procedures in the account of
Balaam, Num. 22–24); it had come to be an alternate name for a
prophet (II Kings 17.13; Amos 7.12; Isa. 29.10). In Israel's vocabulary
'divine' (acquire information from the deity by examining omens;
see the description of a divination procedure in Ezek. 21.26) was a
pejorative term, always used for foreign cultic divination, or in a bad
sense.[h] The terms do not designate different categories in this saying;
Micah uses them all to speak of prophets who conjure up visions on
demand just as pagan diviners create omens (see 3.11). 'To cover
the beard' is a rite of mourning (Ezek. 24.17, 22; cf. Lev. 13.45),
probably an act similar to shrouding the head (II Sam. 15.30; Jer.
14.3). Humiliation and consternation will overwhelm the prophets
because there is no 'answer from God'. The answer of God is an
oracle or act of help for those who lament and appeal to God for
deliverance (see the expression in 3.4; and often in the 'laments of the
individual', Pss. 3.5; 4.2; 20.2; etc.). The situation Micah foretells
will later be described in the laments sung for the fall of Jerusalem
(Lam. 3.9, 14). It is a time when the prophecies of *šālōm* are shown
to be empty deceptions and the prophets are caught up in a catastrophe for which they have no convincing word; in their humiliation
they lose the 'gift' of seeing visions. What the prophets misused will
be taken away from them. Their profession will become as empty of
reality as the oracles they gave.

[8] With a strong adversative (*wĕʾūlām*) and an emphatic pronoun
Micah sets his own mission in the starkest contrast to the practices of
the prophets. The claim he makes for himself is astonishing in its
absolute conviction and scope. The declaration about himself concerns his vocation; it states the capacities which have been given to
him (v. 8a) and the kind of message he is to declare (v. 8b). This twofold structure corresponds to the basic elements of the call-stories of
other prophets of judgment which are generally in first-person style

---

[g] T. Lescow takes v. 6a as a quotation of what the prophets say to those they
harass; the interpretation necessitates the removal of 'therefore' (op. cit., p. 49).

[h] All the instances are listed by BDB, p. 890; on the occurrence and practice of
divination in the ancient Near East and in Israel, see J. Lindblom, *Prophecy in
Ancient Israel*, 1962, pp. 83–95.

and contain the elements of the call by YHWH and the basic message (see Amos 7.14f.; Isa. 6; Jer. 1.4–10; Ezek. 1–2). The reports of their call were used by the prophets to authenticate their surprising message. Verse 8 in the context of the entire saying has that function; its appearance at the conclusion indicates that the saying is set in a controversy which Micah undertakes to end with a declaration of his credentials. His statement in turn becomes a positive norm for his critique of the prophets and their practices. Not the motivation of money, but the endowments of God should be the basis of prophecy. Not *šālōm*, but the accusation of sin, should be the purpose of prophecy. In the book of Micah there is no account of his call as such; this verse can stand in lieu of one as a succinct but complete summary of the basis and intention of his mission. The particular form of the declaration is without parallel in the Old Testament; there is no other first-person claim like it (see the post-exilic echo in Isa. 58.1). In form, v. 8a is a claim of endowment. The nearest parallel in time and language is Jeremiah's statement: 'I am filled (qal as in Micah) with the wrath of YHWH' (Jer. 6.11; cf. also 15.17 with piel). In the Priestly stratum of the Pentateuch there is the statement that Joshua was filled (qal) with the spirit of wisdom by the ordination of Moses (Deut. 34.9). There are several descriptions of the endowments of craftsmen for their trade, using the verb *mālē'* (I Kings 7.14; and from P, Ex. 28.3; 31.3; 35.31, 35). Though no source of the endowments is named here, the pattern of such statements shows that the source is divine. Micah does not speak of his own aptitude, but of capacities which have come upon him for the performance of mission. The gifts are three. The first is *kōah*, power to persevere in the face of opposition and discouragement (Isa. 40.29, 31; 49.4; Ps. 31.11). The third is *gebūrāh*, the courage and might that equips warriors for action surrounded by danger and enemies (Judg. 8.21; Prov. 8.14; Isa. 3.25, etc.). The second, middle term is the discriminating and critical captivity for discerning what is at issue between God and people; it is *mišpāt*, the sense for what is just according to the norms set by YHWH for the social order of Israel. *Mišpāt* is what the leaders in Jerusalem are responsible for (3.1), but they abhor and pervert it (3.9). When the courts and counting houses of the nation fail in justice the prophets must speak for the heavenly court and represent its justice. The prophets have failed. Micah stands in their place endowed with a strength and courage from God that does not flinch from the lonely role of standing against the entire power structure of Jerusalem. The text lists a fourth endowment, 'the spirit of YHWH', which obviously is not on the same level as the other three. The spirit is the extension of the divine personality (A. R. Johnson) who brings and bestows capacities co-ordinate with those which belong to God. The classic portrayal is the description of the 'shoot from Jesse's stump', the future Davidide, upon whom the spirit of YHWH will rest and confer the capacities to rule as God's true regent. A tradent, perhaps prompted by the presence of 'might' in both lists of endowments, has added the phrase 'spirit of YHWH' to state clearly that the endowments are charismatic, the work of YHWH's spirit (note the presence of 'spirit' in several of the endowment forms, Deut. 34.9; Ex. 31.3; 35.31). Micah himself might have avoided the term in his situation (see the comment on 2.11), because of the association between spirit-possession and the prophetic guilds. But the intention of the expansion is a true interpretation of his dependence on the endowment of YHWH.

By his sense for what is just, Micah could discern the crime and sin in Israel's public. The word-pair occurs also in the statement of the reason for YHWH's theophany (1.5a); YHWH comes forth because of the crime of Jacob and the sin of the house of Israel (on the word-pair see the comment on 1.5a). The identity between the purpose of YHWH in his awesome manifestation and the purpose given Micah in his work discloses the co-ordination between God and his spokesman. Micah's indictments which specify what the crime is in Jacob's social order (see 2.1f., 8–10; 3.1–3, 9–11) are an interpretation of the divine significance of the Assyrian crisis. Micah focuses on the sin in Israel, not its gross national product, because it is only in seeing themselves under the judgment of God that the guilty can grasp the reality of what is happening to them in their history.

12. THE TERRIBLE WORD: 3.9–12

9 Hear this, chiefs of the house of Jacob,
    and leaders of the house of Israel—
the ones who detest justice
    and pervert the right (way),
10 building[a] Zion at the cost of bloodshed,
    Jerusalem by means of violence.
11 Her chiefs render decisions for a bribe;
    her priests give instruction for a price;
    her prophets divine for money.

[a] For MT's *bōneh*, the versions assume *bōnē*; but cf. Hab. 2.12.

Yet they lean on YHWH and say,
'Is not YHWH in our midst?
Disaster shall not come upon us!'
12 Therefore, because of you
Zion shall become a plowed field,
Jerusalem a heap of rubble, [b]
and the mount of the house wooded heights. [c]

Jerusalem! What words are adequate to describe the feeling that name called forth in the heart of every Israelite. The city of David, the capital of Judah and residence of the king. And, most of all, the place where the temple of YHWH stands, the mount to which all the tribes go up on pilgrimage. 'Beautiful for situation, the joy of all the earth.' Yet Micah comes from the little village of Moresheth, stands in the midst of the great city and announces its destruction. It will disappear, leaving only a pitiful ruin of rubble in open country to remind men what once was there. The city has been built with bloodshed that cries out to God for the justice its leaders abhor. No surprise that the oracle was remembered! Though it found no early fulfilment, its threat hung over the city for years. There were elders at Jeremiah's trial more than a century later who could quote it (Jer. 26). The saying is an announcement of judgment. It opens with a summons to attention which names the addressees (v. 9a); the summons is similar to 3.1a except for the inclusion of the demonstrative 'this' and 'house of' before Jacob. The indictment (vv. 9b–11) describes the addressees with participles and third-person verbs (so 3.2f., 5; 2.1f.). First, the basic character of their deeds is stated using normative terms as criteria (v. 9b), and then their specific deeds described in a listing which includes priests and prophets with the leaders (vv. 10–11a). A quotation of their confession of faith sets their religion in ironic contrast to their deeds (v. 11b). The announcement of punishment (v. 12) based on the indictment sets in with 'therefore' in direct address style (cf. 2.3; 3.6a). The entire saying is spoken as the speech of Micah.

[9] The addressees are the same chiefs and leaders to whom 3.1–4 was spoken. Their titles (*rōʾš* and *qāṣîn*) and the responsibility attributed to them by Micah (3.1b) indicate that they are the officials of his day who should perform the duties which belonged to the leaders and chiefs in the old tribal society (see the comment on 3.1). Micah

---

[b] *ʿiyyîn*, but *ʿiyyîm* in Jer. 26.18; Ps. 79.1.

[c] The plural *bāmōt* as in 1.5; Symmachus and Theodotion assume a singular and many read *bāmat*.

uses the names, Jacob and Israel, to fix their identity by the 'all-Israel' tradition. Clearly he speaks to Judaeans in Jerusalem (v. 2), but by these names he holds them to the responsibilities which go with their position in Israel's traditions of social order. They have come to think of their authority in terms of their new context in the monarchy and pattern their practices after its use of power, and that is a large part of their problem (on Micah's use of 'Jacob' and 'Israel' see the comment on 1.5b). But their history as Israel under YHWH gives the true definition of their role. Their primary obligation is to know in all situations in the social life of the people what the right decision is and to implement justice (3.1). But their practices are in fact a rejection of their obligation. They detest justice (*mišpāṭ*), the established norms for protecting the rights of the innocent in legal disputes over life and property. Faithfulness to YHWH required that the suits of those in the right, and especially the poor and weak, be upheld, as the Book of the Covenant expressly stipulated (Ex. 23.1–3, 6–8; cf. Deut. 16.19; Lev. 19.13, 15) What happens in Jerusalem's courts is no different from the corruption Amos uncovered in the northern state (Amos 5.7, 10, 14f.; 6.12). By bribery, influence, and lies 'they pervert the right' (literally, 'twist the straight [way]'). The expression means to knowingly follow a course of action that departs from what is recognized to be good, righteous; the teachers of wisdom used the expression to characterize wicked men (Prov. 10.9; 28.18; Job 33.27). The leaders are guilty before law and wisdom, the two great sources from which Israel learned the will of God.

[10] As first evidence for this general indictment Micah cites the way they build Jerusalem by bloodshed and violence. To what hideous business Micah points with this charge is not clear. Violence ('*awlāh*) is the word for the work of Abner's assassins and of marauding enemies of Israel (II Sam. 3.34; 7.10); it is simply a synonym for bloodshed. Probably Micah refers to the unscrupulous and inhuman oppression of the weak because of greed for property (2.2f.) and lust for lavish homes (Isa. 5.8f.). Cases like Ahab's judicial murder of Naboth (I Kings 21) may have become a pattern for building estates. In 2.8f. Micah portrays entrepreneurs who are worse than a conquering army; in 3.2f. he pictures a hunger for property that changes the leaders into cannibals. With such bloody gain the rich built up their proud Jerusalem. It was urban renewal with a vengeance, a new Jerusalem that cost the lives of men. The words of Micah's accusation appear in the form of a woe-saying in Hab. 2.12, 'Woe to him who builds a city at the cost of bloodshed, founds a town by means of violence.' The parallel could be a quotation by Habbakuk: Ier. 26

shows that this oracle of Micah was known in Jerusalem in the late
seventh century. Habbakuk applies the words to the fortifications
built by the Egyptians (?) in Lebanon.[d] It could be that Micah speaks
of fortifications and public buildings erected in Jerusalem with forced
labour during Hezekiah's move toward independence from the
Assyrians. He undertook to secure Jerusalem's water supply by the
excavation of the Siloam tunnel (II Kings 20.20) and expanded
the royal buildings (II Chron. 32.27f.). His leaders would have been
the agents for commandeering labour. The blood spilt over what was
built cried out to God, and that cry would be heard over all the hymns
and prayers of faith that went up from 'the mount of the house'.

[11a] Three similarly formed sentences sketch the corruption of the
city; each sentence has the title of an office as subject, a function as
verb, and a prepositional phrase accusing the officers of performance
for personal profit.[e] An administration of avarice grips the city. The
first sentence concerns the addressees of the oracle. Zion's leaders who
preside as judges sell the justice they dispense. Isaiah also bewails the
bribery which controlled the decisions in Jerusalem's courts (Isa.
1.23; 5.23; 33.15), a blatant disregard for Israel's law (Ex. 23.8;
Deut. 16.19; 27.25) and morality (Prov. 17.8, 23; 21.14; Ps. 15.5).
This subordination of office to avarice has spread like an infection to
the priests and prophets who find the paradigm for their practice in
the leaders of the community. The priests, mentioned only here by
Micah, give instruction (*yōreh*) for a price. One of the duties of priests
was to give instruction about particular problems brought to them,
to point out the way of YHWH (Hos. 4.6; Deut. 33.10). It is possible
that direction in legal matters is also in view here; difficult cases were
brought to the priests to receive instruction from God about their
resolution (Deut. 17.10f.).[f] Prophets complete the triad of greed;
they divine for money. On the practice of divination and the way in
which prophets were manipulating their services, see the commentary
on 3.5. It is not necessary to suppose that these civic and religious
leaders were always openly and crudely corrupt. In a culture
fascinated by wealth and its acquisition the morality of good business
has a compelling power to influence decisions and attitudes in subtle
and indirect ways. Probably it was not 'the fee' for service or profit

[d] So F. Horst, HAT 14, 1954[2], p. 183.

[e] The title of each officer is qualified by a feminine possessive pronoun with
Jerusalem as antecedent; the officials are the actuality of the city and the locus of
her guilt. For similar oracles against the failure of officials with lists of titles, see
Hos. 5.1ff.; Jer. 6.13f.; 2.8; 5.3; Zeph. 3.1ff.; Ezek. 22.23ff.

[f] For a review of the office of priest and its functions, R. de Vaux, *Ancient Israel*,
1961, pp. 845ff.

from work that Micah sees as hideous, but the fact that gain had become the overriding basis of the practices of leader, priest, and prophet alike. Then the obligation to God and neighbour had little chance.

[11b] Alongside the dedication of their vocations to gain, Micah sets their devotion to YHWH. The first measure of the tricolon acknowledges the fact of their faith and the next two in the form of a quotation summarize its content. This piety is attributed, not just to the prophets of the immediately preceding sentence, but to the magistrates and priests as well. They live in a confidence based on YHWH's relation to them. The expression 'rely on' (*niš'an 'al*, literally 'lean on') is a frequent synonym of 'trust in' in the Old Testament vocabulary of faith. 'To rely on YHWH' is used for dependence on divine help in a military situation in all its occurrences (Isa. 10.20; II Chron. 13.18; 14.20; 16.7f.; see Isaiah's 'woe' against those who make alliance with Egypt and 'rely on horses . . . but do not look to the Holy One of Israel', 31.1; this dependence on YHWH in a military crisis appears to be the very policy which Isaiah called for on occasion). The quotation is an appeal to an old confessional motif of Israel's faith. 'YHWH in the midst of Israel' is a spatial way of expressing YHWH's relation to the people he had chosen. In the earlier hexateuchal traditions the theme appears in both Sinai and wilderness narratives. It is the conception of the way YHWH continues to be present with Israel after they leave the mount (Ex. 33.3, 5; 34.9; Num. 11.20; 14.4; cf. Deut. 6.15). 'YHWH in the midst of Israel' was an assurance of help in need; the Israelites tested YHWH at Meribah by demanding water and crying 'Is YHWH in our midst, or not?' (Ex. 17.7). The story of the failure to take Canaan turns upon the issue of 'YHWH in the midst' (Num. 14.42; cf. Deut. 1.42). The motif is connected with the ark and its significance as an objectification of YHWH's presence with Israel in war (I Sam. 4.3; Deut. 7.21; Josh. 3.10). Jeremiah (or the people?) in a time of severe drought pleads, 'But you, YHWH, are in our midst . . .' (14.9). According to Joel 2.27, the return of fertility and plenty after famine demonstrates 'that I am in the midst of Israel . . . I am your God.' Finally, the expression occurs in hymnic material praising YHWH for deliverance from enemies (Zeph. 3.15, 'YHWH's in your midst; you need fear disaster no more,' quite similar to v. 11b; also Zeph. 3.17; Isa. 12.6). The spatial character of the expression made it a particularly reassuring formulation; YHWH is located in the space where the people are, and his person and power are vested in their situation. The third measure is a good summary of the consequence: 'disaster will not

come upon us'. The tangible reference of the confident confession must be the 'mount of the house (of YHWH)' mentioned in v. 12; its addition to the names, Jerusalem and Zion, in the description of punishment implies that 'the house' is an issue. The motif 'YHWH in the midst' is related to Zion as the city of God in Ps. 46.6, a hymn of confidence in the invulnerability of Zion based on YHWH's election of Zion. Whether the full-fledged 'Zion theology' of the hymns of Zion (Pss. 46, 48, 84, 87) was already present among the leading circles in Jerusalem in the late eighth century is a matter of debate.[g] But the language of Micah's saying points to a reliance on YHWH's election that was focused on Jerusalem and the temple, a confidence in his presence which guaranteed security for its residents; it was a faith that Jeremiah would confront in a more dogmatic form a century later (Jer. 7, 26).

The claim to be exempt from disaster ($r\bar{a}^c\bar{a}h$, in this context an antonym of $\bar{s}\bar{a}l\bar{o}m$, v. 5) is not a vague, general hope, but a direct response to Micah's announcement of $r\bar{a}^c\bar{a}h$ as the purpose of YHWH in 2.3, defeat and humiliation by an enemy. The Assyrian crisis probably provides the setting in which the words of Micah and his opponents are to be understood. The leaders confess their faith in this particular language because it is appropriate for confidence in the face of enemies. The theme 'YHWH in our midst' had not always been a slogan of security in Israel's past, nor bound materially to ark or temple; there was an understanding that YHWH's being there was highly conditional on the conduct of Israel, and was a dangerous threat when Israel was disobedient (Ex. 33.3, 5; Num. 14.14; Deut. 6.15; Zeph. 3.5; cf. Hos. 11.9). With that understanding Micah includes this summary of the faith of Jerusalem's leaders in his indictment of them. It furnishes a contrast to their deeds. The faith in itself as one form of the trust in 'God with us' is advocated many times in the OT; it is an indispensable dimension of the biblical knowledge of God's initiative and grace toward his people. But the theological validity of their trust is contingent on the awareness that YHWH is without compromise a God who works justice and expects uprightness, the unanimous position of the eighth- and seventh-century canonical prophets. For leaders who detest justice and build Jerusalem with

---

[g] Compare G. von Rad's reconstruction of a theology of Zion as the background for Isaiah's views (*Old Testament Theology* II, 1965, pp. 155ff.) with G. Wanke's conclusion that the theology was the post-exilic achievement of the Korahites (*Die Zionstheologie der Korachiten*, BZAW 97, 1966). J. J. M. Roberts finds a historical origin for the Zion tradition in the Davidic-Solomonic period ('The Davidic Origin of the Zion Tradition', *JBL* 92, 1973, pp. 329–44).

blood to appeal to YHWH is to invoke a threat that cannot be escaped.

[12] 'Therefore' makes the transition from the indictment to the announcement of punishment. The phrase 'because of you' repeats the accusing function of vv. 9–11 in direct address to emphasize to the audience that they and they alone are the reason for the catastrophe to come. No divine or historical agent of the catastrophe is named; its result is simply described. Around the countryside there were mounds of old ruins where once cities had stood, but now fields and bramble thickets. Jerusalem would become another. The city will vanish, the land revert to agriculture, the site become a *tell* like Ai. Even 'the mount of the house' (an abbreviation of 'mount of the house of YHWH', 4.1) will become a forested height. No listener would miss the implication; the temple will be destroyed. There will be no cultic place to guarantee that 'YHWH is in our midst'. A more absolute 'no' to the faith and future of Micah's audience can scarcely be imagined. The prophecy was not fulfilled in Micah's time. After Jerusalem fell to the Babylonians in the early sixth century, a community lament bewails its partial fulfilment (Ps. 79.1). Jerusalem has never become a deserted ruin to this day. But the prophecy stands as a declaration of YHWH's freedom from any institutionalization of his presence, a freedom manifest in readiness to judge even those who believe in him.

When Jeremiah took up the message a century later (Jer. 7), he was immediately put on trial for his life (Jer. 26).[h] During the trial certain elders of the land recalled and cited v. 12 (Jer. 26.17f.), adding the messenger formula, 'This is what YHWH of hosts has said', to emphasize their understanding that the word was indeed from YHWH. They also had a conviction about what should be done in response to Jeremiah's word, which was at the same time an explanation why Micah's prophecy was not fulfilled. They said that Hezekiah feared YHWH and entreated his favour, and YHWH repented of the catastrophe he had planned for them. It appears that the elders remembered some story like the account of Hezekiah's turning to YHWH during the Assyrian crisis (II Kings 19.1, 14ff.) and took the escape of Jerusalem for the change of YHWH's policy. In the account in II Kings 19, it is Isaiah who plays the role of God's spokesman. If the elders were accurate, Micah also was on the scene and this oracle belongs to some date in the months of the Assyrian attack in 701 BC. For a discussion of this and other problems about the time of Micah's mission, see the Introduction to the commentary.

---

[h] See J. Bright, *Jeremiah* (Anchor Bible 21), 1965, pp. 167ff.

13. 'A CITY SET ON A HILL': 4.1–5

1 This shall happen in the latter days:
    the mountain on which YHWH's house stands
will be established at the top of the mountains,
    be raised above the hills.
Peoples will stream to it,
2   and many nations will come.
They will say,
'Come, let us go up to YHWH's mountain,
    to the house of Jacob's God,
That he may instruct us about his ways
    and we shall walk in his paths;
for from Zion instruction goes out,
    the word of YHWH from Jerusalem.'
3 He will judge between many peoples,
    and decide who is in the right for numerous distant
        nations.
They will beat their swords into ploughshares,
    their spears into pruning hooks.
Nation will not take up the sword against nation,
    nor shall they train for war any more.
4 Each man shall sit under his vine,
    under his fig tree with none to terrify;
for the mouth of YHWH of Hosts has spoken.
5 For all the peoples walk,
    each in the name of its God;
but we will walk in the name of YHWH,
    our God for ever and ever.

4.1–4 is one of the best known texts in the Old Testament. The reason is obvious. At the heart of the passage there is a promise of the end of warfare among nations and the beginning of an era of untroubled peace for every man (vv. 3f.). The appeal of that promise to every sane person is compelling. But in the saying the promise of peace is founded on a prior promise that the reign of YHWH shall become the centre of order for all peoples (vv. 1f.). The longing for peace cannot exist as hope if it is separated from the expectation of the coming divine kingdom. The theological integrity of the prophecy lies in its unity. The text as a whole portrays the way in which the appearance of YHWH's reign on earth will inaugurate an imperial peace that transforms the conditions of life for nations and individuals. In the latter days, the mount on which YHWH's house stands will become the pre-eminent place in the world (v. 1, except for the last colon). The nations will be drawn into pilgrimages which move toward this one centre in order to submit their way of life to the reformation of YHWH's instruction (last colon of v. 1, v. 2). YHWH as king will settle the conflicts between the nations who come (v. 3, first line). They will abandon weapons and war as needless (v. 3, second and third lines). Every individual will be left to live free from the threat of terror (v. 4a). A concluding saying-formula validates the promise as the policy of YHWH of Hosts (v. 4b). In v. 5, there is a liturgical response to the prophecy spoken by the corporate congregation.

As an individual saying 4.1–4 is a promise of salvation to all nations, a vision which expresses a generous and universal hope. In its present literary context other features of the saying are brought into play and the saying assumes further functions as part of the book. It stands in startling contrast to 3.9–12, where the utter destruction of Zion and the transformation of the mount of YHWH into a wooded hill is announced. The recurrence of themes from the oracle of judgment in the salvation-prophecy hold the two together as paired words ('mount of the house' at the conclusion of 3.12// 'mount of the house of YHWH' in 4.1; 'mount of YHWH' and 'house of Jacob's God' in 4.2). The latter word does not cancel the former; both are meant to be heard. The Jerusalem built by bloodshed has no future except judgment. The Zion from which the word of YHWH emanates because it is the manifestation of God's sovereignty shall be the centre of the world. The theme of YHWH and the peoples resumes a concern originally stated in 1.2, where the peoples are summoned to listen to YHWH's witness against them from his holy palace. 4.1–4 introduces the second moment in that witness, when the restoration of YHWH's reign from Zion (4.6–5.4) and the relation of the nations to that reign (5.5–15) are announced (see the Introduction, pp. 27ff.). The universal and generous promise is inseparably connected with YHWH's future purpose for Jerusalem and Israel; it is therefore not only promise but also warning and threat to all who set themselves against God's work through city and people. Such is the spirit of the congregational faith expressed in the confession of v. 5.

The question of the origin and historical setting of 4.1–4 is complicated by the existence of a parallel to 4.1–3 in Isa. 2.2–4. There is no question that both texts record the same saying; they are so nearly identical that the minor differences hardly show in translation. The differences are of the kind which would have arisen in oral tradition and its fixation in writing at separate points: e.g. in Isa. 2.2 (par.

Micah 4.1) the participle 'established' stands at a different place in the sentence, a pronoun is not used as subject of 'be raised', the preposition '*el* is used instead of '*al*, and 'all the nations' replaces 'peoples'. The differences in the other two verses are of the same kind. It can hardly be the case that either is a copy of a literary form of the other. Micah 4.4 is not present in the version in Isaiah and probably represents an expansion of an original saying in the course of the repetition and transmission of the unit. Both versions conclude with sentences of liturgical style (Micah 4.5; Isa. 2.5) which may indicate that the saying was used in liturgical settings and has brought congregational responses from those settings into the two literary contexts.

The question about the source and date of the original saying continues to be a matter of dispute. Some attribute it to Isaiah ben Amoz, some to Micah; others conclude the saying is an independent oracle which has been incorporated in both books in the process of their formation.[a] The last opinion seems to be the one that is most probably correct. The prophecy could hardly have been spoken by Micah. The vocabulary and style of 4.1-4 have no parallels in oracles which can be assigned to him with confidence. The message has no place in the mission of Micah as defined by these oracles and his own vocation (3.8), and it is clearly a direct contradiction of 3.12, the prophecy for which he was remembered a century after it was uttered. The subject of YHWH and the nations is a feature of the final formation of chs. 1-5, and it is most probable that the saying came into the book in this stage of its development (see the Introduction, pp. 27ff.). Isaiah 2.2-4 has no convincing relation to the prophetic activity of Isaiah. Though a 'Zion theology' does figure in his prophecy, the conception of Zion and of the relation of other nations and peoples to the city in 2.2-4 is distinctly different from that expressed in sayings like 14.28-32 and 28.14-18. Nor is 2.2-4 a specific expression of the faith in the invulnerability of Zion against the attack of the peoples which appears in the hymns of Zion and Isa. 17.12-14. The original saying fits best in a post-exilic setting. Prophecy of a positive relation between YHWH's reign and the nations sets in with Deutero-Isaiah (Isa. 42.1-4; 45.22-25; 49.6; cf. also 56.6f; 60; 66.23; 11.10). Other

[a] All of these positions, and variants on them, were supported during the literary critical study of prophecy; see the summary by J. M. Powis Smith in his commentary on *Micah, Zephaniah and Nahum* (ICC), 1911, pp. 83ff. H. Wildberger attributes the saying to Isaiah; see his extensive argument in *Jesaja* (BK X/1), 1972, pp. 75ff. and the other literature cited. For a recent claim on Micah's behalf, see E. Cannawurf, 'The Authenticity of Micah IV 1-4', *VT* 13, 1963, pp. 26-33. The relation of the saying to the Hymns of Zion is explored by G. Wanke, *Die Zionstheologie der Korachiten* (BZAW 97). 1966, pp. 115ff.

oracles which speak of a peaceful pilgrimage of other peoples to Zion are post-exilic (Isa. 60.3f.; Zech. 8.22). Micah 4.1 seems to assume the existence of the temple on Mount Zion. Perhaps the original saying was first spoken after the completion of the temple in 515 BC as an exuberant announcement of what YHWH's reign from 'his house' might mean for the entire world. The oracle would have been incorporated in the book of Micah as the beginning of the second section of chs. 1–5 to serve as its first word of YHWH's witness to the people (1.2).

[1] The temporal phrase 'in the latter days' is a formula used to introduce prophecies of the future (Gen. 49.1; Num. 24.14; Deut. 4.30; 31.29; Jer. 23.20; 30.24; 48.47; 49.39; Ezek. 38.16; Hos. 3.5). The future in mind here is 'eschatological', a time when events transcend the possibilities of the present and manifest the decisive intervention of God to bring history toward its goal in his purpose. History continues, but at a different level under circumstances recreated by God. The focus and centre of events in those days will be the city Jerusalem in its identity as the sacred city Zion with its temple, the house of YHWH. Zion is the reality in the speaker's world which also appears in the future world of the vision. Probably his Jerusalem is threatened and beleaguered, at best a very unpretentious town on a very low hill. But he sees its future in terms of YHWH's choice of Jerusalem to be the place of his abode, the site of 'his house'. Israel's faith in YHWH's election of Zion drew on the ancient Near Eastern traditions about the mountain of God for its articulation, a 'theology' of the city expressed particularly in the psalms of Zion (46, 48, 76).[b] In these psalms Jerusalem is celebrated as the holy dwelling of the Most High (46.4), the loveliest of mounts, the joy of all the earth (48.2). So already the cultic application of the myth to Jerusalem sees the temple mount as the centre of the world. But what the cultic hymns claim to be already true in some sense, this prophecy proclaims as an event to be realized in the future. The myth as claim about the present cannot maintain itself in the midst of the prophetic judgments against Jerusalem, and mythological interpretion of Jerusalem's place in God's way with the world becomes eschatological prophecy. YHWH's house will be established above all other mountains, surely not so much a geographical miracle as a pre-eminence over every other divine mountain and holy place. It is the universal disclosure of the true house of God.

With the elevation of YHWH's house, a movement among many nations sets in toward Jerusalem. The verb 'stream' may be a con-

[b] See the discussions in H.-J. Kraus, *Worship in Israel*, 1966, pp. 201ff.

scious play on the streams said to issue from the holy mount to water the earth (Ps. 46.4; see also Ps. 65.9; Isa. 33.21; Joel 3.18; Ezek. 47); a reverse flow of people begins toward the centre. [2] The summons to pilgrimage will sound in the world: 'Let us go up to YHWH's house' (Ps. 122.1, 4). Israel's pilgrimage practices will spread to many peoples. The notion of 'the pilgrimage of the nations' is heard occasionally in prophetic tradition (Isa. 42.1, 4; 49.6; 55.3–5; 11.10; 19.16–25); Zech. 14.16–19 comes closest to this portrayal, though the motive there is escape from YHWH's curse.[c] The role of the nations here stands in sharp contrast to the psalms of Zion where they are the enemy whose defeat testified to the inviolability of Jerusalem (Pss. 46.6, 8f.; 48.4–7; 76.4ff.).

The quotation placed in the mouth of the new pilgrims tells us why they come so willingly. The magnetic attraction of Zion lies in the instruction (*tōrāh*) which emanates from Jerusalem. The ancient amphictyonic traditions of Israel's central sanctuary, transferred to Jerusalem when David brought the ark there (II Sam. 6) take over to define the significance of Jerusalem for the nations. The relation between the central sanctuary and the instruction of YHWH for life under the covenant goes back to earliest times. Israelites visited the sanctuary not only for praise and sacrifice, but to receive instruction about God's will. Disputes between tribes and the appeal of individuals for justice (see the laments of the accused in the Psalms) were brought to the shrine.[d] *Tōrāh* in this instance is not a general concept for the teachings of YHWH, but specific instruction about a particular case, as the parallel with 'the word of YHWH' suggests. Specific *tōrōt* were usually delivered by a priest, or on occasion through prophets. But no official medium is mentioned here; it is Jerusalem as the place where the word of YHWH can be heard which is the sole centre of interest. The nations will make pilgrimage for the sake of the word of YHWH; they will come to Jerusalem to learn what YHWH's way/path is in the problems they face and the choices they have to make. The 'way' is the course which YHWH disclosed in the oracle of salvation to the accused and oppressed (Pss. 25.4, 8, 12; 27.11; 32.8; etc.; H. Wildberger, op. cit., p. 85). With the elevation of Zion, the life-giving power of YHWH's *tōrāh*, creating justice and bringing salvation, is revealed, and a hunger and thirst for the word of YHWH draws a swelling tide of people to its source.

[3] The first two lines of v.3 identify the setting in which *tōrāh* is given by depicting the role of YHWH. He sits as royal judge on his

---

[c] See G. von Rad, *Old Testament Theology* II, pp. 294–297.

[d] See H.-J. Kraus, op. cit., pp. 188f., where the evidence is summarized.

sacred mount. The office of deciding between plaintiffs, tribes and individuals, which the judge and king has filled within Israel at the central sanctuary,[e] is assumed by YHWH for the whole earth. The nations bring their disputes to him; he determines who is in the right and delivers a decision in his favour. YHWH performs the office which is assigned to 'the shoot from Jesse's stump' in Isa. 11.3f. No human institution is named as instrument; it is simply promised that the court of YHWH will replace the battlefields of the world as a place to settle the hostilities and conflicts among the nations. Warfare, no longer needed, will fade away. Weapons will be converted to tools of agriculture; people will use the scarce and valuable materials of earth to cultivate life instead of crafting death. The conversion from war to agriculture is reversed by the summons to the nations in Joel 3.10 (Hebrew 4.10), where Joel, true to his style, is appropriating and recasting material from the older prophets (see the commentaries on Joel). The theme of the destruction of weapons is a feature of the Psalms of Zion (Pss. 46.9; 76.3), but it occurs there in the defeat of Zion's foes. Here the nations themselves voluntarily convert sword and spear and 'study war no more'.

[4] The scene used to evoke the quality of the peace which ensues is not the myth of paradise (Isa. 11.6f.), but the ideal of the peasant farmer freed from the demands and threats of the military state. The proverbial character of the expressions and the experience of such peace as an occasional interlude is clear from I Kings 4.25 (cf. II Kings 18.31; Zech. 3.10). It is a very poignant, lovely, and real possibility that the farmer should live on his property and enjoy the result of his labour undisturbed. The phrase 'with none to terrify' (*'ēn maḥrîd*) is a feature of descriptions of the restoration of life that YHWH brings about after judgment (Lev. 26.6; Jer. 30.10; Ezek. 34.28; 39.26; Zeph. 3.13). Though v. 4 does not appear in the version in Isaiah, the agricultural imagery follows the conversion of weapons to agricultural implements very naturally and may have been part of an original form of the prophecy. The unit is completed by a concluding messenger formula, which authenticates the prophecy as an expression of what YHWH himself, with his own mouth, has said. The full formula appears elsewhere only in Isa. 1.20; 40.5; 58.14; it is a longer version of 'for YHWH has spoken'.

This picture of what will happen when Zion is raised up and the nations make pilgrimage for the sake of *tōrāh* is restrained and inviting. The result is not a religious empire or a world subject in humiliation to a triumphant Israel. The nations bring their crises to YHWH,

[e] Consult R. de Vaux, *Ancient Israel*, 1961, pp. 150ff.

their disputes are dealt with, and they depart. They are not dominated and incorporated in a power structure, but helped and led to a new policy that makes for life. The vision is not of some final stage of the struggle for power, but of its end, because nations come to see the real answer to their need in the word of YHWH.

[5] After the prophecy is concluded, the words of those who read it and long for its fulfilment are heard. They speak in the midst of a difficult and uncertain history that as yet is undefined by the fulfilment of the vision. The 'we' is the congregation of God's people, the faithful Israel. When they say of their uneschatological situation that all the nations still live in the character and identity given them by the gods they worship, the words are not an easy compromise with theological pluralism, but a realism about things as they are. The time of the pilgrimage to the 'city set on a hill' is not yet. In the meantime faith in the fulfilment of the vision means faithful enactment of it in their life. For them the *tōrāh* of YHWH is already there, and as this unfinished history goes on they can and will walk as those whose identity is created by the election of God.

14. THE CRIPPLED SHALL BECOME STRONG: 4.6f.

6 In that day,
  oracle of YHWH,
 I will assemble the lame;
  the banished I will gather,
  those whom I have hurt.
7 I will make the lame into a remnant,
  and the wounded[a] into a mighty nation.
 YHWH will reign over them
 in Mount Zion
 from now on and forever.

4.6f. is an oracle of salvation promising the restoration of YHWH's ravaged flock under his reign. The limits of the unit are marked by introductory formulae ('In that day, an oracle of YHWH') and concluding phrase ('from now on and for ever'). It contains these elements: the gathering of the banished (v. 6b), their transformation into a mighty nation (v. 7a), and YHWH's unending rule over them in Mount Zion (v. 7b). In vv. 6–7a YHWH speaks; feminine singular

a Reading *wᵉhannahᵃlāh*. MT's *wehannahᵃlāʾāh* is a *hapax* which could mean something like 'the far removed'.

collectives refer to the people. In v. 7b the first person style is dropped
and a plural pronoun is used for the people. 2.12f. is a companion
piece. Both sayings have the same subject and vocabulary, begin in
divine first person style to promise the gathering of the scattered
people, and shift to another style to speak of YHWH's kingship. 4.6
is similar to Zeph. 3.19, a post-exilic addition to the Zephaniah
corpus; the two contain three of the four occurrences of 'lame' in the
Old Testament (the fourth in Gen. 32.31!). The prophecy assumes
the existence of the diaspora created by the fall of Jerusalem, and
uses the term 'remnant' as a fixed notion of eschatological theology.
It belongs to the late exilic or post-exilic salvation prophecies concerned with the recovery of the scattered exiles (cf. the texts cited in
the comment below).

The themes of 4.6f. are related to the literary context in three ways.
4.1–4 foretells the supremacy of Zion over the nations as the site of
YHWH's reign, without mentioning Israel; this oracle introduces
Israel into the picture of that future. The real constituency of YHWH's
reign will be the crippled flock transformed into a strong nation. The
theme of YHWH's reign from Zion (v. 7b) anticipates 4.8–5.4 which
shows how YHWH will restore his dominion centred in Mount Zion.
The theme of the remnant as a strong nation (vv. 6–7a) anticipates
5.5–9 where the remnant is pictured as the mightiest of the nations.
These relationships to the final form of chs. 4–5 suggest that 4.6–7a
was set in its present place and expanded by v. 7b in the final stage of
the formation of these chapters (see the Introduction, pp. 27.ff).

[6] The two opening formulae also introduce 5.10ff.; both are
probably the work of a redactor of this part of the book. Here 'in that
day' is used to place the salvation of the remnant in the same
eschatological time ('in the latter days') as the elevation of Mount
Zion foretold in 4.1ff. YHWH will fulfill his role as shepherd of Israel,
seek out his scattered 'sheep' wherever they have been dispersed
among the nations of the world, and gather them once more into the
flock for which he cares. The rescue of the scattered flock is a recurrent theme of salvation prophecy from the time of the first exile,
and it is often expressed in the same vocabulary and imagery (cf. Isa.
54.7; 56.8; Jer. 23.3; 29.14; 31.8, 10; Ezek. 11.17; Zeph. 3.18f.; Zech.
10.8ff.). The terms for the dispersion are feminine singulars, corporate designations probably reflecting a personification of the population of Judah. The flock is 'lame' (cf. Zeph. 3.19) and 'banished'; the
latter term may have a legal background (see II Sam. 14.13f.); it
belongs to the exilic theological vocabulary as a word for those who
have been cast out by YHWH because of their treason (cf. Deut. 30.4;

Zeph. 3.19; Neh. 1.9; Isa. 56.8). YHWH's rescue of the flock, then, is a work of his power and grace overcoming their weakness and guilt. Indeed, their plight is YHWH's work; it is he himself who has done them ill in judgment. But their future hope lies in the marvellous range of God's work who is both judge and saviour, who wounds and heals (cf. Deut. 32.39; Hos. 6.1; Job 5.18).

[7] The ingathering of the scattered people will reach its climax in their transformation. YHWH will make the wounded into the mighty, the outcasts into a nation, and show himself to be the God who chooses what is small and weak to manifest his glory (Deut. 7.7f.; I Cor. 1.28). The way in which the term 'remnant' (*šeʾērīt*) is used is remarkable. The notion (in profane usage: what remains of any entity after most of it is used or destroyed) is employed in a variety of ways in the theological language of prophecy for the status of the people created by judgment (e.g., Isa. 4.3; 10.20–23; 28.5f.; Jer. 23.3; 31.7; Zeph. 2.7, 9).[b] The term is used in threats (catastrophe will leave *only* a remnant, Amos 5.3; Isa. 7.3 [?]), promises (a remnant *will* survive judgment, Isa. 37.31f.), and as a designation of the surviving community as the object of God's saving activity (Isa. 11.11, 16; 46.3). But here the remnant is created by God's saving activity, not his judgment; 'remnant' has become the name for the eschatological goal of YHWH's way with Israel. The remnant is by character a mighty nation; by reason of their nature they are a supernatural and invincible reality within world history (see 5.7–9). In this literary context 'mighty nation' echoes the 'mighty nations' of v. 3, and promises that Israel itself shall be no less that the nations who are drawn to the house of YHWH when Zion becomes the centre of the world.

The dispersion will not be transformed into a mighty nation in order to resume a political career that is the expression of their own power and will. Instead, they will become the social unit whose existence and character is a manifestation of YHWH's reign over them. The kingship of YHWH celebrated in the 'enthronement psalms' (Pss. 47, 96–99), whose inauguration had been announced by Deutero-Isaiah (Isa. 52.7), will be exclusively their future political structure. For other exilic and post-exilic prophecies foretelling the establishment of YHWH's rule in Zion as the government of the redeemed nation, see Isa. 24.23; 33.22; Obad. 21; Zeph. 3.15. Psalm 146 (see v. 10) depicts the work of YHWH as King.

---

[b] On the theme, see V. Herntrich, *TDNT* IV, pp. 196ff.; G. Fohrer, *History of the Israelite Religion*, 1972, pp. 271, 346f.; and the literature cited in each.

15. DOMINION SHALL BE RESTORED TO JERUSALEM: 4.8

8 But you, Migdal-'eder,
  Ophel of Zion's daughter,
  to you shall come[a]
  the former realm,
  the kingdom[b] to Jerusalem's daughter.

Verse 8 is a brief oracle of salvation composed of vocatives which identify the addressee and a promise. It is marked off within its present literary setting by style and type. The saying is spoken as direct address to a masculine personified place, whereas vv. 9ff. are addressed to the 'daughter of Zion'. Verse 8 is similar in style and type to 5.2 which is adressed to another city, Bethlehem. C. Westermann has pointed to the formal similarity of both sayings to the 'tribe sayings' collected in Gen. 49 and Deut. 33; he suggests that salvation oracles addressed to a personified place are an adaption of the tribe saying.[c] In the time when this promise was made, the realm over which Jerusalem was once capital had been lost. Perhaps the prophet speaks to the site with unusual names, instead of to Jerusalem, because the city itself is still in such a pitiable condition. The historical setting was the exilic period.

The brief promise came into the developing book as the opening unit of the complex 4.8–5.4. It was placed at its beginning as a statement of the theme of the complex, the restoration of Jerusalem's realm. This complex of sayings was formed to be the counterpart of Micah prophecies of the end of Jerusalem. The initial '*But* you . . .' may once have followed 3.12 and its announcement of the city's destruction to introduce the prophetic scenario of the restoration of the old kingdom after the judgment. (See the Introduction, pp. 26f.) In the present literary context it takes up the theme of v. 7b and begins the revelation of the way in which YHWH's reign over the remnant from Mount Zion will be brought about.

[8] The opening emphatic pronoun, the repetition expressed in 'to you' introducing the second line, and the vocative names give the saying a sustained focus on the addressee. The speaker seeks to stir

---

  [a] Omitting *ūbā'āh* as a variant reading.
  [b] On the construct followed by the preposition *le*, GKa 130a. *mamlākūt* for *mamleket* would provide a better parallelism.
  [c] 'Predigtmeditation Micha 5.1–3' in G. Eichholz, *Herr tue meine Lippen auf*, vol. V, 1964, pp. 54ff.

in his audience a readiness to hear his message by creating anew their self-consciousness as the congregation that exists by the promise of YHWH. He invites a 'you' to stand forth and listen, because they remember from the past a role which they can play in God's purpose for the future. *Migdal-'eder* is a place name (see the other names of the type in BDB, p. 154) which means 'citadel of the flock'. Used in names, *migdal* means a fortified tower or castle around which a small population is grouped.[d] The only other occurrence of the full name (Gen. 35.21) refers to a site mentioned in the account of the wanderings of Jacob. The name evokes the theme of Israel as the flock of YHWH (cf. *'eder* in Isa. 40.11; Jer. 13.17, 20; Zech. 10.3); it looks upon Jerusalem as the citadel whose strength gives security to the flock. *'ōpel* (a 'rising', 'hill') in its topographical uses is applied only to the ridge on whose lower reaches to the south the old city of Davidic times was built. In Nehemiah and II Chronicles 'the Ophel' has become the name for the quarter of the city between the temple and David's city. In Isa. 32.14 *'ōpel* is associated with watch-tower and it may be used here as a kind of synonymn to 'citadel of the flock', as well as one of the old names associated with the city. Zion, originally the name for the hill on which the Jebusite and Davidic city of Jerusalem was built, became an alternative name for the city itself. Particularly in the Psalms and in eschatological prophecy the name pointed to the role of Jerusalem as the chosen residence of God, as royal city, and as centre of YHWH's relation to his people.[e] 'Daughter of Zion' (and 'daughter of Jerusalem') is a frequently used personification of the city or its population (e.g. Isa. 1.8; Jer. 4.31; Lam. 1.6; Isa. 37.22; Zeph. 3.14; Lam. 2.13); here because of the topographical terms it is the city which is addressed, though the corporate population is obviously the audience. By this combination of names from traditions of the past the little population grouped around Jerusalem is given a vision of what they have been so that they can hear a promise of the restoration of that past.

The promise is simply to return the former realm, the kingdom over which the Davidides ruled before the overthrow of Judah and the loss of its independence. What the extent of this realm will be or how it will be governed is not said. The salvation promised lies in the restoration of the kingdom itself. The oracle is not simply a nationalist utterance of purely political hopes. The restored realm will be the historical space in which the congregation can have a future. The city at its centre will be the 'citadel of the flock', the historical means

---

[d] On the term and its usage, R. de Vaux, *Ancient Israel*, 1961, p. 235.

[e] See the full discussion by G. Fohrer, *TDNT* VII, pp. 293ff.

by which God creates the possibility for his past purposes to continue
in the eschatological renewal.

16. THE LOSS OF THE CITY IS THE WAY TO REDEMPTION: 4.9f.

9 Now, why do you cry alarm?
    Is there no king with you?
  Or has your counsellor perished,
    that writhing grips you like a woman in labour?
10 Writhe and howl,[a]
    daughter of Zion, like a woman in labour,[b]
  for now you shall go forth from the city,
    and dwell in open country.
  You shall go to Babylon;
    there you shall be delivered.
  There YHWH shall redeem you
    from the hand of your enemies.

This saying is an oracle of salvation addressed to the population of
Jerusalem, personified as 'the daughter of Zion'. It is a prophetic
promise that the present distress, which grips the city with anguish
like the labour-pains of a woman giving birth, is the beginning of a
process which will lead through judgment to salvation. The unit is
the second in the complex organized around the theme 'daughter of
Zion', and the first of three sayings introduced by 'now' which move
from distress to deliverance (see the Introduction, pp. 26f.). Within
the complex its own particular contribution is the revelation that
YHWH's redemption will conclude the painful pilgrimage out of
the city and into the Babylonian exile. The transition in the thought
of the unit between v. 10a and 10b suggests that the saying was
formed in two stages. The first is an oracle of woe, opening with
taunting questions, reproaching and characterizing a population in
distress (v. 9), and foretelling the disaster, loss of the city, which is
about to occur (v. 10a). Here the simile of a woman in labour is
simply a descriptive device to portray the experience of anguish in the
face of an overwhelming military threat. The language and style is
close to sayings of Jeremiah, especially 4.31 and 6.23ff. The saying
must belong to the last days before the fall of Jerusalem to Babylon,

[a] Reading $g^{e\,c}\bar{\imath}$ for MT $g\bar{o}h\bar{\imath}$, 'gush' (of water).
[b] Perhaps $kayy\bar{o}l\bar{e}d\bar{a}h$ has been added from the previous line.

when there was still a king in Judah. In v. 10b the simile is understood in a fuller sense as the birth pangs of a new era and the imperatives interpreted as a summons to a future of hope. The exile
becomes a bridge from the loss of the city to the place of deliverance.
The oracle now sketches a comprehensive scenario of YHWH's way
with Zion's daughter which includes both judgment and salvation.
The expansion is part of the work by which the complex 4.8–5.4 was
formed. The addition gives the original oracle of woe the same pattern
of movement from distress to salvation found in vv. 11–13 and 5.1–4.
(See the Introduction, pp. 7, 26f.)

[9] The introductory 'now' is a device of the arranger of this
section; it is rhetorical and literary in function rather than temporal,
as is the 'for now' in v. 10. The question 'why . . .' does not inquire;
it is a dramatic interrogatory used to depict an astonishing situation.
The outcry is one of alarm and terror as the following line shows,
though elsewhere the shout (*hērīaʿ*) of the daughter of Zion expresses
exulting joy (Zeph. 3.14; Zech. 9.9). The question about the king
seems to imply that there is a monarch in Jerusalem. But he is no
help; he cannot carry out the duty of the king to defend his people.
It is possible that the king referred to is YHWH, as in the lament of
the people quoted in Jer. 8.19, but the scornful 'has your counsellor
perished?' argues for a human ruler. 'Counsellor' is a title for the
king whose wise plans and decisions should provide for the security
of his kingdom; note the attribution of wise counsel to the ideal king
in Isa. 9.6; 11.2; Ps. 20.4. The comparison of a population's panic to
the writhing of a woman in labour is a feature of the language of
Jeremiah (Jer. 4.31; 6.24; 13.21; 22.23; 30.6; 49.24; 50.43; elsewhere
of Babylon in Isa. 13.8; 21.3; cf. Ps. 48.6). In all cases the simile is
used for the terror before an irresistible military assault. Jeremiah's
language in 4.31 and 6.23ff. using the comparison in address to the
'daughter of Zion' is especially close to this text, which probably
belongs to the same situation. The king, then, would be Jehoiachin
or Zedekiah.

[10] The imperatives 'writhe and howl' call upon the daughter of
Zion to recognize her torment as judgment. The prophet speaks not
to promise relief, but to reveal the event which will result from the
situation. On 'daughter of Zion' as a personification of Jerusalem,
see the comment on v. 8. The forced shift of the population from the
city to open country is the prophesied disaster. The identity of 'Zion's
daughter' is bound up with her life in the city. Zion is the city of her
God, the residence of the divinely elected king, the bastion of her
security, and centre of her faith and hope. To have to dwell in open

country symbolizes and enacts the dissolution of her relation to all which Zion represents.

'You shall go to Babylon' adds something different and quite specific to the contrast of city and country. The exile of part of Jerusalem's population after the city's fall is clearly in mind. Babylon is not, like the open country, simply a place of humiliation. Here it is viewed by the twice repeated 'there' as the place of salvation, the predicament from which YHWH will redeem (*gā'al*) Zion's daughter. In its primary function in legal and cultic texts *gā'al* means the procedure of recovering a lost possession. Used for YHWH's action to deliver Israel, the verb often retains something of its original flavour and portrays the rescue as a redemption, a recovery of what was lost and its restoration to its original status. The verb has a massive place in the vocabulary of Deutero-Isaiah as a favourite term for YHWH's role as liberator of the exiles. The language here is similar to Jer. 31.11 (a song later than Jeremiah) and Ps. 106.10, both of which show the influence of the great prophet of the exile.[c] This expansion of the original oracle of disaster carries the scenario of God's way with Israel two steps further, from loss of the city to exile and deliverance there. It sees the pangs of childbirth in the original saying as more than a simile for distress; they are the birth pains of a new phase of YHWH's dealing with Israel. The connection between the end of labour and the return of the lost brethren is clear in 5.3 (cf. the comment), an addition to the promise of the new ruler who will come from Bethlehem.

17. THE THREATENED CITY WILL TRIUMPH: 4.11–13

11 And now, many nations
      assemble against you,
      (who say)[a] 'Let her be desecrated, and let our eyes
          gloat over Zion'.
12 But they do not know
      YHWH's thoughts,
      nor do they understand his plan
          to gather them like sheaves to the threshing floor.
13 'Rise up and thresh, daughter of Zion,
      for I will make your horn iron;

---

[c] See the full discussion of the history of the usage of *gā'al* in J. J. Stamm, *THAT* I, pp. 383ff.

[a] Probably an addition to the poetic line to identify a quotation clearly.

I will make your hooves bronze;
and you shall crush many peoples.'
You [b] shall devote their booty to YHWH,
their wealth to the Lord of all the earth.

4.11–13 is the second of the units introduced by the rubric '(And) now', addressed to the daughter of Zion, and moving from a description of present distress (v. 11) to a promise of its reversal by an event of salvation (vv. 12f.). Its function in its present literary context is to reveal how the problem of the hostile nations will be resolved in the eschatological restoration of the former dominion to Zion (v. 8). The structure of the unit is composed of a pattern of contrasts between the nations (v. 11) and YHWH (vv. 12f.). The nations assemble against Zion, but it is actually YHWH who gathers them. Their intention is to humiliate Zion, but YHWH summons and equips Zion to crush them. They plan to desecrate Zion, but Zion will in the end consecrate all the wealth the nations have gained by warfare to YHWH. The unit is held together by this pattern, the style of direct address to a femine figure, and the connection between the simile of the threshing-floor at the end of v. 12 and the metaphor of the threshing-ox applied to the addressee in v. 13. But there are clues which suggest that v. 13 is a prophetic expansion of vv. 11f., perhaps a summons issued by a prophet who takes up the earlier unit and uses it as a basis for a confident call to the population of Jerusalem. Verses 11f. are spoken as a prophetic saying, but v. 13 is clearly in the style of a divine saying. The former speaks of 'many nations', the latter of 'many peoples'; nations and peoples are brought together in 4.1–5 and by an addition to 5.8. Verse 13 belongs to the traditional type of 'the summons to battle'.[c] Verses 11f. are an expression of the motif of the 'assault of the nations/peoples' against Zion. Motif and type are not combined elsewhere, and this is the only place where the 'summons to battle' is addressed to Israel in prophetic texts. It usually appears in oracles of doom against other nations addressed to the forces who will destroy them. And in all the other occurrences of the 'assault of Zion' motif, it is YHWH who intervenes directly and mysteriously to vanquish them.

The essential plot expressed in vv. 11f. appears in a number of other texts. The nucleus of the idea is: nations (peoples, kingdoms)

[b] MT's verb is first person, probably a reading influenced by the first person verbs preceding. The versions have second person.

[c] See R. Bach, *Die Aufforderungen zur Flucht und zum Kampf in alttestamentlichen Prophetenspruch* (WMANT 9), 1962, pp. 51ff.

are storming Jerusalem (Israel); they are overwhelmed (defeated, eliminated). This notion, developed in a variety of ways and combined with other motifs and elements, appears both in prophetic sayings (the principal examples are Isa. 17.12–14; 29.5–8; Ezek. 38–39 [?]; Zech. 14.1–3, 12–15; 12.2–9; Joel 3.1–3, 9–12) and in the psalms classified as songs of Zion (Pss. 46.6; 48.4f.; 76.3–6). The history and even the definition of the notion is a matter of considerable disagreement.[d] Some think the motif in the songs of Zion to be an Israelite adaptation of an ancient myth from Canaanite times associated with Jerusalem as a divine city, read the prophetic oracles as expressions of this Zion theology applied first to specific historical crises and then generalized in eschatological prophecies as a promise of Zion's ultimate role in history.[e] Others contend that the notion developed from particular prophecies and was transformed into both eschatological expectations and the theology found in the songs of Zion.[f] Micah 4.11–12 presents the assault of 'many nations' as a strategy initiated by YHWH to break their power. In this respect it seems to have some relation to Ezek. 38–39.

Because of the uncertainty about the history and function of the notion it is difficult to know whether vv. 11f. assume a concrete historical setting or simply look forward to some future crisis when YHWH will decisively relieve Zion of the threat of the nations. It is possible that 'the nations' are the neighbouring states who plagued Jerusalem after 587; v. 11b may reflect the setting of Obadiah. The oracle is a re-expression of ideas found in Isaiah's prophecy and employs the language of Jeremiah (see the comment). It is an exilic oracle of salvation which has been included in the complex 4.8–5.4 because its structure of movement from present distress to future salvation fitted the purpose and pattern of the arranger.

The 'summons to battle' (v. 13) looks for the transformation of the daughter of Zion into the irresistible power by which the peoples are overwhelmed. The nearest counterparts of this notion are found in Zech. 12.1–9; 14.14. Its concerns and vision fit in with the portrayal of Israel as the mighty remnant which lives invulnerable among the peoples, the primary interest of the final stage of the formation of chs. 1–5 (cf. 4.6f.; 5.5–9). The verse was probably added as a develop-

[d] The question has been studied in two recent monographs: G. Wanke, *Die Zionstheologie der Korachiten* (BZAW 97), 1966; H. M. Lutz, *Jahwe, Jerusalem und die Völker* (WMANT 27), 1968.

[e] E.g. G. von Rad, *Old Testament Theology* I, 1962, pp. 46f., and Vol. II, 1965, pp. 155ff.; H. M. Lutz, op. cit.

[f] E.g. G. Fohrer, *History of Israelite Religion*, 1972, pp. 342f.; G. Wanke, op. cit.

ment of the original prophecy in this post-exilic development of the book. It extends the promise that YHWH will turn the threat of the nations into their judgment to a promise which looks for the peoples to be brought under the reign of YHWH by the divine power of Israel.

[11] 'And now' is the introductory rubric by which the collector of this section introduces the three 'daughter of Zion' units (vv. 9, 11, 14). The temporal function of 'now' is not so much to designate some one specific occasion as to indicate the general present of distress when the restoration of Jerusalem's former kingdom (v. 8) has not been accomplished. The oracle is a word to any particular crisis brought on by the threat of the nations with that period. 'Many nations' (and the synonym 'many peoples' in v. 13) is an inclusive rather than a limiting term; it is closer to 'all' than to 'some'. It is a category for the political forces whose independent ambitions and power are a threat to Israel and an unresolved problem for YHWH's reign in the world. The terms belong to the language of prophecy in a period when its vision extends beyond the interpretation of the role of specific nations like Assyria and Babylon to the fuller drama of the eschatological time when YHWH's reign will be manifest in all the earth. That YHWH assembles nations both to use them as instruments of judgment and to break their power in a final way is a recurrent feature of that drama; see 'nations, kingdoms' with 'assemble' ('sp, qal and niphal) in Isa. 13.4f.; Zech. 12.3; 14.2; Joel 3.2; and Zeph. 3.8 (which seems to be a revision of an earlier form of the text).[g] In the scene briefly evoked here the powers of history array themselves against Zion, the elect city of God (see the comments on the significance of Zion at v. 8) and the issue is drawn between the pretensions of power politics and the reign of YHWH. The motivation and ambition of the nations is disclosed in the quotation placed in their mouths. They are bent on the desecration of Zion, the profanation of the sacred city, in order to eliminate its role as holy, the chosen place from which God exercises his rule (cf. hnp in Ps. 106.38). They long for the satisfaction of gloating over a defeated prostrate Jerusalem whose humiliation will fulfil their lust for power (cf. $rā'āh b^e$ in Obad. 12f.). Hidden in the words is a profound characterization of the lust that drives restless nations in their politics of power; there is a similarity to the interpretative words attributed to the rulers of earth in Ps. 2.2f. When nations see themselves as the centre of history and seek a destiny that fulfils their power, they can tolerate no Zion; they are gripped with a compelling need to destroy whatever stands in judgment and restraint on their pride.

g See K. Elliger, *Das Buch der zwölf kleinen Propheten* II (ATD 25), 1950, ad loc.

[12] Over against the intention of the nations the prophet sets the hidden purpose of YHWH. The model for this language about the thoughts (*maḥšebōt*) and plan (*'ēṣāh*) of YHWH is the monarch who devises strategies and plans to implement his policy in maintaining his power and extending his realm (e.g. Jer.49.30). YHWH is portrayed as the sovereign whose purpose is the total plan within which nations and earthly kings carry out their strategies; they seek their own ends, but end up fulfilling his goal. See especially Isaiah's oracle disclosing YHWH's plans to use Assyria as an instrument of his wrath against Jerusalem and then to break the Assyrians' power because of their arrogance (Isa.14.24–27 with 10.5–16, 24–27). It is of interest for this saying that the oracles about YHWH's intention for other nations in the book of Isaiah use *'ēṣāh* (5.19; 19.17; 25.1; 46.10f.), while those in Jeremiah use *maḥšebōt* also (Jer.49.20; 50.45; 51.29 has the latter term only). These sayings concern a particular nation, while here YHWH's plan incorporates 'many'. Their assembly for the humiliation of Zion is in fact the secret plan by which YHWH gathers them as cut grain is brought to the threshing floor at harvest time. (Other uses of 'threshing-floor' as an image of judgment occur in Isa.21.10; Jer.51.33; Hos.13.3.) The oracle discloses that what YHWH has done in the past with one nation after another is a proleptic exercise for the way he will now break the power of all who threaten Jerusalem. That revelation is a word of hope to the tiny beleaguered community in Jersualem, which lets them face the threats of the nations in confidence in the sovreignty of their god.

[13] On the basis of the revelation a prophet issues a summons to battle spoken in the first-person address of YHWH himself. The population of Jerusalem is called to be the instrument of the divine plan. The simile of the threshing floor is continued in the imperative 'thresh', a figure of devastation (Amos 1.3). Deutero-Isaiah had promised the exiles that YHWH would transform them into a threshing sledge to thresh 'mountains' (Isa.41.15); here that work is given to the post-exilic community under the figure of the threshing ox equipped for the task by the endowment of YHWH. The horn is a symbol of strength; the hooves tread out the grain from its husks. But the image is not carried through on its positive side. The mission of Zion's daughter is to crush the pretensions of all the peoples who plot the desecration of the city of God.

The final line is both promise and instruction; it shows that the victory of Zion will serve the manifestation of YHWH's reign in the world. Zion's war will not be simply another case of those military ventures which serve the self-interest of those who mount them. The triumph will bring Zion neither booty nor wealth. Instead it will strip the hostile nations of the booty they have amassed in their marauding enterprises and consecrate it to YHWH. This sacred reservation is in effect a political and economic form of confession that YHWH is 'Lord of all the earth'. The title appears in Zech. 4.14; 6.5; Ps. 97.5, and apparently as an addition to the text of Josh. 3.11, 13. The act of devoting (*ḥērem*) booty taken from defeated foes was a feature of the ancient ritual of 'holy war' practices in the times of the conquest and defence of the promised land (see the classic texts Josh. 7; I Sam. 15) in which all gained by the battle was devoted to YHWH as an acknowledgement that the victory was his.[h]

18. THE PRESENT AND FUTURE KINGS: 5.1-4
(MT 4.14-5.3)

1 Now gash yourself, daughter of marauders!
    Siege is set against us.
  With the rod they (shall) strike the cheek
    of Israel's judge.
2 But you, Bethlehem of Ephratha,
    small [a][b] among Judah's clans,
  from you shall come forth for me[c]
    one to be ruler in Israel.
  His origin lies in former times,
    in ancient days.
3 Therefore, they shall be handed over[d] until the time
    when she who is in labour has given birth,
  and the rest of his brothers return
    to the children of Israel.
4 He shall stand and shepherd in the strength of YHWH,
    in the majesty of the name of YHWH, his God.
  They shall dwell (safely), for then[e] he will be great
    to the ends of earth.

[h] On the practice see R. de Vaux, *Ancient Israel*, 1961, pp. 260f.
[a] Perhaps an *h* has been lost following *'eprātāh* and the text should be *haṣṣā'îr*, 'the least'.
[b] Omitting *liheyōt* which overloads the measure and makes difficulties for its sense. Perhaps the word has been introduced from the following line.
[c] Could *lī* be an abbreviation for *lyhwh*? 'For YHWH' would produce a more balanced colon, and the style of divine speech is not present anywhere else in the saying; see v. 4.
[d] Reading *yittenēm* as an impersonal passive.
[e] For *'attāh* of the future cf. 7.10; Isa. 29.22; 49.19; etc.

5.1–4 (Heb. 4.14–5.3, only the English verse numbers are given below) is another saying which moves from grief to hope, from present humiliation to a future redemption. The integrating theme is the figure of Israel's ruler. The current plight of Israel's judge is cause for a summons to extreme measures of lament (v. 1). But a ruler over Israel shall come, whose endurance and goodness and power will establish an untroubled security for 'his brothers' (vv. 2–4). The oracle shifts the focus from Zion and its people (4.8–13) to the royal figure and his role in YHWH's way with Israel, from place to person. For the theology grounded in YHWH's election of David (II Sam. 7) the king was the regent on earth of God's reign, the instrument of his justice and protection, and the source of blessing and peace (expressed in the 'royal psalms', Pss. 2, 18, 20, 21, 45, 72, 89, 101, 110, 132).[1] The king in his faithfulness or failure creates the destiny of the people in the way he fulfils his office. Faith in the 'messianic king' is a form of devotion to the reign of God. Where the divinely chosen king is absent, the community lacks a concrete historical centre and social structure for actualizing their life within God's sovereignty. That crisis is behind the call to self-mutilation in v. 1, and that need is addressed by the promise in vv. 2–4.

Conclusions about the unity and historical setting of 4.1–4 have varied widely.[g] The 'messianic oracle', vv. 2–4, has been taken as an independent unit, as a continuation of v. 1 or other preceding material in ch. 4, and as part of a unit completed by vv. 5f. (or reconstructions of this 'Assyria' oracle). The promise has been attributed to Micah at the end of the eighth century, and dated in the exilic and post-exilic periods.

The decision to hold vv. 1–4 together as a unit for interpretation is based on its similarity to 4.9f. and 11–13. Like them it begins with a 'now' indicating the present time of distress, and then moves to the promise of a future salvation. It is addressed to 'daughter of marauders', a variant of the vocative 'daughter of Zion' which identifies the addressee of the other two. The second poetic line of v. 4 concludes

---

[1] For general discussions of the theology of kingship in Israel, see W. Eichrodt, *Theology of the Old Testament* I, 1961, pp. 436ff.; G. von Rad, *Old Testament Theology*, I, 1962, pp. 318ff.; S. Mowinckel, *He That Cometh*, 1956, especially chs. VI, IX.

[g] See the discussion and literature cited by: C. Westermann, 'Micha 5.1–3' in G. Eicholz, ed., *Herr, tue meine Lippen auf* V, 1964[2], pp. 54–9; T. Lescow, 'Das Geburtsmotiv in den messianischen Weissagungen bei Jesaja and Micha', *ZAW* 79, 1967, pp. 172–207; J. T. Willis, 'Micah IV 14–V 5—a unit', *VT* 18, 1968, pp. 529ff.; M. B. Crook, 'The Promise in Micah 5', *JBL* 70, 1951, pp. 313ff.; the brief proposal by A. Alt in *Kleine Schriften zur Geschichte des Volkes Israel* III, 1959, pp. 375f.

the subject of the promised ruler. Verse 5 begins with an introductory rubric characteristic of the section in 5.5–15 and deals with a different subject (see the comment on 5.5f.). 5.1–4 plays a double role as part of the complex beginning with 4.8. It is not only the third of the 'Now . . .' oracles which move from distress to promise; the opening *weʾattāh* echoes the beginning at 4.8 and returns the style to an address to a masculine personified place, balancing Bethlehem with Jerusalem, and so rounding off the complex.

This double role in the complex is one of the clues that 5.1–4 is not an original unit of speech. The historical setting of v. 1 is the period of the Babylonian siege of Jerusalem (see comment below). It is a prophetic summons to the population to lament. The second line of v. 1 could be either a continuation of the reason (' . . . they strike . . .') or a threat (' . . . they shall strike . . .'). The language and style is close to sayings in Jeremiah. The oracle in vv. 2 and 4 is composed in divine first-person style (so MT), is addressed to Bethlehem (masc.), and promises the appearance of a ruler whose reign will be divinely supported and will inaugurate an era of security for Israel. The language of the oracle is indefinite and mysterious, affording no unambiguous clues to a historical setting. The time of David is viewed as an era of the distant past belonging to 'ancient days'. That the new ruler comes from the people of David's origins, and not his line, may suggest that no Davidide is living or available. If that is the case, exilic times seem the most likely setting. On the uncertain assumption that Isa.9.1–6 and 11.1–9 were spoken by Isaiah, it is conceivable that vv.2 and 4 could come from a time as early as the end of the eighth century. But they belong to a literary context whose organizing material seems to come from the late seventh and sixth century, and that suggests a later date. The style of v.2 is exactly that of 4.8: an introductory 'and you', addressed to a place, emphatic repetition of 'from/to you', and the promise of the restoration of rule (*memšālāh/mōšēl*) meant as a word of salvation to Israel. Similarities in form and function between these two sayings and some of the old 'sayings to a tribe' (cf. Gen.49.10; Deut.33.16) may point to a transformation of the latter into a later type of salvation prophecy. The parallels between 4.8 and 5.2, 4 probably indicate thay they come from the same source, and that their sequence in this literary context is a way of saying that the promised restoration of *memšālāh* to Jerusalem will occur through a coming *mōšēl* from Bethlehem. Verse 3, generally recognized as an addition to the oracle, explains the delay in the appearance of the ruler, and co-ordinates it with the end of the time of oppression and the return of

the 'other Israelites' who live outside Judah. The expansion draws on
the language of 4.9f., and seems to come from the one who gave
chs. 1–5 their final form (cf. the comment below).

[1] As in 4.9 and 11, the introductory 'now' marks the beginning
of a unit and points to a present crisis which is the historical setting
for the prophet's word. The situation is depicted in the second colon:
'Siege (cf. *māṣōr* in Ezek. 4.2; or a siege-rampart as in Deut. 20.20) is
set against us.' In descriptions of a particular historical occasion the
term is used only of Nebuchadnezzar's sieges of Jerusalem (II Kings
24.10; 25.2; Jer. 52.5; Ezek. 4.3, 7; 5.2). It is difficult to locate the
setting more precisely within the protracted course of Judah's
struggle with Babylon,[h] because the reference to Isarel's king in the
next line could refer to several incidents. The saying is addressed to
the population of Zion personified as a woman; but, instead of the
vocative 'daughter of Zion' (4.10, 13), a name is used which is formed
as a play on its accompanying imperative. The word-play is constructed on assonance between imperative and vocative (*titgōdᵉdī
bat-gᵉdūd*) and not on the sense of the words, so it defies reproduction
in another language. *Gᵉdūd* means a band of raiders or marauders
(I Sam. 30.8, 15, 23) and is used poetically for the Babylonian army
as in Jer. 18.22. The feminine personification, 'daughter of marauders', characterizes the population as a people whose identity is given
them by their life under attack; the etymological figure is clarified by
the plain language of the second colon. Compare Jeremiah's feminine personifying vocative, 'you who dwell under siege' (10.17).
Gashing oneself was a practice used by the Canaanites in rituals of
lament in appeal to the deity (I Kings 18.28) and in bewailing the
dead (Deut. 14.1); the practice persisted among Israelites and Jeremiah mentions it three times (Jer. 16.6; 41.5; 47.5). This summons to
an extreme form of lament could be an ironic taunt addressed to a
people who reverted to pagan ways and perhaps wailed appeals to
other gods in their hour of final distress. The present moment is
hopeless; the siege will succeed. Nothing for Jerusalem to do but bow
to the tragedy and bewail her death!

'Judge (*šōpēṭ*) of Israel' refers to a king. *špṭ* is used in its frequent
sense of 'rule' (Amos 3.2; Isa. 16.5; I Kings 3.9; II Kings 15.5; Ps.
2.10; etc.) and the phrase could as well be translated 'ruler of Israel.'
The title *šōpēṭ* may have been selected to create a word-play on rod
(*šēbeṭ*). This particular title, (unparalled in the singular) sets the king
in scornful contrast to the old judges of Israel whose exploits are
recounted in the book of Judges. They rose to the occasion when

[h] See the historical account in J. Bright, *A History of Israel*, 1972², pp. 325ff.

Israel was threatened, and were called 'saviours'. But this king is himself a plaything of the conqueror's arrogance; no help or hope from him (cf. 4.9). Striking a person on the cheek is a way of humiliating a man (I Kings 22.24; Job 16.10; Ps. 3.7; Lam. 3.30). Who is the king? If the verb is a threatening prediction, the two kings who were on the throne after the first siege, Jehoiachin and Zedekiah, are both possibilities. If the humiliation is happening at the time of the saying, a possible construction of the verb, then it is more likely to be Zedekiah, whose capture and torture is reported in II Kings 25.6f.

[2] *we'attāh* followed by a proper name emphasizes the addressee and summons him to an awareness of the identity in which he is to hear the following words. The opening is similar to 4.8 in pointing out a person who is to hear a promise. In the context it functions as an adversative shift, contrasting Bethlehem (masc.) from whom shall come a ruler whose power extends over all the earth to *bat-gedūd* (fem.) who can only lament because Israel's judge is humiliated. The purpose of the double name, Bethlehem Ephratha, seems clear. Both are associated with the origin of David before he became king in Hebron and Jerusalem. David's father, Jesse, was a Bethlehemite (I Sam. 16.1, 18) and an Ephrathite from Bethlehem of Judah (I Sam. 17.12). This double way of putting it reflects a complex history of the relation of the two. Ephratha is sometimes treated as a place (province?) which is distinct from Bethlehem. See Ps. 132.6 and 'the way of Ephratha' as the name of a section of a north-south road (Gen. 35.16, 18; 48.7);[1] also the name in the Chronicler's genealogies (I Chron. 2.19, 24, 50; 4.4). In Gen. 35.18 and 48.7 a comment is appended to the name Ephratha which identifies it as Bethlehem. Ruth 1.2 speaks of Ephrathites from Bethlehem, and 4.11 identifies the two (note the textual problem). Possibly the names represent family groups whose history has long since merged; tradition keeps both names alive. 'Bethlehem in Ephratha' is a possible reading (NEB), or the two names may simply be juxtaposed in the light of the tradition equating them. Either way, the vocative personifies the folk and place from which David sprang as the origin of the ruler to come. Thus the oracle explicitly ignores the Davidic succession and revises the terms of Nathan's founding oracle (II Sam. 7.4–17, especially v. 16). The third line emphasizes the return to the beginning. 'Origin' (*mōṣā'ōt*, elsewhere only II Kings 10.27 with a quite different meaning!) echoes the verb 'come forth' (*yṣ'*) and thinks of children originating in the loins of their father (BDB, *yṣ'*, 1h, p. 423). Bethlehem as the 'parent' of the ruler belongs to a period now viewed

[1] See the map in Y. Aharoni, *The Land of the Bible*, 1967, p. 40.

as an era behind the current order and so belonging to 'ancient days'. The characterization of Bethlehem as 'small(est) (*ṣā'îr*) among Judah's clans ('*elep*)' recalls the procedure by which YHWH selected directly an individual to lead Israel, a procedure that had been replaced by the election of the Davidic succession as bearer of kingship. Gideon protested that he could not save Israel because 'My '*elep* is the weakest in Manasseh and I am *haṣṣā'îr* in my father's house' (Judg. 6.15); and Saul said that he was a Benjamite from the least (*qṭn*) of the tribes of Israel and his clan (*mišpāḥāh*) was the smallest (*haṣṣā'îrāh*) of all the clans of the tribe (I Sam. 9.21). The motif is also present in the narrative of David's selection; he was the youngest (*qṭn*) of Jesse's sons and the last to be considered (I Sam. 16.11). The motif emphasizes the marvel of God's intervention, who brings forth a man to save his people from the most unlikely and unexpected quarter. From such an unlikely source shall emerge one who will specifically belong to YHWH ('to me/YHWH' is emphatic in its sentence). He will serve as ruler (*mōšēl*) over Israel. Perhaps the title 'king' (*melek*) is avoided to reserve the language of kingship for YHWH alone and to subordinate the *mōšēl* to YHWH. His dependence on YHWH is specifically elaborated in v. 4.

[3] Verse 3 interrupts the movement of the saying from promise of a future ruler (v. 2) to a description of his reign (v. 4). Its two prosaic sentences are connected to the promise by 'therefore' which introduces, not some statement of the consequence of the ruler's appearance, but an explanation of its delay. 'They' (the assumed antecedent must be Israel in v. 2) are given up (by YHWH) and left, presumably in the power of their enemies, for the present. The period of dereliction will last 'until the time when she who is in labour (*yōlēdāh*) gives birth.' These words have traditionally been interpreted as a prophecy of the birth of the coming ruler, under the influence of Isa. 9.6; 7.14.[j] But a better guide to their meaning is the use of *yōlēdāh* in 4.9f.[k] In 4.9f., and generally in the Old Testament, *yōlēdāh* is used as a figure for the distress brought on by the attack of enemies; the image is concerned only with the writhing of labour, not an expected birth; see the texts from Jeremiah cited at 4.10; and Ps. 48.5; Isa. 13.8; 21.3. Verse 3 applies the metaphor to the whole period of exile and dispersion. The 'birth' is the end of that term of 'labour' when all the remaining dispersion return to Israel. The verse was composed

---

[j] See C. Westermann's suggestion that this 'calculation' is the result of a 'messianic exegesis' of Isa. 7.14 and the name 'a remnant shall return' (op. cit., pp. 56f.).

[k] On the interpretation of this verse see especially T. Lescow, op. cit., pp. 199–205.

and inserted partly as an apologetic to explain the delay in the appearance of the promised ruler and partly to introduce the motif of the remnant and its return. This motif is the particular interest of those who gave chs. 1–5 their final form (see the Introduction, pp. 27ff.). 'Brother' means member of the people (e.g., Deut. 15.12; 17.15), the fellow Israelites of the *mōšel*. The unexpected ruler has no part in their deliverance; that is the work of YHWH (see 4.10b and 4.6; 2.12). But their return sets the stage for the beginning of his reign as described in v. 4.

[4] The promise of a ruler continues with a description of the power of his reign, full of motifs which echo the portrayal of the ideal king in the royal psalms. The tenure of this king will endure, standing against all the changes and challenges of history (Ps. 72.5). The use of 'shepherd' (cf. 5.5; 7.14) as a name for the office and work of a ruler was an established feature of language about the king across the entire Near East from earliest times. In Israel the persistence and importance of their pastoral culture kept the term from losing its connotations of guidance, protection, and provision for the needs of the people.[1] The coming *mōšēl* will rule, not by his own power, but by the strength which comes from YHWH and by the majestic fame which belongs to the name of his God (I Sam. 2.10). His reign will be an expression, not a replacement of YHWH's kingship. The one explicit soteriological feature of this future reign is gathered up in the expression 'they shall dwell'. That the ruler's power will provide security and stability for Israel (cf. v. 2b) could well be an allusion to this element in Nathan's oracle to David (see II Sam. 7.10). There will be no danger from other nations because the greatness of the coming ruler will be unlimited. He will be known and feared to the very ends of the earth, and his sovereignty will fulfil the hopes for the success of Judah's kings of the past, expressed in the hymns celebrating their destiny in the purpose of God (see Ps. 2.8; 72.8, which is also related as prophecy concerning the future king in Zech. 9.10).

19. PEACE WITH ASSYRIA: 5.5f. (MT 5.4f.)

5 This shall be salvation from[a] Assyria,
    when he comes in to our land,
    and when he treads upon our soil.[b]

[1] See the full discussion by W. Zimmerli, *Ezechiel* (BK XIII/2), pp. 834ff.

[a] Read *mē'aššūr*; haplography of *m*; cf. v. 6b.

[b] Reading *be'admātēnū*, a better synonym in the parallelism and suggested by G. MT has *be'armenōtēnū*, 'on our fortified palaces'.

> We will set over him seven shepherds
> and eight human chieftains.
> 6 They will shepherd the land of Assyria with the sword,
> the land of Nimrod with the bared blade.[c]
> He will deliver from Assyria
> when he comes into our land,
> when he treads within our borders.

Verses 5f. (Heb. 4f.; only the English verse numbers are used below) promise security from attack by Assyria. Indeed, should that classic foe of Israel launch an invasion, the result will be a reversal of the usual roles of the two nations. Israel will establish a military government over Assyria and bring that great power under its hegemony. Several features of the text suggest that the promise is to be read in direct continuity with the promise of the future ruler whose power will be great to the ends of the earth (5.2-4). The demonstrative 'this' (v. 5) could point back to the promised ruler (it could also point forward to the subjugation of Assyria). The pronominal subject of 'he shall deliver' in v. 6b is without antecedent unless it refers back to the ruler. Verses 5f. contain no hint of the way in which Israel will gain power over Assyria; the divine strength of the future ruler (v. 4a) could be the explanation. The use of 'shepherd'='rule' in v. 4a is repeated in v. 6a. But other explanations of these features are possible, and the question of their source and relation to vv. 2-4 has been a major issue in their interpretation.[d]

Verses 5f. have been taken as a self-contained oracle, with necessary emendations (J. M. P. Smith), as the fragment of a longer poem, now equipped with a redactional title in v. 5a (Robinson), as part (only 5a and 6b) of a longer poem which reaches back to 4.8 (Sellin), as a disarranged text of which 6b and 5a complete 2-4 in that order, and 5b and 6a repeat a response of the people to the foregoing oracle (Vuilleumier), as a saying of near apocalyptic brought into the book by a redaction of the fourth century (Lescow, Willi-Plein).

The apparent continuity of vv. 5f. with the preceding oracle results from redaction. The two can hardly compose an original unity, for they are distinct in style and subject. The first is addressed to Bethlehem and speaks of a future ruler through whom YHWH's reign will be manifest on the earth. The second is spoken by Israel in first person plural style and is concerned specifically with the problem of Assyria. Moreover, an unevenness in the content of vv. 5f.

---

[c] *bappetīḥāh* for MT *biptāḥēhā* ('in her gates'); see BHS.
[d] See K. J. Cathcart, 'Notes on Micah 5.4-5', *Biblica* 49, 1968, pp. 511-514.

suggest that an independent oracle has been adapted to this context. In vv. 5b. 6a, it is the corporate group who establish human rulers over Assyria. But in v. 6b the actor is a single person; if 'this' in v. 5a refers back to the divine ruler, he is the origin of salvation from Assyria there also. Verse 6b is largely a verbatim reiteration of the first line of v. 5, which further supports the relationship of 'this one' and 'he shall deliver'. The opening *wᵉhāyāh* of the Hebrew text of v. 5 is the introductory rubric of the rest of the units in ch. 5. An independent oracle has been adapted for this place in the chapter by replacing its opening words with 'And this (one) shall be salvation from . . .' and by adding the echoing v. 6b. The oracle has been crafted to form a transition from the promise of the Messiah at the end of the complex 4.8–5.4 to the block of oracles on the peoples and nations in the eschatological future. (See the Introduction, pp. 27ff.) The occurrence of the catchword 'shepherd' in v. 4 and vv. 5f. made the oracle more appropriate for its position. By revising and locating the saying in this way the redactor has given it a context which turns the fiercely nationalistic character of the original in the direction of the broad sketch of the eschatological reign of YHWH which is developed in chs. 4–5. It prepares for and gives a rationale for the remnant sayings in vv. 7f. The original is not likely to have come from Micah or his time, in spite of the reference to Assyria; the confident claim of a military domination of Assyria make that unlikely. The name 'Assyria' is probably a code-name for any great power which may threaten Israel in the future (see the comment below). No particular military crisis has to be sought as an occasion for the oracle (historical Assyria, Persia, Seleucids, have been suggested). It is, rather, like the following remnant sayings in vv. 7f., the expression of a general eschatological confidence (from the post-exilic period) about the security of the redeemed Israel.

[5] The redactor's addition at the opening means: 'And this (one—the Messiah) shall be (our) salvation from Assyria.' In the present MT 'Assyria' stands outside any expected syntax. 'Salvation' (*šālōm*) means 'well-being', specifically security from threat to the wholeness and prosperity of the nation. The notion is like that of I Kings 4.24 (MT 5.4) which describes how Solomon dominated the nations around about and established *šālōm* with (*min*) them. The redactor could have this tradition as his model for messianic times; not the presence of the picture of peace in Micah 4.4 which also appears in I Kings 4.25 (MT 5.5). The association of the achievement of *šālōm* with the Messiah's reign is a feature of the messianic oracle in Isaiah (cf. Isa. 9.7; 11.6–9). W. Beyerlin finds a messianic title like 'prince

of peace' (Isa. 9.6) in *zeh šālōm*ᵉ and translates 'and he will be Lord of peace'.ᶠ But the reading leaves unsolved problems in MT.

'Assyria' appears to be used as code-name for whatever great power threatens from the north, the direction from which assaults on Israel had always come. The name continued in use, after the demise of the historical Assyrian empire, for whatever great power ruled that territory, e.g. Persia (Ezra 6.22), the Seleucid kingdom (Zech. 10.10f.).ᵍ The prophetic eschatology of exilic and later times on occasion employed historical names of the nations who had figured significantly in Israel's past as symbols for their successors.ʰ The probability that 'Assyria' is a code-name is heightened by 'land of Nimrod' in the parallelism of v. 6b. The name 'Nimrod' appears elsewhere only in Gen. 10.8f. (and I Chron. 1.10 which is a version of it). Nimrod is the son of Cush, founder of cities in Babylon and Assyria; he was the 'first mighty warrior'. 'Land of Nimrod' evokes this tradition and points to the Mesopotamian region as the home of the mighty. The 'Assyria' of the original saying is any power that threatens the Israel of the future. The redaction matches the 'power of YHWH' present in the Messiah (v. 4) against the legendary origin of invasion as the saving solution which will bring peace.

The picture of a military government over 'Assyria' conflicts with the notion of a messianic peace where conflict and force are transcended, but the language of the original saying is left standing. 'Shepherd' is used in its frequent sense of 'ruler'. For 'to set up a shepherd over' (*hēqīm rōʿeh ʿal*), see Jer. 23.4; Ezra 34.23; Zech. 11.16, where YHWH is always the actor. Only in this text is 'Shepherd' used of a ruler from Israel over another nation and in a harsh sense. 'Chieftains' (*nesīkīm*, always plural) in Old Testament vocabulary designates leaders of nations hostile to Israel (Josh. 13.21; Ezek. 32.30; Ps. 83.11), and only here is used presumably of Israelites. That they are 'human chieftains' (*nesīkē ʾadām*) seems to emphasize their role as regents established by the 'we' of Israel; in the context the phrase contrasts with the divine *mōšēl* who rules for YHWH. 'Seven . . . eight' is a numerical sequence which means an indefinite number, 'many'.ⁱ

ᵉ W. Beyerlin, *Die Kulttraditionen Israels in der Verkündigung des propheten Micha* (FRLANT 72), 1959, pp. 34f., 79f.

ᶠ For the linguistic evidence for this meaning of *zeh*, see the literature cited by M. Dahood, *Psalms* II, 1968, p. 139.

ᵍ See J. M. Meyers, *Ezra-Nehemia*, 1965, in comment on Ezr. 6.22.

ʰ See G. Fohrer, 'Die Struktur des alttestamentlichen Eschatologie' in *Studien zur alttestamentlichen Prophetie*, 1967, p. 43.

ⁱ See examples gathered by G. Sauer, *Die Sprüche Agurs*, 1963, pp. 49f.

20. THE REMNANT AMONG THE PEOPLES: 5.7–9
(MT 5.6–8)

7 The remnant of Jacob shall be
　in the midst of many peoples
　like dew from YHWH,
　　like showers upon grass,
　which does not wait on man
　　nor depend upon mankind.
8 The remnant of Jacob shall be among the nations[a]
　in the midst of many peoples,
　like a lion among wild beasts,
　　like a young lion among flocks of sheep,
　who claws when he passes through;
　　he rends and none can rescue.
9 May your hand be raised[b] against your foes,
　and all your enemies be cut off.

5.7–9 (Heb. vv. 6–8, subsequently cited according to English
verse numbers only) contains two brief oracles of salvation (vv. 7 and
8) and a line of liturgical quality (v. 9). The oracles are alike in form;
each is composed of three elements. A first line states the theme ('The
remnant in the midst of many peoples'), a second draws a comparison,
and a third identifies the term of comparison. Though each saying is
formally complete in itself, the two must have been composed as a
sequence. Verse 7 reveals the divine source of the remnant's existence,
v. 8 its irresistible power in comparison to all people. Together they
promise the salvation appropriate to the predicament implied in the
theme: the remnant is engulfed in the sea of history, but as a supra-
historical creation its existence is secure. The unit is probably post-
exilic; Jacob/Israel exists only as a 'remnant' (on the term, see the
comment on 4.6f.), and 'remnant of Jacob' has almost become a
fixed title. Salvation prophecy concerning Israel's power against
other nations seems to set in with Isa. 41.14–16; the nearest parallels
are Zech. 9.11–17; 10.3–12 (cf. also Isa. 11.14; Zeph. 2.9).

Israel's future under YHWH in the midst of the peoples/nations is
the primary interest of the redactor who gave chs. 1–5 their final
shape (see the Introduction, pp. 27ff.). Verses 7 and 8 begin with
the Hebrew verb *wᵉhāyāh*, the opening rubric which marks each of

[a] *baggōyīm* is probably an addition; 'nations' and 'peoples' are frequent synonyms. G has the phrase at the end of the first colon in v. 7 (Heb. v. 6).
[b] Other MSS and the versions support an imperfect *tārūm* instead of the jussive
tārōm.

the units he arranged as a concluding section for the first part of the book. Verse 9 is spoken in direct address to an unidentified 'you', a style which appears in the following oracle (vv. 10–14). The thematic verb ('cut off') of that oracle is also used in v. 9, which thus appears to be a transition composed to attach. vv. 10ff. There are clear echoes of 4.13. In the present literary context vv. 7–9 contribute to the picture of the future Israel which shall be governed by a divine ruler whose power reaches to the ends of earth (v. 4), shall dominate 'Assyria' (vv. 5f.), shall be invulnerable against all peoples (vv. 7–9), and in that security will be dependent neither on military or religious power, but upon YHWH alone (vv. 10–14). There are two other remnant prophecies in chs. 1–5 and each seems to portray one stage in the remnant's salvation: the remnant will be taken into exile by YHWH 2.12f.), rescued and transformed into a strong nation (4.6f.), and live in perfect security among the peoples (5.7ff.).

[7] 'Remnant of Jacob' names the identifiable remainder of the people Israel after the calamities of the sixth century (cf. the standard use of the term as designation in Hag. 1.12, 14; Zech. 8.6, 12). The epithet conveys both tragedy and hope. It acknowledges that the Israel of the present is only a fraction of its former greatness; judgment has occurred. But Jacob has a remnant and the way of YHWH with his elect has not vanished from history. It is the question of the future of that remnant in the midst of the world of nations to which this prophecy speaks. 'Many peoples' is an inclusive term for the numerous political entities whose power and purpose make up the setting for the remnant's future. The term is the language of prophecy which no longer speaks of judgment and salvation in terms of one specific great power or list of neighbouring kingdoms. The drama of Israel's future belongs to the universal; final inclusive statements can be made about it. 'Many peoples', means 'any nation whatsoever'. It is difficult to say whether 'in the midst of' implies that the remnant is scattered among the nations as a diaspora or lives as a little community centred in Jerusalem surrounded by other nations. The latter seems more likely, and is certainly what is meant in this literary context.

Dew is used in some Old Testament comparisons for the beneficial and pleasant (Ps. 133.3; Prov. 19.12). If that were the sense of the simile here, the two verses would contain absolutely contrasting motifs. Verse 7 would speak of Israel as future blessing for the nations and v. 8 of Israel as curse. The sequence has been interpreted as an eschatological statement of the promise to Abraham in Gen. 12.3. But the term of comparison in the third line picks up 'from YHWH' in the comparison and points to the heavenly origin of dew and showers (Gen. 27.28, 39; Deut. 33.28; Zech. 8.12, etc.). As the similar syntax in the next verse shows, the relative sentence in the term of comparison is attached to 'dew/showers'. It is independence of the human realm which the comparison emphasizes. The remnant will be like the dew of mysterious heavenly origin. The existence of the eschatological Jacob will be wholly the work of God, meither dependent upon nor vulnerable to mere human strength.

[8] The lion is one of the favourite images in Old Testament similes (e.g., Gen. 49.9; II Sam. 17.10; Isa. 31.4; Hos. 11.10; etc.) and is used consistently to speak of fierce and fearsome power. The relation between the remnant of Jacob and the nations will be like that between the powerful lion and weaker wild and domestic animals. No people will be able to stand against them. With a different accent this comparison makes the same point as v. 7; the remnant will be utterly secure in the midst of the threats of world history.

[9] Verse 9 could be a prayer addressed to God, but the context makes Israel the expected addressee. As translated above, the line has the form of a prayer of blessing which the congregation would hear and receive as the prophecy was read. The line could be construed as a prophecy ('Your hand shall be raised in'), if the well-attested variant cited in note (b) were followed. The prayer regards the peoples as the enemies of Israel and simply expresses the petition that the divinely given existence and power promised in vv. 7f. should be used in their destruction.

21. THE DIVINE PURGE: 5.10–15 (MT 5.9–14)

10 It shall be in that day,
  oracle of YHWH,
 I will cut off your horses from your midst
 and I will wreck your chariots.
11 I will cut off the cities of your land
 and I will overthrow all your fortresses.
12 I will cut off sorceries from your hand,
 and you will have no soothsayers.
13 I will cut off your images
  and your pillars from your midst.
 You shall not bow down again
  to the work of your hands.
14 I will root out the Asherim from your midst
 and I will destroy your cities.

15 I will take vengeance in anger and in wrath
upon the nations which have not heard.

This oracle announces that YHWH will eliminate chariot-forces, fortifications, divination, and idols (vv. 10–14), and will take vengeance on the nations which do not heed (v. 15). What the oracle says is clear enough, but how it is to be understood is a problem. It is spoken in direct address as the very words of YHWH, but the addressee is not identified. The unit speaks of punitive action at the conclusion of a complex of salvation oracles to which it is clearly attached by v. 9. In v. 15 YHWH's punitive intention is broadened to include 'nations which have not heard'. What they have not heeded is not said, nor is their relation to the 'you', to whom the preceding lines are addressed, clarified.

The saying in its present form is not a rhetorical unit. The original is marked off by lines which begin with the thematic verb 'I will cut off' (vv. 10b–13a); this repetitive sequence reaches a climax in v. 13b where the pattern is broken in order to state the result and purpose of YHWH's action. 'From your midst' in the last colon of v. 13a echoes that phrase from the first colon of the oracle and seems to prepare for this conclusion. In v. 14 the sequence of similarly formed lines resumes, but with a different verb; the Asherim are added to the list of cultic objects to be eliminated, and the item 'cities' from v. 11 (Heb. 10) is repeated to complete the line. The verse was probably added at some early stage in the oracle's history in order to include the detested Asherim among the cultic objects named.

The basic oracle can hardly have come from Micah.[a] In form and style it is quite unlike any other saying in the book. The punishment announced is a purging, in contrast to the judgment of destruction proclaimed by Micah. Concern about idols and horses and chariots as offensive to YHWH is a feature of the early exilic redaction of the Micah tradition (see 1.7; 2.10; and 1.13b). The vocabulary, as the comment shows, is characteristic of the literature of the end of the monarchy and the beginning of the exile. The agenda of the divine purge has partial parallels in Hos. 14.3 ('horses and the work of our hands') and in Isa. 2.6–8 ('soothsayers, horses and chariots, idols'; the unity of the sequence has been questioned); but in both they are

---

[a] It has been often attributed to him, most recently by Weiser and Vuilleumier. A full review of the discussion is given by J. T. Willis, 'Authenticity and Meaning of Micah 5.9–14', *ZAW* 81, 1969, pp. 353–68. Jörg Jeremias connects it with the exilic reinterpretation of Micah (*ZAW* 83, 1971, pp. 343ff.). T. Lescow dates it in the late post-exilic period (*ZAW* 84, 1972, pp. 77f.).

named as the basis for YHWH's judgment of the nation. Here YHWH himself will remove them. This oracle stands in the tradition of the earlier ones, but reformulates their items in a fuller agenda which is now a programme for YHWH's action. The oracle is in fact a kind of salvation saying. It conceives of YHWH's punishment as a purification of his people from all which perverts their relation to him. The saying came into the Micah collection as a reinterpretation of his announcement of Jerusalem's end along with the other expansions which reflect the application of Micah's prophecy to the Babylonian crisis. For other prophecies that YHWH will cut off horses and chariots in his work of salvation see Zech. 9.10 and Hag. 2.22. The oracle's function as a message of salvation through purification explains its presence in chs. 4–5.

Verse 15 widens the area of YHWH's action to include the nations who have not listened. Agaist them he will act, not just to purify, but in wrathful vengeance. The line is a statement of the theme 'YHWH and the peoples/nations' which is the concern of the last major stage in the formation of chs. 1–5. The phrase 'nations who have not heard (šmʿ)' presupposes the opening summons to all the earth to hear YHWH's witness (1.2).[b] So v. 15 not only applies the significance of vv. 10–14 to the nations, declaring that YHWH who removes everything that keeps his people from utter dependence on him will brook no resistance to his reign among the nations. It also concludes the witness of YHWH to the world and stands as the final parenthesis marking off its limits. The full oracle has been connected to the foregoing material by v. 9 which uses a passive form of the thematic verb in a liturgical cry as a transition to this piece. The introduction in v. 10 is also a setting provided by the redactor who repeats the verb (wᵉhāyāh) which introduces the divine saying 4.6.

[10] 'In that day' echoes, along with the same formula in 4.6, the 'It shall come to pass in the latter days' of 4.1 and thus points to the whole drama of YHWH's eschatological redemption sketched in the sayings of these chapters as the period when YHWH will act. The original saying is re-set within the time of YHWH's reign on earth. The thematic verb for divine action, 'I will cut off . . . from among . . .' (wᵉhikrātî miqqereb) with its parallels, sketches a programme of the eradication and removal of things offensive to YHWH's sovereignty. The verb is a feature of a sacral formula for the removal of persons who have violated the holiness of Israel (e.g. Lev. 17.10; 20.3, 5, 6; niphal in Lev. 7.20f., 27; 19.8; 20.18); the removal is not only a judgment upon the persons, but a measure to

[b] T. Lescow, op. cit., p. 58.

preserve the corporate people in the face of YHWH's wrath against the unholy.c Here the action is directed against impersonal objects which pervert a direct and pure relation to YHWH. Horses and chariots are to be eliminated because they can be treated as a substitute for reliance on YHWH alone for security; see Isaiah's polemic against them in Isa. 2.7; 30.15–17; 31.1–3 and Hos. 10.13; Deut. 17.16 forbids them to the king.

[11] Towns, which were generally defended by ramparts, and fortresses will be removed for the same reason.

[12] Sorceries (kᵉšāpîm) is a term for the practice of magic of some sort; just what kind is not clear. The term appears only in Isa. 47.9, 12 and as a figure in II Kings 9.22; Nah. 3.4. It must refer to a method of procuring information from supernatural sources since it is grouped here with 'soothsayers', persons who practiced divination using omens derived from natural or manipulated signs. Soothsaying is abhorrent to YHWH (Deut. 18.10; Lev. 19.26). Both must be removed, not only because they represent techniques for communication with the divine which can be managed by men. They are thus a presumption against YHWH's way of communicating his will only through the law and the prophetic message that comes by his initiative. 'Sorcerers' and 'soothsayers' appear together in a condemnatory list in Jer. 27.9; Deut. 18.10–11.

[13] Prohibition of images (pᵉsîlîm) in the cult of Israel was a basic tenet of Yahwism (pesel Ex. 20.4; Deut. 5.8; pāsîl Deut. 7.5, 25). The standing stone pillar (maṣṣēbāh), found in many shrines and high places during Israel's early history in Canaan, was included in the list of condemned cultic paraphernalia at the time of Josiah's reform (cf. Deut. 16.22; I Kings 14.23; II Kings 17.10; 18.4; 23.14). Pillar is grouped with image in that period (Deut. 7.5, 25; 12.2; Lev. 26.1) and apparently regarded as itself a representative of the deity to be adored as a manifestation of the divine presence. 'The work of (men's) hands' as a scornful epithet for idols was used by Hosea (14.3) and Isaiah (2.8); it became a polemical slogan in the literature of the late seventh century (Jer. 1.16; 10.3; 25.6f.; etc.; Deut. 4.28; 27.15; 31.29; II Kings 19.18; 22.17; Pss. 115.4; 135.15). The contempt in the expression is overwhelming. It was no disclosure of a secret that men made images; but that those who knew YHWH as a God of words and deed should see his presence in what they made could only distort the worshipper's understanding of his relation to God. Verse 13b varies the sequence of lines reciting YHWH's act to state the purpose

────────

c See W. Zimmerli, 'Die Eigenart der Prophetischen Rede des Ezechiel' in *Gottes Offenbarung* (Th B 19), 1963, pp. 162ff.

of his judgment and so sounds like a concluding sentence. Though 'work of your hands', is a phrase which traditionally belongs to the polemic against idols, it may serve here also as a summary category for all the other items as creations and techniques of human independence of YHWH.

[14] Verse 14 adds Asherim to the list of cultic objects and repeats 'cities' from v. 11. Asherah is the name of the goddess who was the consort of Baal in the Palestinian version of the Canaanite pantheon (Judg. 3.7; II Kings 23.4). The name was applied to a wooden post or a tree which represented the female deity in sanctuaries (Deut. 16.21, II Kings 23.14). Asherim were paired with *maṣṣēbōt* (e.g. Deut. 7.5; 17.21f.); perhaps v. 14 is a secondary expansion added to include the other members of the offensive pair. Or 'Asherim' and 'cities' may be paired to represent the categories of military and cultic as a conclusion to the original saying.

[15] In v. 15 the object of divine action is 'the nations' instead of the singular masculine 'you' to whom vv. 10-14 are directly addressed. In the context of v. 15, the oracle in vv. 10-14 is to be heard as the announcement of one function of that judgment; Israel will be purified of all that offends YHWH's sovereignty by YHWH's own action. As for the rest of the nations, if they do not hear the witness and see in YHWH's past mighty actions the manifestation of his rule (chs. 1-3) and respond in submission to his lordship over history exercised from Jerusalem (4.1ff.), then he will take vengeance (*nāqām*) upon them. YHWH's vengeance is a function of his rule as exclusive King in Israel and the world. It is not irrational personal revenge to satisfy a wounded ego, but the exercise of legitimate sovereignty in a punishment which must occur if the rule of God is to be maintained against the self-seeking power and lusts of men.[d] 'In anger and in wrath' are anthropomorphisms to express the inexorable and irresistible certainty of YHWH's defence of his sovereignty. For other portrayals of YHWH's vengeance upon the nations see Deut. 32.35, 41, 43; Isa. 34.8; 59.17; 63.4, 6.

22. GOD'S SALVATION IS HIS JUSTIFICATION:
6.1-5

1 Hear what YHWH is saying:
Stand up. Make (your) complaint before the mountains;
let the hills hear your voice.

[d] See the wide-ranging study by G. Mendenhall, 'The Vengeance of Yahweh' in *The Tenth Generation*, 1973, pp. 69-104.

2 Hear, O mountains, YHWH's case,
   and listen[a] O foundations of earth.
For YHWH has a case with his people,
   with Israel he litigates.
3 'My people, what have I done to you?
   How have I wearied you? Testify against me!
4 For I brought you up from the land of Egypt;
   from the house of slavery I ransomed you.
I sent Moses before you,
   Aaron and Miriam (5) with him.[b]
Remember what Balak, king of Moab,[c] advised,
   and how Baalam, son of Beor,[c] answered him.
. . .[d] from Shittim to Gilgal
   in order to know the saving deeds of YHWH.'[e]

6.1–5 contain a first-person saying of YHWH (vv. 3–5) preceded by a threefold summons to hear (vv. 1a, 1b, 2a). This complex summons serves as an introduction both to the saying and to chs. 6–7. Verse 1a addresses a general audience with a plural imperative to announce that what follows is the speech of YHWH. Verse 1b with its singular masculine imperative and pronoun must be addressed to YHWH's people (vv. 2b, 3) as a summons to Israel to speak before the mountains; it anticipates vv. 6f. where a voice representing Israel responds. Verse 2a addresses the mountains themselves, calling them to listen to a case which YHWH has against Israel; it introduces the divine saying in vv. 3–5. Verse 1a guides the reader to hear vv. 1b–2 as the speech of YHWH in spite of the third-person reference to YHWH in v. 2. It is YHWH who calls Israel into court to plead its case, and YHWH who convenes the mountains and foundations of

   [a] Reading *weha'azinū*. MT's *wehā'ētānīm* ('unfailing streams') probably reflects the other topographical terms in the context and arose by dittography of *m* from the next word.

   [b] *'immō* for *'ammī* ('my people'), which in MT stands as a vocative at the beginning of v. 5. The change completes the parallelism and rhythm of v. 4b, and relieves the overloading of v. 5a.

   [c] 'King of Moab' and 'son of Beor' overload the line in a sequence which appears to be regularly 3+3. The phrases probably were added from Num. 22ff. to identify the names more precisely.

   [d] The measure is too short in the context, and the prepositional phrases can hardly go with the preceding verb, 'answered'; a verb has been lost. The reconstruction of *be'obrekā* ('when you passed over') from *be'ōr* (Weiser, Robinson) would hold two distinct items in the recitation together; see the comment below.

   [e] The name seems to contradict the first-person speech style; some suggest that the final *y* of an original *sidqōtāy* ('my saving deeds') was taken as abbreviation for *yhwh*.

earth to hear his case against Israel. The purpose of the complex introduction is to extend the course of the trial scene portrayed in vv. 2–5 into the following material, so that the voices which speak there will be heard in the context of an on-going legal controversy (see the Introduction, pp. 9f., 32f.). This integrative function of v. 1 identifies it as the contribution of the redactor of chs. 6–7. An original saying lies in vv. 2–5.

The language and style of the saying are drawn from the sphere of legal practice in Israel. It is an example of the type called a court-saying (legal speech, lawsuit speech, *rīb*-pattern) which appears primarily in prophetic material across the history of prophecy from Hosea to Malachi.[f] These sayings can vary in structure and purpose. The classification gathers together units which in different ways evoke the situation of proceedings in a court as their setting-in-life.[g] The speech creates for the audience the drama of a legal controversy as a context in which the particular message is to be heard and understood. In each case the individual use of form and the purpose of the speaker has to be determined. Within the group this saying and several others (Isa. 1.2f; Jer. 2.4–13; Deut. 32) include summons to natural elements, usually heaven and earth, to participate in the controversy and an appeal to items of Israel's normative history (the promise to the fathers, exodus, wilderness, entry into the land). They have been named 'covenant lawsuit speeches' because these features show that the issue at stake in the controversy is the covenant between YHWH and Israel.[h] These formal characteristics stem from the form of treaties used to define relations between a monarch and his client states in the ancient Near East; the natural elements correspond to the cosmic entities named as witnesses and enforcers of the treaty, and the citation of the normative history to the treaty's historical prologue.[i] It is important to remember that such elements

---

[f] Examples are Isa. 1.2f., 18–20; 3.13–15; (5.1–7); Hos. 4.1–3, 4–6; 12.2–14; Jer. 2.4–13; Mal. 3.5. See the analysis in C. Westermann, *Basic Forms of Prophetic Speech*, 1967, pp. 199ff. In Deutero-Isaiah 41.1–5, 21–29; 43.8–15; 44.6–8; 45.20–25; see C. Westermann, *Isaiah 40–66* (OTL), 1969, pp. 17ff. On Deut. 32, G. E. Wright, 'The Lawsuit of God' in *Israel's Prophetic Heritage*, Festschrift for J. Muilenburg, 1962, pp. 26–67.

[g] For an analysis of the terms and forms of legal procedures in the OT, H. J. Boecker, *Redeformen des Rechtslebens im Alten Testament* (WMANT 14), 1964; for a study of the term *rīb* and its role in the lawsuit speeches, J. Limburg, 'The Root *rīb* and the Prophetic Lawsuit Speeches', *JBL* 88, 1969, pp. 291–304.

[h] See H. B. Huffmon, 'The Covenant Lawsuit in the Prophets', *JBL* 78, 1959, 285–295. Undoubtedly the covenant is at issue in others which lack these two characteristics.

[i] On the treaty-form and its uses in the OT, see among others: G. Mendenhall,

of legal and covenant forms are used by a prophet in a genre which
his speech creates. Elements of an entire legal process or a covenant
form are never present. The speaker appropriates a recognized
language and style to create a setting and make the point he has in
mind.

The literary type of 6.2–5 and the themes employed could be
attributed, to speak generally, to an eighth-century prophet. In some
of its features the unit is quite individual; it also has connections
with the recitation of YHWH's deeds in Josh. 24 (cf. vv. 5, 6, 9),
usually attributed to the Elohist, though a Deuteronomic reworking
of the material is generally assumed. But there are a number of in-
congruences between features of this unit and the speech and mission
of Micah in chs. 1–3. None of them alone would be conclusive, but the
cluster makes it difficult to attribute the verses to Micah. Language
and style point to a later period. The verb 'ransom' (v. 4a) used for
the exodus occurs in Deut. 7.8; 13.6; 9.26; 15.15; 21.8; 24.18; II
Sam. 7.23 (deuteronomic historian); Neh. 1.10; and the late Ps. 78.42.
With 'house of slaves' as an interpretative synonym for Egypt, the
verb appears only in Deut. 7.8; 13.16. 'House of slaves' is itself a
favourite phrase of deuteronomic style (see Deut. 6.12; 8.14; 13.11);
5.6 = Ex. 20.2; Ex. 13.14; Josh. 24.17; Judg. 6.8 can be attributed to
the same literary sphere; finally, Jer. 34.13. Moses, Aaron, and
Miriam are named nowhere else in the prophets, Miriam only here
outside the Pentateuch. The three names appear together only in
Num. 26.59 (P^s). The use of all three names in the role of commissioned leaders in the wilderness may result from a reflection on the
attribution of the role of prophet to all three (Ex. 7.1; 15.20f.), which
has a point of departure in Hos. 12.13. The call to remember (v. 5a)
connected with a motif of the saving history and used to enforce the
relation to YHWH is a feature of deuteronomic paraenesis (Deut.
5.15; 7.18; 8.2, 18; 9.7; 15.15; 16.3, 12; 24.9, 18, 22); 25.17 is a near
parallel to v. 5a. The expression 'in order to know' (l^{e}ma^{c}an da^{c}at) is
found only in the deuteronomic history (Josh. 4.24; Judg. 3.2; I Kings
8.60) and Ezek. 38.16; note the similarity of use in Josh. 4.24; I Kings
8.60. The situation of Israel indicated in their complaint against
YHWH that he has wearied them (v. 3), stands in sharp contrast to
Micah's audience and their confidence in YHWH (2.2f.; 3.11). In

---

Law and Covenant in Israel and the Ancient Near East (Biblical Colloquium), 1955; K.
Baltzer, *The Covenant Formulary*, 1964; D. J. McCarthy, *Treaty and Covenant* (Analecta
Biblica 21), 1963. On the relation of the treaty form to the *rib* pattern, J. Harvey,
Le plaidoyer prophétique contre Israël après la rupture de l'Alliance (Studia 22), 1967.

chs. 1–3 YHWH sends a message of judgment to the leaders in Jerusalem; here he seeks to bring all Israel, his people, back to the knowledge of his righteous deeds for them. The language, setting, and purpose of 6.2–5 point to a period in the late pre-exilic or exilic period. The position of the unit at the beginning of the collection in chs. 6–7 fits best with this conclusion. On the question of the relation of 6.1–5 to the following material, see the comment on 6.6–8.

[1] The syntax of the first Hebrew sentence (v. 1a) is unusual; some witnesses to the text support 'Hear the word which . . .' The imperative in the introductory formula is plural, but the addressees are not identified. The formula is naturally taken as the speech of the prophet who in this way introduces what follows as the language of YHWH. Verse 1b with its singular imperative and pronoun is to be read as YHWH's call to his people to participate in the trial he is convening. The verse is the composition of a redactor who draws on the language and style of vv. 2–5 to create an introduction to chs. 6–7. As YHWH's call to Israel to participate in the legal encounter inaugurated in vv. 2–5, the verse anticipates the human voices which will speak, beginning with vv. 6f., and interprets them as speeches in the controversy. The role which v. 1 plays in chs. 6–7 is similar to that of 1.2 in relation to chs. 1–5. On the assumption that the verse is part of an original unit of 'legal speech', some understand the summons as YHWH's instruction to the prophet to sit as 'lawyer' in the court (J. M. P. Smith, Huffmon, Harvey), but there are no parallels to such a feature in other examples of the type.

Israel is commanded to 'stand up' in preparation for speaking and listening as participant (*qūm* as preliminary for speech, Judg. 28.8; Jer. 1.17; in court Deut. 19.15f.; etc.). 'Make a complaint' identifies the kind of speech and the situation; Israel is to state and argue its grievance in confrontation with the aggrieving party in the context of the kind of court proceedings which were traditional in Israel. The phrase 'make a complaint before' (*rîb 'ēt*) usually means 'make a complaint against' (Judg. 8.1; Jer. 2.9; Neh. 5.7; 13.11, 17), but the mountains cannot be the aggrieving party. The preposition *'ēt* means 'in the presence of' here (as in Gen. 20.16; Isa. 30.8; G has *pros*, its usual translation of *'ēl*).[j] Mountains and hills are principal members of the legal assembly before whom the controversy is to be held. The role of cosmic entities in the setting of a *rîb* between YHWH and Israel is a heritage from the type of treaty whose form was used definitively to understand and interpret the covenant between Israel and YHWH. In the ancient Near East certain international treaties

---

[j] See Boecker, p. 102; Limburg, p. 301.

between a suzerain and his client states listed cosmic entities along with gods as witnesses to the terms and executors of the blessings and curses stipulated for keeping and breaking the treaty.[k] In the OT the natural elements are invoked where the covenant between YHWH and Israel is at issue (Deut.4.26; 30.19; 31.28), and as parties to a *rīb* concerning the faithfulness of the parties to the covenant (Deut. 31.1; Isa.2.1; Jer.2.12; Ps.50.4). Their role is that of witness to the original covenant. In the Old Testament they are not regarded as divine or as acting powers; their presence in such texts is a feature of formal speech and their invocation identifies the setting and its function. The appeal to mountains, hills, foundations of earth is a peculiarity of this text; in the texts listed above the elements are always heaven and earth, or simply heaven. Mountains (*hārīm*) and hills (*gebāʿōt*) are standard synonyms in poetic materials;[1] in the book of Micah they appear in 4.1.

[2] In v.2 the mountains are addressed directly in their role as witnesses to the covenant (similarly Deut.32.1; Isa.1.2). 'Foundations of earth', the pillars supporting the world at its nether limits in Hebrew cosmology (Isa.40.21; Ps.82.5; Prov.8.29), appear instead of hills; the longer phrase is probably employed for metrical reasons; 'mountains' is an approximate synonym (cf. Ps.18.8). The variation shows the poetic freedom of this piece from the standard 'heavens and earth'. The subject of the hearing is YHWH's case (*rīb YHWH*); YHWH has a legal controversy with his people (*rīb le YHWH ʿim*). The noun *rīb* in such contexts is the technical name for the process of formal controversy between aggrieved and aggrieving parties in which a judgment concerning who is in the right is sought, or a settlement is worked out.[m] 'Litigates' is an attempt to translate the only occurrence of the hithpael of *ykḥ*. The basic meaning of the usual hiphil is 'to set straight, reprimand', and it is used in the vocabulary of court process (see the participle in Amos 5.10; Isa.29.21) for the

[k] Examples in *ANET*, pp.201, 205, 206; see Mendenhall, p.40; Huffmon, pp. 291ff.; Baltzer, p.14.

[1] See the texts listed under the latter in BDB, p.149.

[m] Discussion continues over the basic meaning of the verb and noun form of *rīb*, whether it means specifically 'accusation, complaint against' (e.g., Limburg, op. cit., and material cited), or more generally 'the process of controversy before a court' (e.g., Boecker, op. cit., especially the summary of positions on p.54). Decision about a particular instance must be guided by accompanying prepositions and the context. For *rīb ʿim*, cf. Hos.4.1 (and the comment of H. W. Wolff, BK XIV.1, 1965, p.39); 12.3; Gen.26.20; Job 9.3. In v.3 YHWH begins to speak in the style of a defendant. In the context of Jer.2.9, another lawsuit saying, YHWH both defends himself (2.5) and accuses Israel (2.6, 13).

one who upholds what is right against its detractors. The niphal in Isa. 1.18 (cf. Job 23.7) is the best guide to the meaning of the hithpael; it refers to mutual legal controversy between YHWH and Israel.[n] YHWH's partner in the case is 'Israel, his people' (see 'my people' as vocative in v. 3). Both name and classification belong to the classic formulation of YHWH's election of Israel: 'YHWH, your God; Israel, my people.' This is covenant litigation. Israel must now be YHWH's partner in legal process, because this folk is partner to his covenant. When YHWH calls them *'ammi* before the cosmic witnesses, he addresses them in the only identity in which he will deal with them, the people whose existence and history is his work and whose supreme obligation in life is to actualize his sovereignty over them. For that reason the covenant lawsuit speeches are so redolent with the language of closest relationship: 'father and children', 'apple of his eye', 'sons and daughters' (Deut. 32); 'sons I have reared' (Isa. 1.2); 'my people' repeatedly (Jer. 2.4ff.).

[3] With the vocative 'my people' the direct speech of YHWH before the court begins. He opens with two questions of the kind which are employed in exchanges between aggrieved and aggrieving parties in the proceedings of a *rib*.[o] The first, 'What have I done (to you)?', is a defensive question, protesting innocence of the grievance alleged by the other party (Judg. 8.2; I Sam. 26.18; 20.1; 17.29; 29.8; cf. Samuel's particular questions in 12.3; the form 'what have you done?' is accusing: Judg. 8.1; II Sam. 12.21; Neh. 2.19). The second, 'How have I wearied (*hel'ētī*) you', is a formal variant of the first, it states the position of Israel, and is the only clue in the vv. 2–5 to the grievance which is at issue in the *rib*. With God as subject and man as object, the verb (hiphil) occurs only in Job 16.7 of Job's exhaustion at God's afflictions. The noun (*tᵉlā'āh*) is used of Israel's weariness under the hardships of Egypt (Num. 20.14), of the wilderness (Ex. 18.8), the oppression of enemies (Neh. 9.32; Lam. 3.5; cf. Mal. 1.13). Deutero-Isaiah describes the exiles as too weary (using *yg'*) for hope and obedience (Isa. 41.27–31; 43.22–24). The evidence is too slender to determine the exact circumstances historically, but the attitude attributed to Israel is plain. They live in circumstances which have exhausted their patience and hold YHWH responsible. Against that weariness YHWH appeals to the events of the saving history to bring Israel to recognition of his saving deeds (vv. 4f.). The attitude is quite unlike that of Micah's opponents and their confidence in YHWH,

---

[n] See H. Wildberger, *Jesaja* (BK X/1), pp. 51f.; and the study of the term by Boecker, pp. 45–47.

[o] On the form and setting of such questions, see Boecker, pp. 26–34.

cited in 3.11; 2.6f. It resembles more that faced by Jeremiah (2.4) and Deutero-Isaiah. The concluding challenge 'Testify against me' is a call for Israel to produce evidence for their grievance, and is often heard in the controversy of the *rīb* (I Sam. 12.3; II Sam. 1.16; Num. 35.30; etc.). YHWH expects no such argument, and none is forthcoming. The question is really an affirmation that right in the case is on his side.

[4] To counter Israel's complaint, YHWH recites the saving history, the classic and normative story of his deeds. The first word of v. 4 plays on 'wearied'; 'I have not wearied (*hel'ētikā*) you; I brought you up (*he῾elītikā*) . . .'; YHWH's works are the rebuttal of the complaint. The recitation is a rather full review of the basic items in the normative history, including the exodus, wilderness, and entry into the land. It cites names and particular incidents, pressing to re-create a fresh awareness of the drama and significance of Israel's beginnings. The appeal to the saving deeds is a frequent feature of YHWH's *rīb* with Israel (e.g. Isa. 1.2; Jer. 2.6f.; Deut. 32.7–14). The cogency and force of the appeal is based on the role which the normative history plays in the covenant form, where its items are cited as the historical prologue, the beneficial acts of the suzerain which create the relation and found the obligations formulated in the covenant. The recitation justifies the claim in the possessive pronoun of 'my people' and places Israel before the gracious work of YHWH which gave her existence and history. YHWH brought Israel up out of Egypt, the primary act of salvation which is so significant that it became the signature, the identity of Israel's God (e.g. Ex. 20.2=Deut. 5.6). The second measure of v. 4a emphasizes the redemptive quality of the event. Egypt was a 'house of slaves'; from its bondage YHWH 'ransomed' (*pdh*) them. *Pdh* means to free someone who is bound by legal or cultic obligation by the payment of a price; in its use for the exodus (e.g. Deut. 7.8; 13.5; Ps. 78.42) no price other than YHWH's investment of self in intervention is in view; the verb has become a metaphor of salvation pointing to the helpless bondage from which they were saved. YHWH brought Israel through the wilderness by commissioning Moses, Aaron, and Miriam to lead them. For similar sentences in recitations of the saving history see Josh. 24.5; I Sam. 12.8; Ps. 105.26, which place the sending (Moses and Aaron only) before the exodus. The notion of leadership in the wilderness ('before you') appears in the somewhat similar Ps. 77.20 (cf. Ps. 99.6). The role assigned Miriam is singular and may be an interpretation of Ex. 15.20f.

[5] YHWH's plea that Israel should remember concerns not just

the item about Balak and Balaam; it indicates the function of the entire recitation. 'Remember' (*zkr*) in such contexts means to recall the past and confront it as present reality, to live and think by events whose force continues from the past into the present. The verb is often used for reflection on YHWH's saving activity (Ps. 77.6f., 12f.; 119.52; 143.5; Deut. 32.7; cf. Ps. 105.5) and approaches the sense of confession of the reality one knows and trusts.[p] The reference to Balak's advice (request) and Balaam's answer does not tell what happened; knowledge of the narrative in Num. 22.24 is assumed. That King Balak employed the seer, Balaam, to curse Israel, who in turn received only a blessing for Israel from YHWH by vision is understood as one of the saving deeds, as in the recitation in Josh. 24.9f. (cf. Deut. 23.4f.; Neh. 13.2). The apparently mutilated reference to Israel's progress from Shittim to Gilgal cannot be part of the Balaam incident; the hexateuchal narrative locates the move after the encounter with Balak. Shittim was the camp of Israel under Joshua east of the Jordan (Josh. 2.1; 3.1; cf. Abel-shittim in Num. 33.49) and Gilgal the camp after crossing the Jordan (Josh. 4.19). The only possible role in the saving history in the preserved tradition is the miraculous crossing of the Jordan which is described as an event like crossing the Red Sea in Josh. 4.20ff.

The purpose of remembering is stated in the final measure: 'in order to know (*daʿat*) the saving deeds (*ṣidqōt*, pl. of 'righteousness') of YHWH'. *Ṣidqōt YHWH* is a summary concept for the acts of YHWH in Israel's behalf in which he vindicated his relationship to his people (the 'victories of YHWH' in Judg. 5.11; the introductory term of Samuel's recitation of the saving history in I Sam. 12.7; cf. Ps. 103.6; Isa. 45.24; Dan. 9.16). The full phrase is unparalleled; 'in order to know the saving deeds of YHWH' appears to be a variant of the recognition formula which connects the proclamation of an act of YHWH with the statement 'and you will know that I am YHWH'.[q] The form is a way of stating a theological axiom of the OT that YHWH is recognized in his historical deeds; they are the revelation of his identity and the occasion of confession actualized in trust and obedience. Such a response is the true answer YHWH seeks in this *rīb*. That the recitation of his deeds for Israel proves that he has not wearied or wronged them vindicates him before the covenant court and belies their complaint. But what he seeks with them is a settle-

[p] See B. S. Childs, *Memory and Tradition in Israel*, SBT 37, 1962; W. Schottroff, *zkr*, in *THAT* I, pp. 515f.; and on *zkr* in legal pleas, Boecker, 106ff.

[q] W. Zimmerli, 'Erkenntnis Gottes nach dem Buche Ezekiel' in *Gottes Offenbarung* (Th B *19*), 1963, see pp. 50 and 86.

ment, a reconciliation expressed in a recognition of faith to replace their murmuring and loss of trust.

23. IT'S YOU, NOT SOMETHING, GOD WANTS:
6.6–8

6 With what shall I meet YHWH,
    humble myself before God above?
Shall I meet him with burnt offerings
    with year-old calves?
7 Would YHWH be pleased with thousands of rams,
    with innumerable streams of oil?
Shall I give my first-born for my crime,
    the fruit of my body for the sin of my soul?
8 He has told ᵃyou, man, what is good,
    What YHWH requires from you.
Nothing but to do justice, and to love mercy,
    and humbly to go along with your God.

6.6–8 is a justly famous text because it raises and answers a fundamental question of faith: What does the sinner do to restore his relation to God? It deals with the issue by juxtaposing two paramount spheres of Israel's religious life. The question is formulated and the answer delivered as though the saying were intended to settle the problem in a comprehensive and final way. The formal structure is composed of questions (vv. 6f.) and an answer (v. 8). The one who inquires is identified only by the general vocative 'man' (v. 8a). The subject of the inquiry is stated in an opening thematic question (v. 6a); the man seeks instruction about the means to be used to set his relation with YHWH right. He must take some initiative. He has become unacceptable to God because of the sin of his life (v. 7b). He assumes that an acceptable sacrifice will lead God to accept (*rṣh*) him, and needs an authoritative declaration specifying the correct one. Verses 6b–7 develop the thematic question with a list of proposals which steadily escalate in extravagance. The answer is announced in direct address by a speaker who appeals for the authority of his answer to a declaration already made and known concerning the requirement of YHWH. But the response does not answer the specific inquiry; it shifts instead to the question of what is good and lists as its definition a threefold description of conduct. The unresolved

---

ᵃ G assumes a passive ('it has been told') which would fit the context better.

tension between question and answer contains the message. The question is focused on 'with what', on external objects at the disposal of the questioner. The answer is focused on the questioner himself, on the quality of his life.

The style of the unit comes from the practice of seeking and receiving direction (*tōrāh*) from an official person who is authorized to instruct concerning the general and particular will of YHWH. The official was usually the priest.[b] Here the setting-in-life assumed by the style is the situation in which a layman, aware of his predicament because of sin that endangers his status before God and knowing already that a sacrifice of atonement is requisite, seeks to learn which one is adequate.[c] The sphere of competence to which the question is addressed is the responsibility of the priest to evaluate sacrifice and declare which in the situation is acceptable for the purpose for which it is brought.[d]

While the answer completes the formal structure, it does not offer the expected information about the acceptable sacrifice. Instead, it breaks with the setting-in-life and function of the type being used and creates a structure of content which is in effect a polemic against sacrifice and a rejection of the inquiry as misplaced. Sayings putting sacrifice and conduct in opposition belong to the tradition of prophetic preaching, and appropriate formal elements of cultic language to make the contrast (cf. I Sam. 15.22f.; Amos 5.21–24; Hos. 6.1–6; Isa. 1.10–17; Jer. 6.19–20; 7.21ff.; 14.11). The undertaking to comprehend what YHWH requires under the one term 'good' and to summarize his will by the use of two or three concepts arose in the prophetic attempt to confront Israel with the whole will of YHWH, instead of individual commands and laws.[e] See the comment on v. 8.

In its present literary context the unit contains a response to the divine speech in vv. 3–5 and continues the *rib* initiated there to settle affairs between YHWH and Israel. The individual who speaks in vv. 6f. represents Israel. His role is anticipated and commanded by v. 1b.

[b] For a summary of his functions and literature on the question, see H.-J. Kraus, *Worship in Israel*, 1966, pp. 93–101.

[c] For discussions of the type and setting-in-life, see J. Begrich, 'Die priesterliche Tora' in *Gesammelte Studien zum Alten Testament*, 1964, especially pp. 249ff.; K. Koch, 'Tempeleinlassliturgien und Dekaloge' in *Studien zu Theologie der alttestamentlichen Überlieferungen*, eds. R. Rendtorff und K. Koch, 1961, pp. 45ff.; T. Lescow, *Micha 6, 6–8 (Arbeiten zu Theologie*, First Series, no. 25), 1966, pp. 9ff.

[d] See G. von Rad, *Old Testament Theology* I, 1962, pp. 246ff.; and the literature cited there.

[e] G. von Rad, *Old Testament Theology* II, 1965, pp. 186f.; G. Fohrer, *History of Israelite Religion*, 1972, pp. 192ff.

He speaks in response to YHWH's defence of himself which in its validity becomes an accusation against Israel as the other party in the trial. He is brought to the recognition of his sin (v. 7b) and anxiously inquires in questions (directed to the court?) what sacrifice would be adequate to repair his estrangement from YHWH. The pronouncement in v. 8 (from the court?) recalls and outlines the requirement which has always been the appropriate response to YHWH's saving deeds—not sacrifice, but a life submitted to the will of God.

The kerygmatic symmetry between vv. 1–5 and vv. 6–8 binds the two closely together, and they have often been viewed as components of an original unit of speech (e.g., Weiser, Vuilleumier, and among the studies cited in the comment on 6.1–5, Huffmon, Harvey). But the two are quite distinct literary types and there are no examples elsewhere in the Old Testament of their combination in a rhetorical unit. The language and sphere of thought shifts from the legal to the cultic. YHWH is not answered directly, nor does he speak. The vocative, 'man', addressed to the one who raises the question in vv. 6f. is a surprising shift from the vocative 'my people' (v. 3) in the previous unit. The sequence is better understood as the work of the compiler who set v. 1 at the beginning of chs. 6–7 and here extends the drama of the trial between YHWH and Israel into the following material.

Unlike the similar sayings of Amos, Hosea, Isaiah, and Jeremiah cited above, this one does not seem to be addressed to a particular audience in a specific historical situation. It has the marks of a much more general and final statement about the subject. The questions list a series of proposed sacrifices in an ascending order of extravagance calculated to exhaust the option of approach to God through sacrifice. The answer looks back on a declaration that seems to have become tradition and considers the matter settled. The general vocative 'man' points to any individual concerned with the problem. The style of priestly torah and the tradition of the prophetic opposition to the cult have been used to compose a powerful and conclusive word on sacrifice and obedience that is more doctrine than specific message. These characteristics and the position of the unit after vv. 1–5 and within chs. 6–7 indicate that the composer was not Micah but a prophet of a later period.

[6a] Verse 6a is the basic question. Its opening interrogative, 'with what', indicates the procedure which the questioner believes he must follow. See the use of the interrogative (bammāh) in inquiries about the proper offering for specific occasions of dealing with God

in I Sam.6.2; II Sam.21.3; Gen.15.8. The question is based on a specific assumption and thinks only with the possibilities which that assumption allows. In dealing with God, it is God who is the problem; something must be done for him to change his attitude. The assumption should not be too easily dismissed as pagan and assigned to the corruption of Israel's religion. It could grow out of such sentences as 'You shall not appear before me with empty hands' in Israel's oldest normative tradition (Ex.23.15; 34.20) and was reinforced by the growing importance of cultic sacrifice in Israel's religious development. The basic issue was always whether the offering represented an event in the life of the worshipper himself or left him untouched and was calculated only to affect God. What happens to whom in the offering of sacrifice? The questioner wants 'to meet YHWH with. . . .' (*qiddēm bᵉ*) and 'to abase oneself before . . .' (*nikkap lᵉ*). Coming before YHWH in the shrine where he is present and where sacrifice can be offered is clearly in mind; but the verbs are not the usual ones for approaching the deity. They characterize the approach in a highly particular way. 'To meet (someone) with . . .' (*qiddēm bᵉ*) evokes the picture of an approach to another with gifts meant to achieve a favourable reception (Isa.21.14; Deut.23.5=Neh.13.2; see the story of Jacob's preparation to meet Esau in Gen.32.13ff.; in a cultic context, Ps.95.2). 'To abase oneself' depicts the intention of the approach in terms of submission and self-humiliation (the only case of the niphal of *kpp*; qal for 'bowing down' in distress and humiliation, Pss.57.7; 145.14; 146.8; note the context of Isa.58.5). The abasement is a way of confessing the absolute sovereignty of YHWH; it acknowledges the distance and contrast between self and the 'God of heaven' (the title *'ᵉlōhē mārōm* only here; cf. the similar expression in Ps.93.4. *Mārōm* stands for the high heaven where YHWH is and from which he helps the distressed, Pss.7.8; 68.19; 144.7; Isa.58.4; Lam.4.13).

[6b–7] Verse 6b repeats the first verb of v.6a and begins to list possible answers to the interrogative 'with what?'. The list ranges across a variety of sacrificial offerings, though it is obviously not complete. The list is comprehensive in its illustrative character. The sequence has an ascending intensity of number and value which exhausts the possibilities available in the practice of sacrifice and leaves no stone unturned in the search for the 'thing' to be used to arrange a propitious encounter. The burnt offering (*'ōlāh*) is the only specific type of sacrifice mentioned; apparently the other items are objects to be offered as or with the *'ōlāh*. The burnt offering was a sacrifice in which the entire animal was consumed by fire on the altar and 'sent up' to God. It was used on a variety of occasions with different intentions. Here it is brought as a gift and its purpose is propitiation. A calf could be used for sacrifice after it was eight days old; a calf a year old would be more valuable (Lev. 22.27). The ram could also be used for the *'ōlāh* (Gen. 22.13; I Sam. 15.22; Isa. 1.11). Solomon is reported to have sacrificed a thousand offerings (I Kings 3.4; 8.63); perhaps he is the model of extravagant piety in mind here. The escalation of the proposal continues with 'innumerable rivers of oil' to be poured upon the altar to accompany the sacrifice and raise its value (Ex. 29.2; Lev. 2; etc.). The list of possibilities reaches its climax in the proposal to offer the first-born child. The proposal to offer the first-born child to YHWH is astonishing, and meant to be. The special claim of YHWH on the first-born is clearly stated in Israel's oldest normative tradition, and its redemption by a substitute offering just as clearly stipulated (Ex. 22.28; 34.20; cf. 13.2, 13). Reported cases of human sacrifice in Israel are rare, are told as exceptional cases, and regarded as the result of extra-YHWHistic influence (Judg. 11.34; II Kings 3.27; 16.3; 21.6). The prophets who mention the sacrifice of children condemn it as the effect of foreign religion (Jer. 7.21; 19.5; Ezek. 16.20; 20.26; Isa. 57.5; cf. Deut. 12.31). Deuteronomy and the Holiness Code prohibit it as an explicitly non-YHWHistic practice (Deut. 18.10; Lev. 18.21; 20.2–5). The proposal is not drawn from the recognized range of possibilities in the cult of Israel. It is rather a function of the escalation of the list and reaches beyond the options available in Israel's cult to exhaust the total cultic enterprise by citing its most desperate measure. Perhaps it reaches back to the story of Abraham and Isaac for the supreme test that a man fears YHWH (Gen. 22.1ff.), to raise a possibility that was removed at the beginning of Israel's history with YHWH.[t]

The desperate questions are a quest for the sacrifice which YHWH will accept (*rṣh*). The term belongs to the technical vocabulary of the priest who evaluates sacrifice and declares which is accepted, e.g., whether it serves the purpose for which it is brought. If God through the office of the priest 'accepts' the sacrifice, the one who brings it is accepted and the purpose he has in view is accomplished (cf. *rṣh* in Lev. 1.4; 22.23ff.; II Sam. 24.23; Hos. 8.13; Jer. 14.12; etc.; see G. von Rad, op. cit., pp. 26off.). The necessity of the offerings lies in guilt before YHWH. In v. 7b the questioner speaks of 'my crime' (*pešaʿ*) and 'the sin of my life' (*ḥaṭṭaʾt napši* only here, probably means 'my very own sin'). On burnt offerings to make atonement for sin, see the pro-

[t] On the question of human sacrifice in Israel see R. de Vaux, *Ancient Israel*, 1961, pp. 441–6; W. Eichrodt, *Theology of the Old Testament* I, 1961, pp. 148ff.

cedures described in Lev. 4–5. What wrong is in mind is not said; 'crime' and 'sin' as synonyms in a parallelism are frequently used as a general category for acts which violate YHWH's norms for the sacral and social spheres (e.g. Micah 1.5; 3.8; 7.18f.; Gen. 31.36; Ps. 54.4). But particulars are not important here, the question concerns all who fall into the category 'sinner' and therefore seek to repair their standing with YHWH.

The answer ignores both the substance and desperation of the questions with what seems a studied disdain. The proposals and the assumption on which they are based are simply disregarded. The anxious uncertainty about which sacrifice is replaced by a calm certainty about what YHWH requires. The concentration on the thing to be offered is shifted to a focus on the quality of life that is lived. Good is what YHWH requires and what is good is the one thing needful to know. That answer does not revert to divine first-person style or use any other device to authorize itself. The declaration belongs to tradition and one needs only to be reminded.

To what proclamation and what setting the appeal to the past refers is difficult to say.[g] Probably the answer rests on a memory of what earlier prophets had said. The prophets spoke of YHWH's requirements under the theme of 'good' (Isa. 1.17; 5.20; Amos 5.14f.; Micah 3.2) and on occasion gave brief generalizing summaries of YHWH's will composed of two or three elements (Isa. 5.7; Amos 5.24; Hos. 4.1; 6.6; 13.7). Wisdom also advocated this other way; Prov. 11.27 and 12.2 advocate devotion to good as the way to gain YHWH's acceptance ($r\bar{a}\d{s}\bar{o}n$), the programme in view here as an alternative to the cultic route (see also the wisdom psalms, Pss. 37.2, 27; 34.14ff.).

The surprisingly indefinite and inclusive vocative 'man' ($'\bar{a}d\bar{a}m$) is not intended to identify the questioner with humanity in general or to address him in some other identity than that given by his relation as an Israelite to Yahweh his God (cf. $'\bar{a}d\bar{a}m$ in Ezek. 20.4; 13.21). The vocative rather reflects the generalizing and paradigmatic intention of the saying as a whole; its teaching is meant for any *man* in Israel.

'To do justice' ($mi\check{s}p\bar{a}\d{t}$; on the term see the comment on 3.1, 8) is to uphold what is right according to the tradition of YHWH's will,

---

[g] W. Beyerlin, *Die Kulttraditionen Israels in der Verkündigung des Propheten Micha*, 1951, p. 51, points to Deut. 4.13 and Ps. 147.19 and concludes that the verb *higgīd* refers to the continuing proclamation of the amphictyonic law in the cult; T. Lescow, after a study of analogous uses of the verb, believes its setting-in-life is the sphere of prophetic speech (op. cit., pp. 23ff.).

both in legal proceedings and in the conduct of life. Amos equates 'good' with the advocacy of justice in the court in the gates (5.14f.); Isaiah sets it in contrast to cultic performance (1.17); Jeremiah gives a summary of the content, emphasizing the central intention of maintaining the rights of the weak (7.5f.; cf. 22.3ff.). It is this concern with the claim created by the condition of the helpless as an obligation upon conduct which is meant in the expression 'to love mercy' (*ḥesed*). Such justice is based on the kindness and mutuality which recognizes the needy and responds in brotherly identification. 'To love mercy' is to choose and devote oneself to acts of that recognition.[h] *Ḥesed* was a primary theme of Hosea's prophecy and he used the term both for God's devotion to Israel in spite of the nation's faithlessness (e.g. 2.19), and also for the conduct God sought from Israel (e.g. 4.1f.; 6.6). The third item is unique to this passage and must have been coined as an inclusive summary of the series. The traditional translation is 'to walk humbly (*haṣnēaʿ*) with your God'.

The term *ṣnʿ* appears elsewhere only in wisdom texts (Prov. 11.2; Sirach 16.25; 35.3); there and in this context it indicates something of a measured and careful conduct.[i] It is a way of life that is humble, not so much by self-effacement, as by considered attention to another. The humility lies in not going one's own way presumptuously, but in attending the will and way of God. Israel's God performs and seeks justice and mercy; the 'humble' walk with him in that course. Understood in this way, the third item is not a separate requirement, but the final and most inclusive of an ascending series from the concrete to the general. The specific requirement is to do justice which is a way of loving mercy, which in turn is a manifestation of walking humbly with God.

So at a profound level the answer does call for sacrifice, but a kind quite different from that proposed by the question. It is not sacrifice of something outside a person which can be objectified as a means to deal with God. It is rather a yielding of life itself to God and his way, 'repentance' of the most radical sort. What YHWH requires is not the life of some thing, but the living of the man who stands before him. The saying makes that one point. It does not deal with the guilt of 'man' or the problem of whether 'man' can do what God requires.

[h] The term *ḥesed* is so plastic in usage that its exact definition is notoriously difficult. See the varying emphases on mutuality and graciousness in the discussions of N. Glueck, *Ḥesed in the Bible*, 1971; and H. J. Stoebe, *THAT* I, pp. 599–620.

[i] KB translates 'act cautiously, carefully'; H. J. Stoebe suggests 'to be discerning, circumspect' ('Und demütig sein vor deinem Gott', *Wort und Dienst, Jahrbuch der Theol. Schule Bethel* 6, 1959, pp. 180ff.) G translates 'be ready/willing to walk with your God'.

For the one who teaches here, the fact that what is good is known takes precedence over all else.

24. GUILT AND PUNISHMENT UNDER THE COVENANT: 6.9-16

9 Hark! YHWH calls to the city
  (and he who heeds your name shows sound judgment),
  'Hear, O tribe and ªassembly of the city:ª
12 Her rich are full of violence;
  her residents speak deceivingly;
  all their speech is treachery.
10 Shall I forget ᵇ ᶜthe treasures won by wickedness,
  and the despicable use of an ephah that is too small?
11 Shall I approve anyone with false scales,
  with cheating weights in his pouch?
13 So I have begun ᵈ to smite you,
  to lay waste because of your sins.
14a You shall eat, and not be satisfied.
15 You shall sow and not reap.
  You shall tread olives and not anoint yourself with oil,
  grapes, and not drink wine.
14b ᵉSemen into your womb you will take,
  and not bring forth;ᵉ
  and the ones you bring forth,
  I will give to the sword.
16 You have followedᶠ the practices of Omri,
  every deed of Ahab's house;
  youᵍ walked in their counsels.

ª *mōʿēd hāʿîr* for MT's *ūmī yeʿādāh*: *ʿod*. The text at the end of v. 9 and beginning of v. 10 is in bad repair and a conjecture is necessary. Some vocative is expected; G's text points in this direction. Another possibility: 'and whoever assembles in the city' (*ūmī yiwwāʿad hāʿîr*, Plein).

ᵇ *haʾeššeh* for MT's *haʾiš* (?). MT makes no sense and the reconstruction furnishes a parallel to the opening verb in the next line.

ᶜ Omitting MT's 'house of the wicked' (*bēt rāšāʿ*) as an explanatory note concerning the location of the treasures; it overloads the colon.

ᵈ *haḥillōtī* for MT *heḥelētī*; cf. G.

ᵉ The language of the line is extremely difficult; *yešaḥ* is a hapax and the root of *tassēg* is uncertain. The above translation omits the *wᵉ* before *tassēg* and revocalizes *taplīṭ* as a piel; it depends on M. Pope, *JBL* 83, 1964, pp. 270f. and n. 4, where Arabic and Ugaritic cognates are used to establish meanings. See his full discussion of the history of the problem.

ᶠ *wattišmōr* for MTG *wᵉyištammēr*; so some Greek translations.

ᵍ MT's verb is plural.

So I will turn you into a cause of horror,
and her residents into an object of derision;
you[g] shall bear the scorn of the peoples.'[h]

6.9–16 is a divine announcement of guilt and punishment. The
entire saying is composed in first-person style (vv. 10f., 13f., 16). An
introductory formula (v. 9a) identifies the addressee as 'the city', and
a summons to hear the message (v. 9b), which is apparently spoken
by YHWH, makes the identification more specific with the vocatives
'tribe and assembly of the city'. Verses 10–12 itemize the social crimes
that characterize the city's population. Because of them YHWH
has already initiated a punishment (v. 13) of frustrating all the normal
processes by which life is created and sustained (vv. 14f.). Verse 16
repeats the scheme of accusation and proclamation of punishment;
this time the sin is aping the practices of the rulers of the northern
kingdom (v. 16a), for which the city shall be so devastated that all
who look on it shall be horrified (v. 16b).

There are features in the unit which encumber interpretation in
spite of the apparent clarity of type and arrangement. The text is bad
enough at points to require conjectural readings (see notes a, b, and
c), though the context of the obscurities gives general guidance to
what is being said. A better arrangement of the order of the sentences
seems possible. Verse 12 should follow v. 9; its feminine singular
pronouns are then preceded immediately by their antecedent, 'the
city', and the identification of 'the rich' as the guilty group would
introduce the characterization of their activity in vv. 10f. The first
poetic line of v. 14 is separated from its parallel in the first line of v. 15.
The person, and gender, and number of pronouns and verbs desig-
nating the addressees in the Hebrew text shift in bewildering fashion.
These difficulties have led to different conclusions about the unity,
source, and date of the passage. After reconstruction of order and
text some attribute the saying to Micah (Weiser, Vuilleumier), or
hold the possibility open (J. M. P. Smith). Others see only an arrangement of fragments (T. H. Robinson), or a redaction of several pieces
into a new unit (T. H. Lescow, *ZAW* 84, 1972, pp. 193ff.). The
present saying is hardly an original unit of speech as it stands. But
vv. 9b–15 do compose a unit whose features are consistent with the
type of an announcement of judgment. Verse 9b is its opening summons (see comment on v. 9). The indictment (vv. 10–12) is in third-
person style, and the feminine pronouns in v. 12 refer back to 'city'
in the phrase 'assembly of the city'. The proclamation of punishment

[h] *'ammīm*, cf. G. MT has *'ammī*.

(vv. 13–15) is in the style of direct address, as is often the case in the genre; its second person masculine singulars refer to the collectives 'tribe' and 'assembly'. The oracle was addressed to Jerusalem in a period when a citizens' assembly was responsible for its affairs, and disasters which are interpreted as punishment have already begun (v. 13). The time is likely to be late in the Babylonian crisis. The first introductory formula in v.9a was added when vv.9b–15 were set at the beginning of 6.9–7.12, the first phase of the formation of chs. 6–7; 'the city' as addressee anticipates the feminine personification of Jerusalem who appears in 7.8ff. (see comment on v. 1 and the Introduction, pp. 31ff.). Partly because of the confused state of its text, v. 16 presents unusual difficulties. It contains some features which suggest that it was introduced in the final compilation of chs. 6–7 (see the comment and Introduction, pp. 32f.). 'Walking (*hlk*) in the counsels of Omri and Ahab' is the opposite of 'going along (*hlk*) humbly with your God' (6.8). Suffering the scorn of the peoples is the punishment from which the song of hope in 7.8–10 expects deliverance. Being made a cause for horror (*šmm*, a motif picked up by the redactor from 'to lay waste' in v. 13) is the judgment which will be extended to the earth and its inhabitants (7.13, note the motif *šmm* there in a verse which is also redactional).

In its final literary context the oracle now stands as the point in the alternation of divine and human voices where YHWH accuses his partner of sin and announces the judgment which falls on the partner first and then on the other nations of earth. God requires justice, mercy, and submission of life to his way (6.8). Instead there is wickedness, violence, and a style of life patterned after Omri and Ahab (vv. 10–12, 16). So God begins with his own the devastation because of sin (vv. 13, 16b) which will lead to their confession and repentance (7.1–10). Then the same devastation and humiliation will be extended to the whole earth (7.13, 16f.). The identification of the partner in the *rib* as a city and its inhabitants prepares for the feminine figure who begins to speak at 7.1 and remains in view up to 7.12.

[9] This introductory line contains internal inconsistencies of style which suggest that it is the result of several stages of formation. There are three sentences. The first introduces the saying as a speech of YHWH addressed to the city, which as antecedent would require feminine singular pronouns and verbs. The second is a remark addressed to YHWH expressing reverence for what is said in his name. The third is a summons to hear, expressed by a masculine plural imperative addressed to the collective nouns 'tribe and assembly

of the city', which are masculine. This summons appears to be the introduction to the original announcement of judgment which follows in vv. 10–15. The feminine singular pronouns (v. 12) in the indictment have 'city' in the phrase 'assembly of the city' as antecedents. The announcement of punishment shifts to direct address, as is often the case in this type of saying, and its second masculine singular style assumes the collectives 'tribe and assembly' as antecedents. The indictment speaks of the sins of the city's inhabitants; the announcement of punishment is addressed to the corporate group and the assembly responsible for its life. What is the explanation of these vocatives, which are unique in such a context? Does 'tribe' indicate an audience which is composed only of the tribe of Judah? And 'assembly of the city' a situation in Jerusalem when the king is not there, or no longer effectively responsible? 'Assembly' (mōʿēd) seems to be used as in Isa. 14.13; Num. 16.2; but nothing is known of such a body as a regular feature of Jerusalem's urban life. Perhaps the setting is the extraordinary times of the Babylonian crisis. Verse 13 indicates that the covenant curses have already been invoked and their effect is being felt.

The second sentence is the contribution of a scribe who inserts a reverant observation directed to YHWH himself that it is only sound judgment (tūšīyāh, a term from the vocabulary of wisdom–Prov. 2.7; 8.14; 18.1; Job 6.13; etc.) to heed words spoken with the signature of YHWH's name. The sentence is to be compared to sentences of similar character like Amos 5.13; Hos. 14.9 (Heb. v. 10).

The first sentence as a form of introduction has no parallels in prophetic literature. It portrays YHWH in a way that somewhat resembles personified wisdom who appeals in the city for a hearing (Prov. 1.20f.; 8.1ff.). 'The city' must be Jerusalem; see the definite designations in Jeremiah, Ezekiel, Lamentations, Trito-Isaiah. The assumption of this sentence that YHWH speaks directly to the city is not borne out in the summons in v. 9b or in the following saying (vv. 10–15). It is rather a feature of the first phase of the formation of chs. 6–7, being the original introduction to the complex 6.9b–7.12. It anticipates the response of the feminine personified city in 7.1–10 (see the Introduction, pp. 10, 32f.).

[10–12] The indictment is directed against those who enrich themselves by dishonest trade. In rhetorical questions YHWH protests that he cannot tolerate such wickedness. Three ways to cheat in buying and selling are listed. In measuring, a seller could use an ephah smaller than standard. In weighing for sale or purchase a merchant could use unbalanced scales or stone weights of irregular sizes, one set for buying and another for selling. These ways of defrauding are listed together in Old Testament references and in such summaries seem to have been a topic for instruction about wickedness and righteousness (see Prov. 20.10, 23; 11.1; Deut. 25.13f., Lev. 19.36. For other prophetic sayings using the topic, Amos. 8.5; Hos. 12.8). It is interesting that though 'the rich (people)' as a class appear frequently in Proverbs and Ecclesiastes, they are mentioned elsewhere in prophetic material only in Jer. 9.23 (cf. possibly Isa. 53.9). The speaker regards their dishonesty as 'violence' and 'injurious deception' against those who are defrauded. By using such language to characterize dishonesty, he puts such practices in their broadest social context. The injury is more than economic; it damages the lives and status of persons in the fabric of society and destroys that fabric.

[13] The announcement of punishment opens with an emphatic 'So I also . . .' ($w^egam'^an\bar{\imath}$), which correlates the divine action with the acts of wickedness described in v. 12. The violence and treachery of the rich against their victims justifies corresponding measures of punishment. What the violent visit on their fellows is 'sin' against God. The 'you' directly addressed is the group (the 'tribe and assembly' of v. 9) of whose existence the city is an expression. The oracle views the city as a corporate identity responsible for the commercial crimes and cultic apostasy which invite judgment. God's response is already evident as the oracle is delivered and the messenger points to events now in progress as the onset of God's smiting. The effect of the punishment will be to turn the city into a waste ($ha\check{s}m\bar{e}m$), a theme echoed in the 'horror' ($\check{s}amm\bar{a}h$) of v. 16. The historical circumstances seem to be those created by military invasion and siege. Reference to the sword (v. 14b) and to an outcome of international disgrace and public humiliation point in that direction; all the particular disasters foretold in vv. 14f. could occur in the course of conquest by an enemy.

[14–15] How the 'laying waste' will occur is depicted in a series of sentences which foretell the frustration and failure of the activities basic to life. Such sentences are 'curses' which tell how life will be diminished instead of augmented. 'Futility curses' with a pattern and function similar to these appear in two contexts in the Old Testament. They are present singly and in little series in connection with YHWH's covenant with Israel as the sanctions he will invoke against the nation for breaking covenant (Deut. 28.30–31, 38–40; Lev. 26.26) and they are used, as here, by prophets to announce measures taken by YHWH to punish Israel (Hos. 4.10; 9.11f., 16;

Amos 5.11; Zeph. 1.13; Hag. 1.6).[1] The curses are, then, not an attempt to sketch an accurate picture of external events, but a code to interpret disaster as YHWH's reaction to breach of covenant. The fertility of wives, fields, orchards and vineyards will become means of bitter frustration; the blessing turns into cursing.

[16] The Hebrew text of v. 16 contains a confusion of styles. Translated as the text stands, it reads: 'And he (an impersonal passive?) follows the practices of Omri, and every deed of Ahab's house; you (masculine plural) walked in their councils. So I will turn you (masculine singular) into a cause for horror, and her inhabitants into an object of derision; you (masculine plural) shall bear the scorn of my people.' Except for the first verb, the styles all appear in vv. 9b–15. The scheme of guilt and punishment is also repeated, and it seems likely that the verse was composed as an addition to the original, repeating its styles and structure. The features which connect it with the final redactor of chs. 6–7 are cited above.

Instead of listing particular sins, the speaker characterizes deeds by putting them in a category identified by the names of Omri and Ahab. This way of speaking assumes a tradition that the practices and policies of Omri and Ahab are so evil that the invocation of their names can serve as a final indictment. Such a view of these two kings of the state of Israel appears in the Deuteronomistic history, and v. 16 may have been composed in circles where that tradition was established (see I Kings 16.25–33). The sin of the Omrides to which that document points in horror is apostasy to Baal and idolatry (repeatedly, II Kings 10.18; 21.3, 25f.; cf. 8.27).

The concluding tricolon depicts the outcome of YHWH's punishment. The city will be left in such devastation that the sight horrifies any who behold it. The surviving population will be a laughing-stock to its enemies; it will suffer under the contemptuous scorn of other peoples. The picture of the ruined and disgraced city was frequently used to portray the totality and bitterness of YHWH's judgment. It appears in the versions of the covenant curses in Lev. 26 (see v. 32),[j] in I Kings 9.6–9 as punishment for apostasy (as here), and often in prophets of seventh-sixth century (Jeremiah, Ezekiel, and once in Zephaniah). The picture and the particular vocabulary of v. 16b are particularly at home in Jeremiah; 'object of derision'

---

[1] On the 'futility' curse in the ancient Near East and OT, see D. R. Hillers, *Treaty-Curses and the Old Testament Prophets* (BO 16) 1965, pp. 28f. and his general discussion in *Covenant: The History of a Biblical Idea*, 1969, pp. 131–42.

[j] The possible relation of the picture to the treaty-curses is discussed by Hillers, *Treaty-Curses*, pp. 76f.

($$\check{s}^e r\bar{e}q\bar{a}h$$) appears only in Jeremiah (19.8; 25.9, 18; 29.18; 51.37, in all these texts with 'horror' [$\check{s}amm\bar{a}h$]), and in II Chron. 29.8. The sentence 'bear the scorn of the peoples' appears in Ezek. 37.15. The verse uses established language and tradition to connect the guilt and punishment of Jerusalem with that of Samaria, and so introduces an echo of the Samaria-Jerusalem pattern present in the redaction of ch. 1 (see the introduction to ch. 1).

25. THE LONELINESS OF THE FAITHFUL: 7.1–6

1 How I sorrow!
   For I am like the gatherer^a of summer fruit,
      like the gleaner^b of the vintage,
   when there are no grapes to eat,
      none of the early figs I crave.
2 The faithful have vanished from the earth,
      not one human being is upright.
   All lie in wait to shed blood,
      each hunts his brother with a net.
3 ^cTheir hands are good at doing evil;^c
      the official demands . . .^d;
   the judge . . .^d for the reward;
      the great speak only of what they want.
4 They twist^e (4) their good like a briar bush,
      ^ftheir uprightness like a thorn hedge.^f
   The day^g of their punishment^h has come;
      now their confusion is at hand.
5 Don't rely on a neighbour;
      don't trust a friend.
   Even with her who lies in your bosom
      be guarded in what you say.

^a Vocalizing $k^e{}^{\prime}\bar{o}s^e p\bar{\imath}$; see *HAL* and G.
^b $k^e{}^{\prime}\bar{o}l\bar{e}l$ for MT $k^e{}^{\prime}\bar{o}l^e l\bar{o}t$.
^c Reading $l^e h\bar{a}ra^{\prime}\ kapp\bar{e}hem\ h\bar{e}t\bar{\imath}b\bar{u}$.
^d Both sentences appear incomplete, though the sense seems evident; perhaps the two are to be taken together in sense: 'the official demands a favourable decision, and the judge decides to get the reward.'
^e Reading $y^e{}^{\prime}aww^e t\bar{u}$.
^f Reading $y^e \check{s}\bar{a}r\bar{a}m\ kims\bar{u}k\bar{a}h$.
^g Omitting $m^e \check{s}app\bar{e}yk\bar{a}$, 'your watcher'?
^h MT has a second singular masculine suffix, which possibly resulted from adjustment to the preceding word.

6 For sons treat their fathers like fools;
   daughters rebel against their mothers,
   daughter-in-law against mother-in-law;
   a man's enemies are the people in his family.

Verses 1–6 are a lament bewailing the evil times in which the singer lives. The opening cry of sorrow establishes the mood. The singer uses a metaphor to evoke the helpless hopelessness he feels as he looks about him (v. 1) and then states his basic theme in general assertions about the absence of 'the faithful' (v. 2a) and the presence of hostility (v. 2b). His present evil world is described in two movements, focusing in turn on the public sphere and its officials (vv. 3f., a section of text in bad repair) and on the sphere of the family (vv. 5f.). The original lament (or all of it included in the collection) seems to end with v. 6. Verse 7 does seem to continue the unit because of its continuity of style and opening adversative which sets hope in God in contrast to the hopelessness of mankind. But the connection is redactional (see the comment on 7.7 below).

Questions about the unity of the passage have been raised because of the shift in the subject and style of the description of the times (cf. vv. 1–4 and 5–7) and the apparent climax at the end of v. 4, where the arrival of punishment is announced (Robinson, Lescow). But inclusion of public and private wrong in a descriptive lament occurs in pieces like Jer. 9.2–6; the shift from third-person portrayal to imperative warnings is simply a versatility of style; and the punishment which has come includes the desperate situation in which even the most intimate relations are perverted.

The one who laments is not identified, nor is his description of his circumstances sufficiently specific to establish a historical setting with confidence. The tone and attitude of the piece is not congruent with the stance of Micah during the reign of Hezekiah. Those who assign the lament to Micah must extend his career into the reign of Manasseh to find a more appropriate setting (Weiser, Vuilleumier). The portrayal of public and private decadence is composed of traditional themes and could have been composed in various periods. Similar laments about general wickedness appear in Pss. 12 and 14=53, and sweeping descriptions are heard in the post-exilic Isa. 57.1–2 and 59.4–8. Perhaps the unit also was composed during the discouraging instability of the early post-exilic period.[1] There is some evidence in the language of the unit that points to this time (see the comment below).

[1] See the description of the situation in J. Bright, *A History of Israel*, 1972², pp. 365ff.

However, in its present literary context the lament is given a continuity with the surrounding material and the singer takes on an identity. The lament is the response to the announcement of judgment in 6.9–16. The speaker is the city to whom the announcement is made (6.9), the feminine figure (Zion) who turns to YHWH in hope (7.7) and asserts her confidence in YHWH's salvation (7.8–10). The function of the lament is to acknowledge the justice of the judgment upon a population lacking in justice (7.2b–4) and in faithful devotion (7.2a, 5f.). The city is thus portrayed as an identity with a conscience and consciousness which transcends that of her own population. She acknowledges the rightful norms of justice and loyalty set forth in 5.8 and clears the ground for the resumption of the submissive walk with God expressed in the following psalm of confidence (7.7–10).

[1] The opening cry sets the tone for vv. 2–6; it is an exclamation of anguish over the helpless situation in which the speaker finds himself (Job 10.15). The world of his daily life has become a frustrating prison; change and help must come from beyond. He uses a metaphor to portray how empty of any support or encouragement he finds his surroundings. He is like a hungry man in the midst of stripped vineyards and bare trees, when the fruit has all been gathered and the vintage is over. Verse 2 states the theme for which the metaphor stands. The human environment of the speaker looks like a wasteland; good men have vanished and all carry murder in their hearts. The first term used for the missing type or group is 'the faithful' (ḥāsīd), an adjective which designates those who live out their relation to YHWH with singleness of purpose; they practice ḥesed as a way of life, enacting loyalty to God by their faithfulness to the rights of all with whom they deal. The term is at home in the language of the prayers in the Psalter (25 of 32 occurrences) and appears elsewhere in the prophets only in Jer. 3.12 where it applies to God. As the designation of a type or group it belongs to a time when personal loyalty to YHWH has become an explicit and self-conscious issue.[j] In this context ḥāsīd furnishes the norm assumed by the second term, 'upright' (yāšār). The second line of v.2 supplies the antithesis to ḥāsīd. The activities of all men are nothing more than an ambush and hunt in which their fellows are the quarry. Human relations are an occasion for violence instead of a structure for practising faithfulness. The two movements in vv. 3 and 5f. describe more specifically how this is so.

[3–4] The text of vv. 3f. is quite unclear. Apparently undamaged

[j] See H. J. Stoebe, *THAT* I, pp. 618ff., and the literature cited there.

words and phrases indicate that the verses deal with a recurrent subject in the prophetic portrayal of wrong, the corruption of public officials and leaders upon whom justice and order depend (cf. Amos 5.7, 10; Hos. 5.1f.; Isa. 3.14; Micah 3.9ff.). The first colon of v. 3 is spoken in biting irony: 'They can do well only at doing evil' (Sellin, see the similar expressions in Jer. 4.22; 13.23). Official (*śar*), judge, and 'great one' are listed; they function for their own gain exclusively. Any who expect goodness from them end up entangled in a thicket of intrigue and avarice ('briar' and 'hedge' together in a metaphor in Prov. 15.19). Verse 4b speaks of the punishment (if the text is correct) and confusion (cf. the word in Isa. 22.5) of these treacherous leaders. Hope for relief from God through his punishment of the guilty is a feature of laments (see Pss. 12.5; 14.5f., for similar statements within laments). Bad leaders make bad times worse.

[5–6 The second movement of the description of the times turns from the public to the personal private sphere. Again, the intent of the language is to portray an area of human relationships devoid of any faithfulness to the other (v. 5), and filled with hostility (v. 6). The shift to the style of direct address simply creates variety in the description. The list of those who cannot be trusted moves through structures of increasing intimacy: neighbour, close friend, wife. The stability and harmony of the basic family unit was of such crucial value to the Israelite (cf. Ex. 20.12; 21.15, 17; Deut. 21.18ff.; Lev. 20.9; Prov. 20.20) that its disintegration by insolence and rebellion seemed the worst manifestation of times of woe. See Jesus' use of these lines to indicate the radical seriousness of the crisis which his presence among men provokes (Matt. 10.21, 35f.; Mark 13.12; Luke 12.53).

26. LITERARY ANALYSIS OF 7.7–20

This second section of the second part of the book is marked by a pervasive anticipation of the salvation of God. Its language confidently proclaims that YHWH will transform the judgment of his own people into a salvation in which their sin is overcome and their enemies are brought to submission to him. The section is composed of four distinct literary units, identifiable by style and subject. In vv. 8–10 a feminine voice sings of her confidence that YHWH will change her punishment to salvation and vindicate her in the presence of her enemy. Verses 11–13 address a promise of the restoration of walls, borders, and population (?) directly to the feminine figure. In

vv. 14–17 the people of YHWH appeal to him to take up his role as their shepherd in a way that shall compel the nations to acknowledge his power. Verses 18–20 conclude with praise from the people of their God who is incomparable in forgiveness.

The four units thus seem to be paired. The first two make a sequence of proclamation of trust and answering promise which feature the feminine figure. The second pair form a sequence of prayer and praise spoken by the corporate group. There seems to be a progression of thought in the arrangement. The first piece speaks of a *deliverance* which the enemy will *see*. The second promises and details that *deliverance*. The third prays for the *deliverance* to occur as renewal of the people and as revelation which the nations shall *see*. Then in the final unit the 'theology' of the whole is stated in praise of God's forgiveness. Faith in the God who 'does not persist in anger, but delights in mercy' (v. 18) is the only basis of the confidence of the sinner who looks for salvation (v. 9). The restoration of the people will be the concrete form of that forgiveness. The wrath of God against the sinner (v. 9) will pass to those who scorn God's reign (v. 10) and ignore his requirements (v. 13) in all the world, and will bring them also to dread and awe (v. 17). In this unity, the section concludes 'the trial' opened at the beginning of this second part of the book (6.1). Israel is brought to a faith that accepts God's judgment on its sin and looks for a salvation that vindicates his relation to them and to the nations.

7.8–20 is connected to its foregoing literary context in several ways. Verse 7 is clearly transitional. It introduces the shift from the mood of 6.1–7.6. It states the theme of the following unit, so much so that it could be the opening line of vv. 8–10. Yet its initial adversative ('But I . . .') introduces a contrast with the lament in 7.1–6, particularly with vv. 5f., and clearly assumes its presence. The first-person speech of v. 7 continues the style of the lament, suggesting to the reader/hearer that the feminine figure of vv. 8–12 begins to speak at 7.1. The reader is thus guided to the conclusion that the speaker is the personified city summoned to hear (6.9) YHWH's announcement of judgment given in 6.9–16.

These features of style and arrangement have led to recurrent consideration of 7.7–20 as a special problem and to hypotheses about its formation and relation to the foregoing material. As early as 1903, B. Stade recognized the similarity of the language to that of many psalms and pointed to the liturgical character of the material.[a]

---

[a] 'Micha 1, 2–4 und 7, 7–20, ein Psalm', *ZAW* 23, 1903, pp. 163–71.

K. Marti thought two psalms had been woven together and distinguished them on the basis of purely stylistic criteria; B. Duhm found three psalms in vv. 8–10, 11–13, and 14–20.[b] Though some have persisted in treating the block as a result of purely redactional compilation of independent pieces and fragments with no inner coherence,[c] the ground had been prepared for the analysis of H. Gunkel.[d] Using the form-critical principles and criteria he had developed in his study of the psalms, Gunkel identified four units of different types arranged in two pairs. The first is composed of a song of trust (vv. 7–10) sung by a personified Zion and a divine oracle addressed to her (vv. 11–13). The second contains a lament of Israel (vv. 14–17) and a hymn of assurance of a future deliverance sung by the congregation (vv. 18–20). The whole is an artistically constructed poem composed to be rendered as a 'liturgy' by different singers. He concluded that the poem suited the historical circumstances which also are reflected in the material assigned to Trito-Isaiah. The setting for the liturgy would have been one of 'the days of dole' in the early post-exilic community in Jerusalem. His contribution has been the foundation for most subsequent studies,[e] but response has not remained unanimous. Bo Reicke added 7.1–7 to the liturgical pattern whose setting he related to the suffering and restoration of the king.[f] O. Eissfeldt read the liturgy as a composition designed for Israelites living in the north in the Assyrian province created in 722 BC by the Assyrians and attributed it to Micah who here expresses his hope for the salvation of the remnant left of the northern kingdom.[g] T. Lescow in his study of the redaction history of chs. 6–7[h] concluded that the original framework on which 6.9–7.20 was built up was a prophetic liturgy of penitence from the early exilic period, composed of a prophetic summons to repentance addressed to Zion (6.9–12), a lament of Zion (7.1f., 5f.), a song of Zion's confidence (7.7–10a), and a hymnic conclusion (7.18–20). The rest of the material was added

[b] Ad loc., KHC, 1904.

[c] E.g. J. M. P. Smith in ICC; T. H. Robinson in HAT, 1954, who concludes that the section is built upon an independent lament (vv. 8–10) by the addition of fragments of other pieces.

[d] 'The Close of Micah: A Prophetical Liturgy' in *What Remains of the Old Testament*, 1928, pp. 115–49.

[e] E.g. A. Weiser in ATD, R. Vuilleumier in CAT.

[f] 'Liturgical Traditions in Mic. 7', *HTR* 60, 1967, pp. 349–67.

[g] O. Eissfeldt, 'Ein Psalm aus Nord-Israel: Micha 7:7–20', *ZDMG* 112, 1962, pp. 259–68; also in *Kleine Schriften* IV, 1968, pp. 63–72.

[h] 'Redaktionsgeschichtliche Analyse von Micha 6–7', *ZAW* 84, 1972, pp. 182–212.

in long process of redaction which was completed about 330 BC.[1]

The work which has followed Gunkel's study has not overturned the general validity of his analysis. There is an over-arching unity in vv. 7–20. Three of the units are luturgical in type, and the fourth fits easily into a cultic context. There is a progression of content which manifests a coherence. The clues to historical environment contained in the text consistently point to the early post-exilic period (see comment below). On the other hand, there are no convincing reasons for including any of the foregoing material with vv. 7–20 in a longer original unit. Even though a first-person style does begin at 7.1, the content and language of 7.1–6 has no demonstrable connection with the liturgical block that argues for an original unity. The same holds true for the announcement of judgment in 6.9–16.

It is, however, difficult to reach a confident conclusion about the character of the unity in vv. 7–20. It is possible that the unity of the different parts lies in some such liturgical setting as the one postulated by Gunkel, but so little is known about the components and patterns of Israel's worship on such occasions that it is impossible to be certain whether the features which hold vv. 7–20 together are evidence of an original liturgy or the result of compilation and arrangement of material in a literary process of forming the book (surely a process which a liturgical pattern could have influenced).

In the comment below the conclusion is reached that some parts of the text are the compiler's work. Verse 7 is a seam which joins vv. 8–20 to the foregoing material. Verse 13 expands the promise of salvation addressed to Zion so that it includes judgment on all the earth. Verse 15 has been extended with a phrase which makes sure that the wonders which YHWH will work in the coming time are understood to be a resumption of the exodus history. In v. 17 'to YHWH our God' is an extra colon which makes sure that 'you' is understood to refer to YHWH and not Israel and to provide a specific identity for the pronoun and class noun (you/God) at the beginning of v. 18.

These features open the possibility that the arrangement of vv. 7–20 is the work of the compiler of chs. 6–7. What appears to be a progression of thought in these verses from one unit to another includes a variety in subject and language in the units which point to differing origins. The continuity of content is far from precise. The basic core of the material was probably the pair of units featuring the feminine figure (vv. 8–10, 11–12). The compiler added v. 13

---

[1] For another recent study of the problem with a very full bibliography see J. T. Willis, 'A Reapplied Prophetic Hope Oracle', *Supp. VT* 26, 1974, pp. 64–76.

to make the transition to vv. 14–17, and 'to YHWH our God' to tie vv. 18–20 to the growing block. Verse 7 was his seam to connect the whole to the first section of chs. 6–7. The unity then could be the result of the compiler's conception of the second part of the book as a whole.

27. THE DECISION TO WAIT: 7.7

7 But I – for YHWH I watch;
   I wait for my salvation through God;
   my God will hear me.

In v. 7 the on-going controversy between YHWH and Israel takes a decisive turn. The first-person voice representing the people, which had before spoken in frantic frustration (6.6f.) and despairing lament (7.1–6), suddenly begins to speak of a confidence in God that is sustained to the end of the book. The verse is dealt with separately to emphasize its connecting and transitional role in the literary form of chs. 6–7. In concludes 7.1–6 whose first-person style is continued. The opening 'But I . . .' clearly states a contrast with the lament which surveys the human scene and finds no cause for hope. In a world where even neighbour and family are not to be trusted (vv. 5f.), only God is left. But *he is* there. The assertion discovers and proclaims the one who can be trusted. But the verse also belongs to the following song of confidence (vv. 8–10); it shares its style and states its theme. So in its context the verse is a unifying element which has a function in both literary units on each side of it. This suggests that the verse was introduced as a connecting transition in the compilation of chs. 6–7. It has been assigned to 7.1–6 (Weiser, Vuilleumier), but its language is clearly identified with the genre of 7.8–10; the line is similar to the 'confession of trust' which interrupts the laments of the Psalter to voice the reasons for holding the troubles of life up to God in prayer (e.g., Pss. 13.5; 31.14; 52.8; 71.14; etc.). It has been treated as the first line of 7.8–10. But the *waw*-adversative which begins the line never appears at the opening of a lament of an individual or a song of confidence.[a] Such assertions of trust are heard in Jeremiah's 'confessions' (Jer. 11.20; 12.3; 20.11) and perhaps the model for the use of the verse in this location is to be found there as well as in the

---

[a] On the *waw*-adversative in the laments, see C. Westermann, *The Praise of God in the Psalms*, 1965, pp. 70ff. H. Gunkel, op. cit., pp. 123ff., claims that the confession of trust opens a lament, but none of his examples contains the adversative.

Psalms in which such an assertion makes the transition from descriptions of need to prayer and praise. Here the question of the speaker's identity is answered by the literary context. It is the voice which speaks in response to YHWH in the trial which he has convened in history, sometimes masculine and sometimes feminine (as in vv. 8–12).

In a present full of violence and betrayal the speaker turns to a future in which he can hope. With a magnificent counter-assertion he claims the way of the ḥāsīd (cf. 7.2) for himself and reaches toward the reality of God for salvation. He watches the future for an act of God (Ps. 5.4) as besieged men watch the horizon for the appearance of relief. He does not give up and surrender to depression, but 'waits', the most powerful form of action by the helpless (Pss. 38.15; 42.5, 11; 43.5; 130.5) who express in their waiting the knowledge that God comes to them in the form of salvation (Pss. 18.46; 25.5; etc., almost always in 'confessions of trust'). He speaks of his anguish in no void; he will be heard by one whose hearing is identical with helping (Ps. 4.3; and often in psalms of lament). The power that perfects itself in weakness flows from the certainty with which he says 'my God'; the possessive is a simple but complete utterance of his personal contact with one who is reliable (Pss. 3.7; 5.2; 7.1, 3; etc.). 'My God' is a way of saying, not that God belongs to him, but that he belongs to God. He holds to the election of Israel, actualizes its promise in his hope, and commits himself to the help of God.

28. THE EXODUS FROM DARKNESS TO LIGHT: 7.8–10

8 Rejoice not over me, O my enemy!
  Though I have fallen, I shall arise.
  Though I sit in darkness,
    YHWH will be my light.
9 YHWH's rage I bear
    because I sinned against him,
  until he pleads my case
    and defends my right.
  He will bring me out to the light;
    I shall see his righteousness.
10 My enemy shall also see,
    and shame will cover her,
  she who says to me,
    'Where[a] is YHWH your God?'

a 'ayyēh for MT 'ayyō.

My eyes shall see her;
Now she will be trampled
like mud in the street.

These verses are a song which tells what the singer expects from the God upon whom she (!) waits (v. 7). Its twofold theme is stated in v. 8a: confidence in the face of an enemy who for now has the upper hand, and confidence in anticipation of the deliverance of God. Verses 8b–9 describes the deliverance as an exodus from darkness to light. Verse 10 returns to the theme of the enemy whose scorn will be answered and punished in the course of God's deliverance. In style and function the unit is like the 'songs of trust' (Pss. 4; 11; 23; 27.1–6; 62; 131) which appear to develop independently the element of the assertion of confidence from the lament. The language is predominantly psalmic, as the comparisons in the comment below indicate. Though the poem opens with direct address to the enemy (v. 8a), the style is rhetorical and dropped immediately (cf. v. 10). Like most of the songs of trust the unit identifies no audience specifically, and probably was spoken before the community as confession. In contrast with the other songs of this type, the piece contains some peculiarities which identify the singer as a personification of a corporate group and indicate that its setting is national history. Both speaker and enemy are feminine figures (the possessive pronoun in 'your God' in v. 10 and the word for 'enemy' are feminine). The gender represents the dramatic personification of corporate groups as women. The speaker could well be Jerusalem; the city is represented as speaking in liturgy (Lam. 1.9, 11–16, 18–22; 2.20–22) and in prophecy (Isa. 49.14; Jer. 3.4f.; 4.31). A likely identity for the enemy is Edom (see the comment on v. 8). Verse 10 clearly identifies the enemy as national rather than individual. The unqualified confession of sin and acceptance of punishment in v. 9 looks back on the Babylonian victory over Judah as confirmation of the prophetic indictment of Judah for sin. The song thus fits the circumstances after the fall of Jerusalem when the fragile remnant left in and around the city was constantly harassed by neighbouring peoples. The confidence expressed in the psalm suggests the late exilic or early post-exilic periods. It could have been used in liturgies of repentance at the ruined sanctuary. On the question of its relation to the rest of vv. 7–20, see the introduction to this section above.

[8] With the courage of confidence Zion addresses the historical instrument of her distress and warns her enemy against any cele-

ᵇ See H. Gunkel's convincing demonstration, op. cit., pp. 117–29.

bration of her humiliation. Petitions to be spared the shame of the enemy's joy are a feature of laments (Pss. 35.19, 24; 38.16), and here certainty of an answer rises to defiance of the foe's derision. The enemy, a recurrent figure in the laments (Pss. 13.2, 4; 41.11; and in plural often) is a feminine figure only in this text; the gender corresponds to that of the speaker and represents also the personalization of a corporate identity. The reference is probably to Edom, the treacherous agent of Jerusalem's bitterest humiliation after her fall to Babylon; see the similar phrase in Obad. 12, and in general (e.g. Isa. 34.8ff.; Ps. 137.7; Obad. 10–15). Zion's basic confidence about her destiny is stated in a reversal of the locution for final disaster, 'fall and rise no more' (Amos 5.8; 8.14; Jer. 25. 27). Verse 8b uses the paired metaphors of darkness and light, to point to the source of Zion's faith. Now she sits in darkness (Pss. 35.6; 143.3; Lam. 3.2, 6); in the visible circumstances of her plight the human eye can see no objective possibility of help. Yet in that darkness, YHWH's 'light' is visible to the eye of hope (Ps. 27.1). Faith's grasp of YHWH's reality and way gives meaning to the misery (v. 9a) and promise to the plight (v. 9b).

[9] The knowledge of YHWH lets Zion accept her distress as the effect of his 'rage' (za'ap of YHWH elsewhere only Isa. 30.30). She may appear to be in the power of the enemy, but she experiences his punishment of her. The justification of that judgment is acknowledged with simple and unqualified confession: 'I have sinned against him' (Pss. 41.4; 51.4). That is the voice of a community that has learned the message of the pre-exilic prophets by heart and found in the fall of Jerusalem the truth about themselves. Now it is said in a liturgy of contrition without reservation. Because that is so, their testimony to YHWH does not have to stop with judgment. Their contrite acceptance of his wrath is both appeal and anticipation that YHWH's judgment will reach its purpose in their salvation. To describe that transition they use language of a court of law to interpret the history of judgment as a process in which the judge marvellously becomes advocate and defender. He will plead their case (Pss. 43.1; 119.154; Lam. 3.58; the theme balances rîb in 6.1f.) and defend their right (Pss. 17.2; 9.4; 140.12). This outcome to their trial before God will occur as an event of salvation. God will lead them out (yōṣē', the traditional verb for the exodus) in a new exodus from darkness to light. And here 'light' is a profoundly interpretative word for the possibility of 'seeing' created by deliverance. In witnessing their salvation they will 'see' the 'righteousness (ṣᵉdāqāh) of God'. Sᵉdāqāh is used here in the sense it has in Deutero-Isaiah (Isa. 45.8; 46.13;

51.6) and in the psalmic speech about God's saving victory (Pss. 5.8; 31.2; 98.2; etc.) and by Paul in Romans. God's righteousness is the action he takes to vindicate his election of his people, the deed that is right in accord with the norms he sets for himself in the purpose of that election. That is the light which overcomes darkness, and that is what lies at the basis of Zion's hope which turns punishment into anticipation. Her confidence is not in herself—she has sinned and that characterization is total—but in the righteousness of God.

[10] God's righteousness occurs as concrete visible event; the enemy also will see the deliverance. The salvation of Zion shames the enemy because it is an overwhelming response to their scornful question 'Where is YHWH your God?' The mocking thrust is always spoken by the pagan nations (Joel 2.17; Pss. 42.3, 10; 79.10) to the faithful in trouble. It questions the reality and effectiveness of YHWH because his people are humbled, so the glory of YHWH is at stake in the destiny of his people (Ps. 115.2). In their salvation God vindicates himself before the nations. Because the enemy has elevated her temporary triumph into arrogance against YHWH, her humiliation will become a revelation of the victory of Zion's God.

29. THE DAY OF RESTORATION: 7.11–13

11 A day to rebuild your walls!
    The day^a when ^bboundaries shall be distant^b!
12 The day when they^c shall come to you^d
    from Assyria to^e Egypt,
    and from Egypt to the River,
    ^ffrom sea to sea and mountain to mountain.^f
13 The earth will become desolate because of its inhabitants
    as a result of their deeds.

Verses 11–12 are the exultant cry of one who sees the approach of a new time. The word 'day' stands at the beginning of the first

^a *hū' wᵉ* for *hahū'*; cf. v. 12a.

^b The meaning and correctness of MT's *yirḥaq-ḥōq* is uncertain. Word play (Gunkel) or corrupt text? The above translation follows MT; see the comment. If *r* and *d* have been confused, the reading might be *yidḥaq-ḥōq*, 'the set time (Job 14.13) presses hard'.

^c MT's verb is singular, but context requires plural.

^d MT's pronoun is masculine—feminine would be consistent with v. 11.

^e *waʿᵃdē* for *wᵉʿārē*.

^f MT's word sequence makes no sense though the meaning in this context is clear; read *mîyām ʿad yām ūmēhar ʿad har*.

three measures to establish an intensity of excitement and immanence about the theme. And each measure names one change whose occurrence will give the distinctive content to the time which makes it new, a different day. The third measure is extended with a succession of adverbial phrases which expand the sphere of its event to the outermost limits of the world. Such seeing belongs to vision; its hope is founded on revelation; the language is the speech of prophecy. The announcement is in the style of direct address to a feminine person. Her identity is known from the preceding song of confidence; the figure is personified Zion and the prophecy concerns her walls and boundaries and population. The oracle is a divine answer to 7.8–10 and describes the salvation for which the song hopes. In looking forward to the rebuilding of the city's walls, the oracle anticipates the work of Nehemiah (445–433 BC). It assumes the existence of a widely spread diaspora. Its historical setting is the same as that of vv. 8–10, probably the first half of the fifth century.

In style and subject v. 13 reads like a literary expansion of the oracle. The line is more prose than poetry. The rubric of 'the day' is dropped. It speaks of a world-wide devastation which will befall all the earth as punishment. In the literary context it anticipates the prayer for the humiliation of the nations in vv. 16f. and echoes themes from 6.16. The line was probably introduced in the literary compilation of chs. 6–7.

[11] A day when the wall of Jerusalem could be rebuilt would be a new time. The anguish and shame felt by the Jewish community over the ruined defenceless city is evident in texts like Neh. 1.3ff. Rebuilding the walls would mean infinitely more than urban repair. The razing of the walls (*gādēr*) had entered Judah's language of faith as speech about the judgment of God (see *gᵉdērāh* in Pss. 80.12; 89.40). The motif of rebuilding belongs to pictures of salvation which developed after the destruction of the city (Isa. 60.10; Ps. 51.18; see Jer. 31.38–40; Pss. 69.35; 102.16; 147.2). In Ezra's prayer the gift of a *gādēr* is listed as an act of salvation (Ezra 9.9). The second event (v. 11b) is described in one terse phrase of uncertain text or meaning: *yirḥaq-ḥōq*. Some render 'the border will be distant' (Weiser, Robinson) and compare the phrase to Isa. 26.15 where the widening of Judah's territory is promised. But *ḥōq* does not seem to be used elsewhere with the meaning 'territorial borders'; it is used frequently in the sense of a limit or boundary set to restrict or contain (Isa. 5.14; 24.5; Jer. 5.22; etc.). The phrase might mean that Jerusalem will live in a world without limits which separate her life from the nations, and so prepare for the movement of people freely from all the world

to her (v. 12).ᵍ Another solution more frequently adopted is to translate *ḥōq* as 'set time' (Job. 14.13), amend the verb to read *yidhōq*, and
render: 'when the time presses near'. The measure would then be
simply a statement that the prophesied day is imminent.

[**12**] The second event of 'the day' will be a movement of people to
Jerusalem from every part of the earth. Who 'they' are is not specifically said. But the coming of Judah's own people from Assyria, Egypt,
and every other direction is described in similar language in Isa.
11.11–16; 27.12; Zech. 10.8–12. The announcement speaks of this
return of the dispersed rather than the pilgrimage of the nations to
Zion (Isa. 2.2f.; 60.3; Zech. 14.16). 'From sea to sea and from
mountain to mountain' encompasses the whole earth (Zech. 9.10;
Pss. 72.8; 107.2f.). The rebuilding of the ruined walls and the recovery
of the scattered people together symbolize the complete end of the
time of wrath and the restoration of what once was.

[**13**] In the very day when Zion is being rebuilt and repopulated
the earth will become a devastated wasteland as punishment for the
deeds of its inhabitants. There will be a complete contrast between
Zion and the rest of the world; the one will manifest the marks of
salvation, the other the scourge of judgment. Verse 13 echoes motifs
of 6.16b which describes the judgment of Zion (desolation, inhabitants, deeds) and may be an expression of the concept of the eschatological reversal—the city/land which was an island of humiliation
in the midst of powerful nations will become an island of salvation in
the midst of a world under judgment. The motif of the desolation of
the world appears at the conclusion of the theophany in Nahum 1.5,
but v. 13. is closer to the portrayal at the beginning of the 'Isaiah
apocalypse' (Isa. 24.1, 3) and its emphasis that destruction comes
upon disobedience (24.5f.).

30. LET THE HISTORY OF SALVATION RESUME: 7.14–17

> 14 Shepherd your people with your staff,
>   the flock of your inheritance,
> who dwellᵃ alone in scrub
>   in the midst of fertile land.

ᵍ See the discussion in I. Willi-Plein, *Vorformen der Schriftexegese innerhalb des
Alten Testaments* (BZAW 123), 1971, pp. 107f.

ᵃ The versions assume a plural *šōkᵉnē*. But MT's singular masculine *šōkᵉnī* may
depend on the antecedent 'your people' (masc.) in spite of the intervening feminine
'flock'.

> Let them graze in Bashan and Gilead
> as in ancient days.
> 15 As in the days when you went forth from the land of Egypt,
> let us see[b] wonders.
> 16 May the nations see and be ashamed
> in spite of all their power.
> Let them lay their hand on their mouths,
> their ears be deaf.
> 17 Let them lick dust like a serpent,
> like things that crawl on the earth.
> Let them come trembling from their strongholds
> to YHWH our God;
> Let them dread and fear you.

This is a prayer to YHWH in his royal office as shepherd of his people, appealing to him to intervene on behalf of his 'flock' by resuming the deeds of the salvation history. In MT the style of direct address to YHWH is dropped at two points. In v. 15 YHWH is obviously the subject of 'I will show him,' but the reading is incongruent with the context (see the comment below). In v. 17b 'to YHWH our God' is a clarifying addition. The prayer unfolds in two movements. Verses 14f. petition for the restoration of 'the pasture' of the flock, and vv. 16f. seek an end to the power and pride of the nations. The verbs in vv. 16f. could be translated as future assertions instead of jussives, understanding the second part as an answer to the petition in vv. 15f. But the 'you' in v. 17 must refer to YHWH; such a petition is an expected element in the type to which the unit belongs (cf. Ps. 83.9–18). The prayer is a 'lament of the people' (cf. Pss. 44, 74, 79, 80, 83). The petition to YHWH as shepherd, the appeal to the classical tradition of YHWH's deeds, the circumstances of distress because of foes, the appeal for restoration and relief are all recurrent features of the type.[c] The lament maintains the style of petition throughout and absorbs the other customary elements of the type into the petition. There are no concrete indications of the circumstances in which the lament was composed other than the metaphorical description of severely restricted territory (v. 15) and the implied subjection to the nations (vv. 16f.). These clues point to the post-exilic community, perhaps in the first half of the fifth century.

Read within its literary context the prayer continues the sequence of liturgical material which begins at v. 7. It appeals to YHWH to

---

[b] *har'ēnū* for MT's *'ar'ennū* ('I will show him') which assumes the line is divine first-person style.

[c] See C. Westermann, *The Praise of God in the Psalms*, 1965, pp. 52ff.

enact the salvation which vv. 8–10 confidently expect and which is promised in vv. 11–13. The prayer repeats the twofold concern of both the previous units: restoration of God's people and God's vindication of himself against others. While the feminine figure of Zion speaks and is addressed in the preceding units, the first person plural appears in the prayer (vv. 15, 17; albeit both uncertain texts); the congregation speaks as a corporate body. But the continuity of content is not precise. Verses 8–10 are concerned with relief from a particular enemy; vv. 11–13 look for the rebuilding of the city and the coming of many from all the world. Here the restoration of territory is the concern. Whether these shifts represent the progress of an original composition or point to a pattern created by compilation of independent units is discussed above in the introduction to 7.7–20.

[14] The petition begins with language drawn from one of the most important ways in which Israel spoke about its relation to YHWH, the picture of YHWH as shepherd and the people as flock (Pss. 100.3; 95.7; 28.9; 23). The picture goes back to a continuous metaphor of the ancient East: the king is the shepherd of his people. In his role he guides and protects, exercising dominion for the welfare of those he rules. The metaphor is particularly appropriate in laments (Pss. 74.1; 80.1) because it appeals to the responsibility which belongs to YHWH in his office as King and rests the hopes of the people for help on the integrity of his kingship. The appeal is strengthened by the people's characterization of themselves as YHWH's 'inheritance'. The term *naḥᵃlāh* 'belongs to the sacral body of law dealing with the tenure of land, and originally designated the heritable land alloted by Yahweh to the clan or family'.[d] It came to be used for the people as the special possession of YHWH, a metaphor of the value of Israel to YHWH created by his election (Ps. 33.12; see also Pss. 68.9f.; 94.5, 14; 78.68; 71; etc.). The circumstances of the appeal seem very much like those reflected in the similar language of Isa. 63.17 and Joel 2.17; the people and their land are in the hands of enemies who violate YHWH's heritage. The second line of v. 14 gives the only direct description of their distress. The flock is isolated in grazing ground overgrown by scrubby thickets (*yaʿar*; cf. 3.19; Isa. 7.24f.; 21.13) and cannot enjoy the good pasture of fertile land (*karmel*; cf. Isa. 29.17; 32.15). The image reflects a historical situation in which the nation's territory is confined to the hill country with the good grazing and farming land in the possession of others.[e] Bashan and

---

[d] G. von Rad, *Old Testament Theology* I, p. 224.

[e] O. Eissfeldt translates v. 14b as a vocative addressed to YHWH ('O you who

Gilead were territories on the east of the Jordan which were famous as prime grazing areas. Acquired during the conquest, they had not been in the possession of Israel since their loss in the eighth century. The prayer looks back to that time as 'ancient days'. Their restoration to Israel would represent the full recovery of national life. What the petition seeks is what the salvation prophecies in Jer. 50.19 and Zech. 10.10 predict.

[15] The MT of v. 15 says, 'As in the days when *you* went forth from the land of Egypt *I* will show *him* wonders.' The three pronouns seem inconsistent within the sentence and with the context. Something has brought disorder into the text. In the rest of the Old Testament YHWH never 'goes forth from (*yāṣā' min*) Egypt', though of course Israel does (Ex. 13.3; 23.15; Deut. 11.10; Ps. 114.1; etc.). YHWH goes forth in theophanies, often to do battle with his and the people's enemies (Judg. 5.4; Isa. 26.21; 42.13; Ps. 68.7; etc.; see comment on Micah 1.3). Possibly the line originally read, 'As in the days when you went forth, show us wonders'; the deeds of YHWH in winning the land in the conquest period were in mind. Someone inserted 'from the land of Egypt' to be sure that the rather vague expression was understood as a reference to the classical saving history. Then a scribe assuming that 'you' meant Israel, took the line for divine speech and changed the verb. Or perhaps a unique reference to 'YHWH's going forth from Egypt' led to the same change. The victories which brought Israel into historical existence were the 'wonders' (*niplā'ōt*) which made up the classical history of salvation (Ex. 3.20; Judg. 6.13; the *niplā'ōt* are compiled and recited in psalms like Pss. 78, 105; 106; and 107 for the purpose of appealing for the resumption of the 'miracles' of salvation in post-exilic times). The prayer yearns for the sight of marvellous deeds as a revelation that YHWH's rule determines the history of his people.

[16] With v. 16 the prayer shifts its focus from YHWH's people to the nations. But the intention of the appeal does not vary; it continues to seek the salvation of Israel. The nations whose power and pride frustrate YHWH's manifestation of his rule through his history with his people must be vanquished. What the flock 'sees' as a miracle of salvation, the nations will 'see' as the intervention of a power greater than theirs. From of old YHWH's deeds brought terror upon the foes of his people (Ex. 15.14–16) and the prophets of the

---

dwell alone in a wood in the midst of Mount Carmel') and locates the origin of the psalm in the north after the fall of Samaria ('Ein Psalm aus Nord-Israel', *ZDMG* 112, 1962, pp. 259–68; also in *Kleine Schriften* IV, 1968, pp. 63–72).

exile looked for YHWH's new salvation to effect victory over the nations (Isa. 45.16f., 24; 49.22f.; cf. 64.2). Historical salvation cannot occur without changing the circumstances of history; the laments of the community in distress plead for YHWH's victory as an inevitable manifestation of his reign (especially the quite similar language in Ps. 83.9–18). The sight of YHWH's 'coming forth' will be so overwhelming as to leave speech and hearing dysfunctional. 'To lick the dust' is a posture of humiliation in powerlessness (Ps. 72.9; Isa. 49.23; cf. Gen. 3.14). The nations will desert their fortifications in recognition that their might is of no use, and they who made others grovel will know the dread and awe which comes upon those who behold the manifestation of the divine (cf. Ps. 18.45).

31. GOD'S VICTORY OVER SIN: 7.18–20

18 Who is a God like you,
　　taking away guilt,
　and passing over crime
　　for the remnant of his inheritance.
　He does not persist for ever in his anger
　　for he delights in mercy.
19 He will again have compassion on us,
　　will subdue our iniquities.
　He[a] will cast into the depths of the sea
　　all our[a] sins.
20 You will show faithfulness to Jacob,
　　mercy to Abraham
　as you have sworn to our fathers
　　from days of old.

The book, which begins with a portrayal of YHWH's advent in wrath, concludes with praise of his mercy. Verses 18–20 are a hymn of praise composed to be sung by the congregation (first person plurals in vv. 19f.). It begins in the style of direct address, shifts through participial clauses to third-person style (vv. 18f.), and returns to direct address at the conclusion (v. 20). The stylistic transition is common in the type, and not an indication of redaction or compilation. The content of the praise is a continuous description of the

---

[a] MT has 'you will cast . . . their sins'. An uncertainty about the person of verb and pronoun appears also in the versions and is probably due to the hymnic shift from second to third and back.

way in which God deals with his sinful people. The hymn does seem
to contain a twofold movement. Verse 18 describes what YHWH is
known to be like, characterizes him. Verses 19f. project that knowledge in expectation of what he will do. Each movement reaches a
climax in a statement of the basis of God's action. He is a God who
delights in mercy (v. 18c), who has given his oath to the fathers to
show them mercy (v. 20b). The whole is a response to the active
mercy (*ḥesed*) of God which he enacts in overcoming the sin of his
people.

The song sounds like a hymn composed on the text of the theological
formula: 'YHWH, a God compassionate and gracious, slow to anger
and abounding in mercy and faithfulness' (Ex. 34.6; Neh. 9.17; Pss.
86.15; 103.8; 145.8; Jonah 4.2). The clues to the historical setting of
the hymn are similar to those found elsewhere in vv. 8–20. The congregation names itself 'the remnant of God's inheritance' and sees its
sin as the basic problem to be overcome by God's salvation. They
live in the post-exilic period and look back on the disasters of the
sixth century with an understanding that they live under God's
judgment which only he can remove.

In its literary context the hymn states the theology which under-
girds all of vv. 7–17. It resumes the acknowledgment of sin expressed
in v. 9. Its anticipation of coming salvation (vv. 19f.) gives it a prophetic function that is consonant with the expectation vibrant
throughout the section. It states the basis for that hope, which has to
this point gone unexpressed, in its celebration of God's mercy. And it
interprets the entire drama of restoration represented in the three
previous units as an enactment of the forgiveness of god.

[18–19] The praise of God sets in with a rhetorical question which
is in effect a proclamation that YHWH is incomparable. The style is
direct address, because the exultant question is a response to what
YHWH does, usually his majestic manifestation of might against
enemies and in behalf of his people (Ex. 15.11; Pss. 35.10; 71.19;
77.13; 89.6; 113.5). Here praise responds to YHWH's capacity to
deal with sin, the recurrent central theme of the hymn. All three of
the Old Testament sin-words are used (iniquity, crime, sin), perhaps
to comprehend the totality of the phenomenon which the Old
Testament designated by these words, any incongruence between
the purpose of God and the life of the people. The hymn piles up
expressions for this forgiving work of God which show how real sin is
and how difficult it is to speak precisely of what God does about its
thereness: 'he removes it' . . . 'passes over it' . . . 'casts it into the
depth of the sea'. The last two expressions portray forgiveness as a

battle and sound like a reminiscence of the victory of the sea (Ex. 15.5); they show that the hymn regards even forgiveness as the work of majestic powers, a 'miracle' of the might of God.

The congregation names itself the 'inheritance of YHWH', a term for their identity as his possession (see the comment on 'flock of his inheritance' in v. 14). They are now but a remnant; the decimating judgment of fall and exile has passed and they are what is left. Their praise of him as the one who passes over *their* crime is not intended as a presumptuous claim that his forgiveness is for them alone, but rather a celebration that as the remnant created by his judgment their very existence is the work of his forgiveness. They are there at all because 'he does not persist in his anger' (cf. v.9). The time of wrath is finished and to describe what now will be the hymn uses a second and lovely anthropomorphism: 'he will again have compassion on us.' Compassion (*rḥm*) is the tender care lavished by a stronger on the need of one who is related to him in some way. The anthropomorphism belongs to the picture of YHWH as father and kinsman of his people (Hos. 11.1–4; Ps. 103.13). The change from anger to compassion and the victory over their sin are the manifestation of a characteristic which Israel has learned belongs to the nature of YHWH himself: 'he delights in mercy (*ḥesed*)' (cf. Jer.9.24). *Ḥesed* is the gracious conduct which makes the most and best of a relationship, the deed which brings a relationship to its fulfilment, even when the partner is weak or fallible. YHWH's *ḥesed* is his work to fulfil his election of Israel in spite of their frailty, a work the Psalms repeatedly speak of as his deliverance, salvation, and forgiveness (e.g., Pss. 6.4; 85.7; 86.5; 103.4f.).

[20] In v. 20 *ḥesed* is combined with faithfulness (*'emet*) in the familiar hendiadys[b] used so often in the Psalms as a word-pair for YHWH's beneficient history with Israel. Gracious faithfulness will form the future of the remnant. Abraham and Jacob are used as characterizing names for the people as the corporate objects of YHWH's election (the former only here in the Old Testament). The invocation of the names of the patriarchs also prepares for the following reference to the fathers. The hymn concludes with an appeal to the very beginning of Israel's history and the oath by which YHWH initiated it. That oath created the relation which *ḥesed* fulfils and *'emet* maintains. A recitation of Israel's entire history as an expression of YHWH's oath is developed in Ps. 105 (cf. vv. 8–11), the only use of the motif in the Psalter. There and in all its other occurrences (Gen. 22.16; 26.3; 50.24; Ex. 13.5, 11; 33.1; Num. 11.12; 14.16, 23;

b N. Glueck, *Ḥesed in the Bible*, 1967, pp. 54f. and n.82.

32.11; Deuteronomy and Joshua; Judges; Jer. 32.22) the content of the oath is gift of the land. Undoubtedly the restoration of the land is in view here, which fits in appropriately with vv. 13–15. Israel's sin brought them to the confined existence of a beleaguered remnant in a ruined city. YHWH's victory over their sin will give them back their life, and the land will become the sacrament of his forgiveness.